D0580915

THE
FISHERMAN'S
VADE
MECUM

G. W. MAUNSELL

The Fisherman's

Vade Mecum

THE COMPLETE HANDBOOK
ON FISHING FOR TROUT,
SEA TROUT, SALMON AND PIKE

ADAM & CHARLES BLACK
LONDON

FIRST PUBLISHED 1933
SECOND EDITION 1936
REPRINTED 1938, 1941, 1942,
1944 AND 1948
THIRD EDITION REVISED AND
ENLARGED BY
WILSON STEPHENS, 1952
FOURTH EDITION REVISED BY
ROY EATON, 1959
REPRINTED 1963, 1967, 1972, 1977

ISBN 0 7136 0559 6

A. AND C. BLACK LIMITED
35 BEDFORD ROW, LONDON WC1R 4 JH

PRINTED IN GREAT BRITAIN BY
LEWIS REPRINTS LTD.,
MEMBER OF BROWN KNIGHT & TRUSCOTT GROUP
LONDON AND TONBRIDGE

PREFACE

For many years I have been in the habit of making notes of what I have learnt and observed during a day's fishing. I did this for my own information, instruction and guidance, and I arranged these notes under separate headings, adding to them, from time to time, items that interested me in *The Field*, the *Salmon and Trout Magazine*, the *Fishing Gazette*, etc. On seeing these notes, some of my friends were kind enough to encourage me to publish them, some even going so far as to say that such a volume would supply a long-felt want.

Every angler is entitled to consider that his own ways and methods are best, so long as he can catch fish with them, and most fishermen will agree with the dictum of that great angler T. E. Pritt: 'One of the charms of angling is that it presents an endless field for argument, speculation and experiment.' So doubtless there are many who will prefer to adopt different methods from those advocated in this little book. To these I would say that the notes which I have made are those which I myself have found successful or helpful in catching fish, and I record them merely in the hope that they may be helpful to others.

Most of the illustrations have been drawn for me by my friend Mr. J. A. Rennie. I am deeply grateful to him for the time and trouble he has devoted to this task, with such eminent success. I must also thank

Mr. W. A. Hunter, author of *Fisherman's Pie*, for allowing me to use the illustrations on pages 108, 110 and 148. Messrs. C. Farlow and Co. Ltd., have generously lent me the block of the illustration on page 292.

Much of the chapter on 'Natural Flies' is, by his permission, based on Mr. C. A. N. Wauton's admirable book *The Flyfisher's Entomology*, and some of the 'Notes on Fly Casting' are the result of instruction I received many years ago from Mr. Reginald Hughes at Perivale.

G. W. MAUNSELL.

London, 1933.

CONTENTS

Book I
TROUT FISHING

Book II
SALMON FISHING

Book III
SEA TROUT FISHING

Book IV
STRIKING, PLAYING, LANDING

Book V
CASTING AND SPINNING

Book VI
PIKE FISHING

Book VII
SUNDRIES

CONTENTS
Book VIII
THE SALMON FAMILY

Book I

TROUT FISHING

Book I : TROUT FISHING

Part I

WET FLY FISHING

SECTION I

Notes for a Beginner

Before you 'go fishing' you should acquire some knowledge of the following three things (if you don't, you spend your time trying to learn them, and this hampers your fishing):

1. Learn how to use your rod and how to cast a fly.

2. Get someone to point out to you the places in a stream where fish usually feed and rest. Try also to acquire a knowledge of their habits and natural history.

3. Get someone to show you the standard artificial flies and to explain to you what they represent; and also roughly the type, size, and colour suitable for certain weather, water, and light conditions.

SECTION 2

Greasing the Line

Unless of course you wish to fish deep, it pays to grease your line when fishing in a lake or when fishing *upstream* in a river. Some of the advantages are:

1. You can recover the line off the water easier

2. You can shoot your line better (*see page* 226)

3. The line is less liable to become waterlogged

4. In wet weather the line is less liable to stick in the rings (*see also pages* 34 and 371).

SECTION 3

To Sink a Fly, Cast, or Line

To sink a fly:

1. Dip it in glycerine

2. Wet it in your mouth

3. Wet it well and then press it between your fingers.

To sink a cast :

1. Rub it with soap or a piece of lead
2. Rub it with glycerine
3. Draw it through the gills of a fish

To sink a line :

1. If you rub a line with Fuller's Earth this removes all traces of grease and makes it sink well.

2. Rub it gently with soft mud, wet clay, or any substance soluble in water.

SECTION 4

Stream Fishing

a. PRELIMINARIES

1. If you have time, walk over the water and pick out likely spots.

2. Choose which bank to fish from (this depends chiefly on the wind). You must also consider the position of the sun, the presence of bushes, etc., on the banks, the water conditions (the best side from which to fish, likely stickles and currents), and the windings of the river.

3. Find out what fly is on the water and try to match it.

4. Find out what the fish are feeding on.

5. Find out what stage of the rise is on, 1st, 2nd, or 3rd stage (*see page* 47).

6. Consider what are the weather, wind, light, and water conditions, and decide on type, size, and colour of your fly.

7. Decide if you will fish up- or downstream.

4

8. If unsuccessful, don't linger too long in any one place.

b. GENERAL NOTES

1. Keep out of sight as much as you can. A high bank, hedge, wall, or trees behind you help to make you less visible to the fish.

2. Remain as steady and motionless as you can. Fish soon detect any movements of the body, legs, or arms.

3. Move slowly, tread lightly, be silent, and keep as low as you can.

4. Avoid casting your shadow or that of your rod on the water.

5. Try to keep behind your fish.

6. Your first cast over a fish is your best chance.

7. Note carefully the landmarks of a rise (*see page* 27, Note 6).

8. Keep your fly in the water and your hook sharp.

9. When casting over tall sedges or rushes on the river bank, it is better to recover the line by pulling it through the rings than by trying to lift it back with the rod, there is less chance of the fly catching up.

10. Remember that a road is simply a highway over the land and the public has no right to fish in private water from a public highway or from a bridge.

c. WEATHER CONDITIONS

Wind (*see page* 46): An upstream breeze when fishing upstream, and a downstream breeze when fishing down, are an advantage.

A steady breeze to cause a ripple is always useful.

A changeable *squally* wind is bad for any sort of fishing.

Water (see page 40) : When the temperature of the water is warmer than the air, fishing is better than when the water is colder than the air.

A rapidly falling or a rapidly rising water is bad for fishing (*see page* 43).

A normal height and colour of the water is best.

The second or third day after a flood, when water is clearing, is usually a favourable time.

The threat of floods, heavy rain, or storms, always puts fish down.

Water at a temperature of 50° to 60° is about right for trout fishing.

Light (see page 44) : When there are gleams of sunshine between clouds, or when the light is dull and diffused, expect good fishing.

When there is a strong glare on the water, fishing is seldom good. This glare is often caused during bright sunlight when heavy white clouds are about.

Barometer (see page 39) : A steady or rising barometer is better for fishing than when it is variable or falling.

Mist or Fog, etc : Fishing is seldom good during a fog, or when there is a mist like smoke close over the water, or where the mist hangs low on the hills.

'Close rain' is bad for fishing, 'open rain' does not interfere with it (*see page* 307).

A 'soft' day is better for fishing than a 'hard' day (*see page* 319).

General. There is often a rise of fish just after a change of wind, light, or weather.

On the approach of stormy or unsettled weather nearly all animals (including fish) cease feeding and take shelter (*see page* 317).

Just before and during a thunderstorm trout do not usually take well. After the storm has passed, you have a good chance of a fish with a wet fly.

Fishing is never good on a day when the water appears full of light and you can see the stones, etc on the bottom very clearly and your line and cast are very visible in the water (*see page* 44).

d. WHEN TO FISH UP- OR DOWNSTREAM

Stream fishing is of two sorts:

(*a*) *Upstream*, using a short line, usually one fly (with kick) casting to individual fish
(*b*) *Downstream*, using a long line, usually three flies (with a good entry) (*see page* 10).

Usually best to fish *upstream*

1. With an upstream wind
2. In bright weather
3. In clear low water
4. Where the current is not too swift

Usually best to fish *downstream*

1. With a downstream wind
2. On a dull day with a breeze
3. With a swift current
4. When the water is clearing after a flood

Always fish upstream if wind and water conditions permit.

It often pays to start fishing upstream and to come back again over the same ground fishing down.

e. NOTES ON FISHING UPSTREAM

Some advantages of fishing upstream are:

1. When casting you are behind your fish, and unseen.
2. Your fly floats down naturally, with no drag on it.

B 7

3. You can cover every yard of the water with a short line.

4. When you hook a fish, you play him downstream and do not disturb the water above you.

The usual method is

1. Cast upstream with a short line (say about 8 yards from the rod top to the fly).

2. Raise the rod top as the fly drifts down towards you, or draw in line through the rings, keeping a fairly tight line between rod top and fly.

3. Allow the fly to swim down naturally, no drag – give no motion to the fly.

4. In a swift current you must make frequent casts. Fish the cast well out; fish often take a fly close to your feet in the shallow water. Strike quickly and gently to the rise.

5. When wading keep low, move slowly, glide forward foot by foot, cause no ripple, no splashing, no rapid movements of the body.

6. With a bright light and clear water, try the sides of the broken water at the head of the runs.

7. With a breeze, try the easy water at the tail of a run. In the gravelly shallows is always worth trying.

Other methods :

1. The wet fly oil method. Cast upstream, short line, thin line, one fly.

Oil line and cast (except last 18 in. of cast), to make it float. Rub soap, glycerine, etc, on the last 18 in. to make it sink about 6 in.

Watch the cast for a rise.

Fish slowly, strike quickly.

8

This method is worth trying

  (*a*) When fish are rising short
  (*b*) When fish are bulging
  (*c*) In a strong light, clear, calm water.

2. Try fishing the dropper upstream, short line, two or even three flies.

No oil on flies, cast or line: the tail fly may be glycerined to make it sink.

Raise the rod top when drawing the flies towards you, keeping all line off the water and the top dropper only on the surface.

This is best with a wind or in broken water.

3. Try two flies, one floating and one sunk.

It is best to have the *tail* fly well oiled and floating, the other fly about a yard up the cast on a 3 in. dropper glycerined or well wet to make it sink.

The reel line and cast must be greased to float (except about a foot of the cast each side of the dropper, which can be rubbed with glycerine or soap to make it sink).

Cast upstream into pools and very easy water.

Watch the floating fly.

Strike at once.

This is a useful method in a still pool or in a lake.

4. A cast made up of a nymph fished wet on the tail and a dry fly on the dropper is sometimes a good combination. A hatch of nymphs being a gradual affair, at times the fish will be taking both duns and nymphs.

By watching the dry fly you can detect the slightest touch at the nymph and strike quickly (*see also page* 64).

f. NOTES ON FISHING DOWNSTREAM

The chief disadvantage of fishing downstream is, the line pursues an unnatural course across and against the stream and is rather conspicuous. The fisherman is also easily seen by the fish. This can be partly avoided by using a long rod, a thin line and casting a long line.

When fishing down, you miss many fish that rise to the dropper which you would hook if you fished upstream. You are also more liable to prick a fish as the tendency is to pull the hook out of his mouth.

The usual method is

1. Cast a fairly long line especially in shallow water.

2. You can have three flies, 1 yard apart, on a 9-ft cast. The flies, especially the tail fly, should have a 'good entry' (*see page* 56).

3. Do not grease your line or cast. A greased line fished down and across causes 'drag' (*see page* 28).

4. Cast across and slightly downstream, allow your flies to swim round with the current unchecked (when they represent nymphs or dead flies). But when they represent small fish or beetles, etc (such as butcher, Alexandra, or small salmon flies) still allow them to swim round with the current, but give them a little jerky or trembling motion with the wrist.

5. When the line has come round and is straightened out in the stream, hold it still for a few seconds, then draw it in a few feet and let it fall back again. Try also letting the stream take out the line foot by foot until you have say 30 yards of line out.

6. Fish usually follow the fly round, and do not take it until the line has straightened out.

7. Camouflage yourself as much as possible, keep off the fishes' skyline, and tread lightly on the bank.

   Cast first under your own bank with a 'cross country' cast, then try midstream, then under opposite bank.

   A *cross country cast* is made by standing well back from the bank and casting a short line to a fish under your own bank, allowing the gut cast only to fall beyond the edge of the bank (*see also page* 5, Note 9).

   Move on about 3 yards and cast again, etc.

8. Cast a straight line, try to avoid having much belly in it (sometimes this cannot be helped when the current is strong in midstream).

   A fly is not fishing properly until the line is fairly straight in the water.

9. To fish deep, cast rather upstream and across; this gives the fly time to sink, but is liable to cause a belly in the line.

   With a strong midstream current, it pays to cast almost downstream to avoid the belly in the line.

10. Mind your shadow and that of your rod, also the glitter of your rod.

    Face the sun if possible when casting.

    When the sun is behind you the water in front of you should be 'broken' either by currents or by a good breeze so as to obscure your shadow.

    In any case your shadow must not fall within 5 feet of a fish.

11. When wading keep low, tread lightly, move slowly, and cause no ripples on the surface of the water.

12. Fishing downstream, a fish generally hooks himself, so strike very gently, as you have a tight line and are striking against the stream.

g. WHEN TIED UP IN A BUSH

1. Try a gentle pull in the direction of the wind.

2. Throw a stone attached to a string over the branch and pull it down to you.

3. When fishing only one fly, try reeling up until the fly touches the rod top, then twist the rod to right and left.

4. Lower the rod, point it at the fly, reel in slowly or pull in line through the rings. The fly may drop clear; it is an even chance.

5. When caught up in a bush on the far side of a stream try lowering the top of the rod and letting the stream take the line. This may cause the fly to fall clear.

6. When hopeless and you must break, reel up all you can and pull on line direct through rings.

When caught in the bottom *see page* 249.

h. WHERE TO CAST IN A STREAM

It is very important for a fisherman to have a knowledge of the haunts and habits of trout.

It is more important to the wet fly fisherman than to the dry fly man (who casts to a rising fish).

The seasonal movements of trout in a stream are roughly as follows:

In November and December they are busy spawning in the higher reaches.

In January and February they drop downstream
exhausted and rest in the pools and sluggish
water.

In March they appear in the gravelly shallows
(1 ft deep), and in the tail of, and at the sides
of, easy currents.

In April (under normal conditions) they take up
their place or 'pitch' in the stream, at a spot
where plenty of flies and food are passing.
When several trout are in a pool, they take up
their position in order of size, *viz* the largest
in front where the food enters and the others
behind.

In the early autumn they congregate at the
mouths of tributaries, etc, preparatory to
moving up to spawn.

The 'pitches' or spots chosen in April for the
season, are roughly where the current is easy and
passing food is plentiful, *viz :*

1. At the sides of stickles or currents.

2. In the eddies on the edge of a run, behind
   and between weed patches.

3. In the pools and bays made by the stream.

4. In the irregularities of the river bed which
   offer shelter from the current, behind stones,
   etc.

5. In the 'hang of the stream,' *i.e.* the smooth
   water above a rapid run.

6. In the 'eye of the stream,' *i.e.* the first eddy
   or pool after it commences to become rapid
   water.

7. In the tail of the stream when the current
   begins to get easy and normal again.

8. Where two currents of water meet at the
   mouth of a small tributary, below a weed bed

or obstacle. Where two currents of wind meet under the lee of an island or clump of trees.

9. All fish prefer shade to a strong light. In strong sunshine they seek the shade of trees, bushes, banks, bridges, etc. It pays to cast into the shade and draw your fly into the sunshine.

In rising water trout search for food in the middle of the stream.

In a strong flood they go to the sides and under the banks for shelter, until the flood subsides.

In falling water they gradually take up their pitches in the stream.

In low water and bright weather trout seek the shade of the banks and bushes.

In a normal breeze they move to the bank on to which the flies are blown.

In a strong wind they seek the sheltered places where the insects congregate, *viz* on the lee side of trees, bushes, banks, walls, etc.

When the temperature of the upper surface of the water is cold they keep to the bottom in the deep pools.

SECTION 5
Lake Fishing

a. PRELIMINARIES

1. To fish on a lake you must have a steady wind from some quarter.

2. From a boat the wind decides what bay or shore you will drift along.

3. From the shore it is easier to cast with your back to, and across, the wind.

4. Try to find out what fly or water insect the fish are feeding on and match it.

5. Decide the following:

(a) Whether you will use one, two or three flies on your cast.

(b) Whether you will use large, medium or small flies.

(c) Whether you will fish deep or near the surface.

(d) Whether the colour of your flies should be in harmony with, or in contrast to, the surroundings.

(e) Whether your flies should be deceivers or attractors (*see page* 57).

(f) Whether you will work your flies in the water quickly or slowly (*see page* 20, Note 4).

6. When being rowed out in the morning to the fishing ground, instead of sitting in the stern of the boat doing nothing it is worth while trying to find out whether the fish are lying near the surface or not and whether your flies should be fished fast or slow.

As you sit in the stern, cast a long line across and beyond the oar; the flies when they alight will rest idly for a moment, then they will gradually move with the tug of the boat until they are finally dragging along behind it. Fish may take the fly when it is quiescent or slowly sinking or swinging round with the boat, giving you some indication as to whether your flies should be fished fast or slow.

If you don't rise anything, you have anyhow been occupied, and the chances are the fish are not lying near the surface.

b. GENERAL NOTES

1. You must have a steady wind to cause the boat to drift.

2. The boat should drift slowly and evenly.

3. Where the wind permits, drift parallel to and about 20 yards off the shore. An experienced boatman is a great advantage.

4. In a very strong wind when the boat drifts too fast on top of your fly, try hanging a heavy stone attached to a rope over the windward side of the boat as a drag, or use a drogue on the windward side. A *drogue* is merely a cone-shaped canvas bag with a couple of stout lines attached, this checks and controls the drift of the boat; or if the oars work on a thole pin put an oar in the water on the leeward side pointing towards the bows of the boat, this checks the drift.

5. The weight in the boat should be evenly distributed or the boat will not drift properly. Put stones with the lighter weight to balance.

C. BOAT EQUIPMENT

1. When wet fly fishing on a lake from a boat, I prefer to use a light 14-ft rod because you can work the bob fly better and cover more water than with a shorter rod, also you are sitting down in the boat and have more command over your flies.

If, however, you must use a 9 or 10-ft rod it is best to cast standing up in the boat.

2. A light line (level or tapered) is best; your flies work better and more naturally. In a wind a heavy line causes a splash, and is rather conspicuous. Of course, with a heavy line you can cast better into the wind, but when boat fishing you seldom have to do this.

3. A rubber cushion is useful.

4. Nailed boots are a nuisance as you may step on your line. Rubber soled shoes are better.

5. It is easier to cast when sitting on a board resting on each gunwale than when sitting in the stern seat of the boat. Do not sit with a leg each side of the board or seat of the boat. It is best to sit facing the stern and cast sideways, because when you hook a fish you can turn and bring him to windward without having to lift one leg over the seat which may cause trouble when playing a big fish.

6. When lake fishing, the glare off the water is sometimes very trying. As a protection, glasses or spectacles fitted with Crookes glass are a great comfort. (Crookes glass cuts out the harmful rays of the sun.)

d. WEATHER CONDITIONS

1. On a lake you must have a wind of some sort to make the boat drift, and the direction should suit the shore or bays you want to fish. The shore against which the wind is blowing (the lee shore) usually provides the best sport.

When the wind is blowing *across* the entrance of a bay or small inlet, a very likely place for a big trout is along the dividing line of the calmer water inside the bay and the rougher water outside.

2. A steady wind which raises a nice ruffle on the water is best (a soft, mild, S or W wind is preferable).

3. A diffused light through clouds with some gleams of sunshine are favourable conditions.

4. A steady rise of water in a lake usually means good fishing.

5. Squalls from any quarter are bad.

    A shifting, unsteady, or close wind is bad.

    A wind which raises white horses is bad.

6. Bright sunshine with heavy white clouds about, producing a glare on the water, is bad.

7. If you commence catching small fish in the morning the chances are you will continue to do so all day.

8. If you have good sport in the forenoon, don't expect much in the afternoon.

9. The temperature of the water is important. The actual direction of the wind is quite a secondary consideration. Certainly a N or E wind usually cools the water while a S or W wind usually warms the water.

10. See also weather conditions on a stream (*page 5*).

e. WHERE TO CAST IN A LAKE

1. In a lake trout move about to feed; a spot where you find them one day may be deserted the following day. (In a stream trout wait for the current to bring them food.) As a rule the best feeding grounds are in the shallower parts of a lake, although along a rocky shore the banks of which go down sheer into fairly deep water, is a very likely place for a big fish.

2. They usually feed up-wind, or they select a locality (a bay or along a shore or off a point) and cruise about there in search of food.

In deep water they cruise in rather large circles.

In shallow water they cruise in smaller circles.

3. They appear to move about according to plan, regulated by

    (*a*) Times of day
    (*b*) Seasons of the year
    (*c*) Direction of the wind
    (*d*) Desire for food
    (*e*) Favourable feeding grounds

4. A trout travels about the same rate as the ripple of his rise, so when you see a rise, cast up-wind outside the outer ring of the ripple.

5. Cast on the shelf between the deeps and the shallows, in from 3 ft to 10 ft of water; a gravelly rocky bottom is a favourable place.

6. Cast carefully during any change of wind, light, temperature, or weather; a change often brings on a rise of fish.

7. In a strong wind cast in the sheltered spots, *viz :*

    (*a*) behind a point, and in the tail of the wind well past the point

    (*b*) behind islands or groves of trees in the tail of the shelter

    (*c*) in sheltered bays and nooks.

8. Cast near streaks of foam caused by the wind.

9. Cast at the mouth of a stream where it enters the lake; try carefully where the current of the stream ceases. Most lakes have a river or inflow of water at the top end and an outflow at the lower end.

The top end is generally the best for fishing, as it usually has a soft bottom with some silt and plenty of weeds to harbour good fish food.

10. Always cast on both sides of a sunken shoal or bar in the lake.

11. To fish the shallows properly the day should be dull, and cloudy with a breeze.

On a bright calm day on a lake it is little use fishing in say 2 or 3 ft of water.

12. In a good hatch of fly (especially Mayfly), study the 'line of fly,' *i.e.* the direction in which the fly are blown. Example: off, say a wooded point, the 'line of fly' and the lay of the fish in an ordinary breeze is roughly thus, and NOT directly under the shelter of the point.

f. NOTES ON FISHING FROM A BOAT

1. Do not cast directly down-wind, cast slightly to right or left.

2. Try to keep a fairly tight line with no belly in it. Never lose control of your line or flies.

3. When casting, cause your flies to fall lightly – no splash.

4. Work your flies according to the wind and light conditions at the time:

> On a calm or bright day work them fairly quickly;
> On a windy or dull day work them much slower.

When using flies with gold or silver tinsel bodies I think that they should be worked quicker than brownish or other dull-coloured flies.

5. On a 'soft' day (S or W wind, diffused light, balmy weather) it often pays to fish your tail fly well sunk and neglect the droppers.

On a 'hard' day (N or E wind, bright light, cool crisp day) try fishing the dropper bobbing along the surface.

6. In a very strong light try fishing deep, as fish sink towards the bottom to avoid the glare of strong light (*see also page* 44).

7. When fish are coming short, do not draw your flies along surface; try sinking them a few inches; fish can see them better and are less likely to miss them.

8. When fish are very stiff, try letting flies hang quietly in the water for a little with the bob fly just touching the surface, then draw them in towards you very slowly, with the bob fly dribbling along the surface.

9. Try drifting directly down-wind, using a fairly short line, drawing the droppers along the surface; commence by giving a jerky motion to the flies, then draw them slowly towards you. If you can, draw your flies along the trough of the waves and not across them.

10. Try rowing slightly up and across the wind thus: and casting from the stern seat, make your flies sweep round or, so to speak, comb the arc A B. Row slowly; if you row too much into the wind, the man in the bows does not have much of a chance. If only one fisherman is in the boat, try keeping the boat almost up-wind and cast over the stern. The boatman can then 'hold' the boat, letting it drop down-wind slowly: this gives you a second cast over a fish that has risen and you have missed.

11. Try casting a long line and shooting it; keeping the rod top low, draw in line through the rings, work the rod top to give life to flies; fish deep and fish the cast out, sometimes a fish will follow the fly up to the boat.

Be careful of the spare line coiled in the boat, as when you hook a fish you are handicapped until you get your line back on the reel again.

12. Try rowing almost up-wind about 20 yards from the shore, and casting across the wind among the rocks and weeds along the shore.

13. In a dead calm try casting a long line into the shallows along the shore – one fly – sink it well; *or* try three small flies on a fine cast, in the deep water; sink the flies well, and draw them in with jerks.

14. Two casts over a rising fish are enough. With a good wind a boat does not alarm fish. It may do so

in a calm. The vibrations of a motor frighten trout (*see also page* 177).

15. When you hook a fish, coax him to the windward side of the boat, play him and land him to windward. If you try to land him to leeward the boat is liable to drift over him.

16. When you get a rise do not hurry the strike (*see also page* 185). With a head and tail rise a fish generally hooks himself in a lake.

17. When the boat is drifting there is usually a calm patch in front with two well defined currents where the wind takes charge again. If you find fish are taking in this calm area, it should be well tried before casting in the rest of the reachable water, as in certain lights the flies appear to shew up better in certain parts of the area in front of the boat.

18. Fishing from a boat is not entirely the chuck and chance it game that it is sometimes thought to be.

The man who will catch most fish is he who concentrates on what he is doing and tries the different methods mentioned in this sub-section, until he finds out what method suits the moods of the fish.

For instance he might begin by trying:

   (*a*) Fishing close to the surface, drawing the flies fast and then drawing them slowly

   (*b*) Dribbling the dropper along the surface

   (*c*) Throwing a long line, fishing deep and drawing in through the rings, etc etc.

A man who is continually talking or thinking of something else while fishing is badly handicapped.

g. NOTES ON FISHING FROM THE SHORE

1. Wade in (if necessary) and cast rather across the wind, not directly down-wind.

A wind from some point behind you is an advantage.

2. Fish between the deeps and shallows in about 3 to 10 ft of water.

3. Try in the small bays, off points, by weed beds, at the mouth of a stream, round rocks, etc.

4. Your flies should be at least a yard apart on the cast. Have the top dropper well up the cast (say 2 ft from the reel line).

On a calm day or when many weeds are about use only one fly.

5. The usual method is, after casting allow your flies to sink a little, then draw them towards you, giving some motion to the flies (*see page* 18, Notes 4 and 5).

6. Try wading out and casting towards the shore with a long line to within a foot or so of the bank.

7. It often pays (even on a bright still day) to cast a very long line, letting the flies sink well, and then draw in the line slowly through the rings (a tiny bit of lead on the cast is useful to sink it).

8. Try the 'wet fly oil tip.' Sink the fly and 18 in. of the gut cast. Oil the rest of the line and cast. Let the fly remain still for a little, then draw in the line very slowly about a foot at a time (*see page* 8, Note 1).

9. Try the tail fly floating and the dropper sunk. Allow the flies to remain still on the water for a little, then draw in line slowly about a foot at a time (*see also page* 9, Note 3).

10. On a windy day with rough water, try fishing the top dropper only and neglecting the others.

11. Do not strike too quickly with cruising fish in a lake – give them time.

Book I: TROUT FISHING

Part II

DRY FLY FISHING

P

SECTION I
General Notes

1. In dry fly fishing, the object is how best to cover a fish with your fly after having chosen the best point from which to make your attack, while in wet fly fishing the object is to search every yard of the water with your fly.

2. Skues very truly said : ' There are days and hours when the wet fly has not a chance against the dry fly, and there are days and hours when the dry fly has not a chance against the wet fly.'

3. There are two sorts of dry fly water, *viz :*
   (a) The chalk stream, where there is plenty of insect life and fish have to move only a foot or so to obtain their surface food
   (b) The mountain stream, where food is scarce, the current strong, and fish have to search well and work hard for their food.

4. On arrival at the waterside do not be in too great a hurry to begin. It pays to sit down for a few minutes and see what is happening (*see also page* 4,).

a. PRELIMINARIES

Equipment. For dry fly fishing it is best to have a light and fairly stiff rod. In comparison with a wet fly rod the power should be more in the butt. It should recover quickly, have a good pick-up and an easy power of propulsion.

The line should be tapered for the last 4 yards and the centre should be thicker than the centre part of a tapered line used for wet fly fishing. It is convenient to keep one well greased tapered line for dry fly fishing only and to have another line (tapered or level) for wet fly fishing.

A tapered gut cast is very necessary for dry fly fishing. 5 ft is usually long enough, with a longer gut cast accuracy is more difficult, especially if there is any wind.

SECTION 2

Notes on the Dry Fly Method

1. When casting, bend down or kneel, conceal yourself as much as you can, make use of bushes, reeds, foliage, etc, to screen you from the fish.

2. Keep well behind your fish, and out of sight; you should only be able to see the surface of the water; when you can see the bottom the chances are the fish can see you.

3. Keep as still as you can, avoid rapid movements of the body or legs. When necessary move slowly and tread lightly.

When wading, make as little ripple as possible.

Mind your shadow and that of your rod and line.

4. Cast deliberately and accurately to a spot well above the fish and let the fly float down over him naturally.

Make your fly fall on the water lightly (like thistledown). Do not cast so that your line, gut cast and fly, all strike the water at the same time.

Don't raise your hand when the fly falls on the surface as this is liable to cause drag on the fly.

Your first cast is your best chance.

If you make a bad cast, let the fly float down well behind the fish before picking it off the water.

Never cast a longer line than is absolutely necessary.

5. In rapid water, it is usually best to fish upstream with a short line, keeping as much of the cast off the water as you can, and using a good floating fly of the buzz variety.

Avoid having any slack line, by drawing in line with the left hand as the fly floats down, or by raising the rod top.

In very rapid water it pays to float your fly even for a foot or so.

6. When you see the rise of a good fish, mark the place by taking note of the position of a bush or bunch of herbage on the bank; you may want to come back and try him again. A method sometimes adopted by an expert angler on the Irish lakes, when fishing over a bar or bank some distance from the shore, is to tie a thread to a small stone and attach a cork, thus marking the spot.

7. At a waterfall, when other methods fail, it often pays to float a large hackled fly in the eddies by the sides of the falling water.

8. When wading or fishing from the bank, it is a good plan to stand quite still for a few minutes and watch for rising fish; they often move when the water is quiet and undisturbed.

9. In a lake, when fishing from a boat, it is best to anchor the boat and to cast across or into the wind as close as you can (avoid casting straight down-wind).

10. If a fish refuses your fly, it is probably through one of the following causes:

(*a*) The fly is the wrong pattern or size
(*b*) The fly has been badly presented
(*c*) The fish has seen you, your movements, or your shadow.

11. The gut near the fly sometimes curls up into a little arch; opinions are rather divided as to the cause of this arch. It usually occurs when the gut is very dry or of inferior quality.

To remove it, rub it with a bit of india rubber or moisten it well and straighten it out with the fingers.

12. When dry fly fishing and you want to lift the line off the water before making another cast, do not jerk it off suddenly or you will cause considerable strain on the rod; it is better to lift up the rod almost vertical and then make a little flick forward with the top just enough to make a wave in the line. This frees the line from the surface and helps to make it come away easily. This is one of the many tips which G. E. M. Skues has given to fishermen. (To pick off a sunk line, *see page* 210.)

SECTION 3

Notes on Drag

1. When your artificial fly travels faster or slower than the pace of that part of the stream on which it is floating, or when it takes a direction more or less across the current, it is said to drag.

2. One of the chief troubles you have to contend with in dry fly fishing is trying to avoid drag on the fly, until it has floated well below the rising fish.

When casting directly upstream or on still water, drag is not very troublesome.

3. When you are fishing in still water, a deliberate drag or movement of the fly for a *few inches* is often useful to attract a feeding fish.

4. It is not always the dragging fly that frightens the fish, it is more often the zig-zag or unnatural movement of the cast on the surface of the water which causes a fish to become suspicious and puts him down.

5. When fishing in running water, it does not always pay to cast a beautifully straight line.

Some methods of casting a dry fly in order to try and avoid drag are described on pages 227, 228.

SECTION 4

Striking

1. Striking a fish is largely a matter of temperament and practice, an excitable man or a nervous man will always strike too quickly or too hard.

2. More fish are lost by striking too soon than too late.

3. A dry fly strike disturbs the surface and alarms fish much more than the wet fly underwater strike.

4. It is very difficult to lay down rules as to when to strike, the conditions connected with each rise vary so much (*see also pages* 185 *et seq.*).

The following notes may be helpful:

(*a*) Your strike may be fast or slow, but always let it be deliberate.

(*b*) Never strike in a hurry, control yourself at the crucial moment of the rise; probably more fish are lost by momentary lack of personal control than by any other mistake.

(*c*) Never make your strike a 'snatch' or a jerk. Just 'tighten,' 'lift,' or 'draw' on the fish. It is the 'snatch strike' that breaks the gut cast.

(*d*) Always try to tighten on a fish when he is going down after taking your fly – not before. When possible it pays to strike with a downstream horizontal movement of the rod instead of a vertical movement.

(*e*) In slow water strike slowly, as fish here are apt to be deliberate.

In fast water strike more quickly, fish are quicker and more energetic than in a slow flowing stream.

(*f*) With big fish, strike slowly and firmly.

With small fish, strike quickly, especially in
shallow water.

(*g*) If a fish lets the fly pass over him and follows
it downstream, give him time to get it properly
in his mouth before you strike, it is easier for
him to eject it when he is moving downstream
than when he takes it moving upstream.

(*h*) When a trout rising to a dry fly makes just a
little dimple on the surface it is best to strike
quickly.

5. Striking from the reel. This method is all right
under certain conditions (*see page* 186).

(*see page* 186)

SECTION 5

The Qualities of a Dry Fly

Selecting a Fly. Search the stream, bushes, eddies
and the scum, and find out what natural fly the fish
are feeding on; put up an artificial which is similar
in type, size and colour.

Should your imitations of the natural fly fail to
deceive the fish, try some fancy fly to attract him,
such as: a Wickham, a variant, a tup, a black hackle,
a hackle fly of mixed colours. When trout are not
feeding they are more likely to take patterns which
bear no very close resemblance to the natural insect.

The qualities of a dry fly in order of importance are:

(*a*) Form and size
(*b*) Buoyancy
(*c*) Transparency
(*d*) Colour

(*a*) The correct *form* and *size* are the most important qualities in a dry fly.

Trout recognise a fly chiefly by its silhouette or
form, and by the relative size and shape of certain
parts, much more than by its colour, etc.

In a full or rough water, or when fishing upstream in rapid water, you can use a fairly large fly, which should float well out of the water. It is important that a dry fly should fall on the water properly cocked (floating with wings upright). A winged fly is liable to fall on its side or upside down, while a hackle fly, no matter how it falls, will stand upon its hackles. Further, transparency and prismatic lights are better represented by hackles than by feathers. So I think hackle flies are best suited for all dry fly fishing.

(*b*) *Buoyancy.* A dry fly should be built to float well and to dry soon.

It should almost bounce off the water when thrown on the surface. Oiling a fly only renders it waterproof and makes it float longer.

Stiff cock's hackles are best. They should be bright, with spring in them.

The hackles should not be too thickly put on so as to obscure the body of the fly; they should glisten and shine when held up to the light; it adds to their attraction if the centre is darker than the ends.

(*c*) *Transparency.* Hold a natural fly up to the sun and even the transparent body will shew up some sort of colour.

It is important to try to copy this translucent misty colour in the artificial.

Hackle flies represent this transparent effect better than winged flies, as the hackles let the light through better and there is gleam and sparkle in the fibres.

(*d*) The *colour* of an artificial dry fly is really the least important quality, because its colour as seen by the fish changes under the varying conditions of light, etc. The colour is affected by:

    1. The position of the sun at the moment and the amount of reflected light. (The reflection of light off the water causes an artificial fly

floating on the surface to appear much lighter in colour than when it is in the hand.)

2. The background of clouds, sky, etc. It is difficult for a fish to distinguish the colour of a fly by transmitted light (when the light is behind it). If a trout can distinguish the colour of a fly which is opaque it must be the ventral portion.

3. The colour of the bottom and surroundings affect the appearance of the fly as seen by the fish, in a minor degree.

It is a fact that the wings of most natural flies are darker on a dull cloudy day than on a bright sunny day.

There is a great number of patterns of artificial flies on the market.

Avoid filling your fly box with a large variety of patterns; it is better to decide on a few standard patterns and have two or three sizes and dressings of each. These should be quite sufficient for ordinary purposes.

The following are five useful day patterns: medium olive, red quill, iron blue, black hackle, sedges.

For the evening rise: No. 2 red upright or quill, blue upright or quill, tup, blue-winged olive, orange quill No. 2.

After sunset try larger flies, *viz* No. 4 Wickham, coachman, white and brown moth, sedges.

SECTION 6
Notes on Certain Artificial Flies

Here is a rough list of artificial flies which are worth trying during a hatch of certain natural flies. This list is only given as a help in selecting what fly to put up.

It will be noticed that the colours of some of the artificials suggested do not resemble those of the natural insect at all.

During a hatch of *olives* try:
  A dark, medium or light olive
  Blue dun, or quill
  Greenwell
  Hare's ear (gold twist)
  Ginger quill
  Red quill

During a hatch of *iron blues* try:
  An iron blue dun
  Jenny, ruby or claret spinner
  Black hackle red body
  Blue upright red head

During a hatch of *pale wateries* try:
  Pale watery dun or spinner
  Blue upright
  Blue quill

During a hatch of *blue winged olives* try:
  b.w.o dun or spinner
  Orange quill, No. 2
  Red quill, No. 2
  Sherry spinner
  Pheasant tail

During a hatch of *sedges* try:
  A dark, medium, or cinnamon sedge
  A silver or a Kimbridge sedge
  A Welshman's button

During a hatch of *March browns* try:
  A March brown
  A large red spinner

During a rise of *gnats* try:
  An olive, ruby, brown or green gnat
  A black gnat

The following are useful flies to have in your box in case of need: alder, Wickham, variants red and blue, half stone, tup, governor, black hackle.

During a rise of any kind of *dun* its spinner pattern will often be taken better than the dun pattern.

Example:

During a rise of olives try a red quill

    ,,   ,,   iron blues try a jenny spinner, or a claret spinner

    ,,   ,,   b.w.o. try a No. 2 orange quill, or a sherry spinner.

If you know there are fish in a pool but none of them are moving or rising to anything, and you are in doubt as to what fly to put up, just try a red quill or a tup.

SECTION 7

Greases for Line, Cast and Fly

To make your line, cast and fly float properly is very important in dry fly fishing.

Animal or vegetable oils or greases are much better than mineral oils (*i.e.* paraffin or vaseline).

A grease is much better than an oil, as most liquids are liable to leave a film on the water.

The best and safest grease for all purposes is Aspinal's Mucilin (solid).

SECTION 8

Greasing the Line

Always see that it is quite dry. Never grease a wet or even a damp line.

First of all rub the line down with a dry rag to remove any grease, grit or scum from it.

Then rub down about 10 yards of it with mucilin on a rag; go over the line twice and it will float well.

When fishing in still and sheltered water (especially during a dry summer), a scum composed of oil and other greasy matter collects on the surface and a greased line soon gathers it up, causing the line to sink in a most annoying way. Wind also collects scum under certain conditions. The only thing to do is to clean off the scum with a dry rag or a bit of amadou, re-grease it, and begin again.

The reason for this is the skin tension at the surface of the water is destroyed by the coalescence of the grease on the line and the oily scum on the water, causing the line to sink.

For a similar reason, if you want to sink a line, rub it with glycerine, soap, slime or other substance soluble in water·

Always clean your line well with a dry rag every evening after a day's fishing.

Never put away a line with grease on it.

SECTION 9

Drying the Line

During continuous rain, fog, or in very damp weather, a line often gets heavy, semi-waterlogged, sticks in the rings, or won't float well, and no amount of waving it backwards and forwards in the air will dry it.

The only thing to do is to rub it down well with a piece of amadou until dry before you attempt to re-grease it.

SECTION 10

Greasing the Gut Cast

Just rub it down two or three times with solid mucilin on a rag.

Whether you grease the whole of the cast or not depends a good deal on whether you are fishing:

35

    (*a*) In still water, or

    (*b*) In running water.

    (*a*) When fishing in still water, your fly is usually on the small side, and is required to float for some time at the end of a fairly long line. In this case it is better to grease the whole cast up to the fly, so as to make it float on the surface.

    The recovery of the line is easier and cleaner, also the fly is not pulled under water at recovery.

    When, however, the sun is low, and the whole cast is floating, the glint reflected off the sides of the gut is rather conspicuous, and is seen by the fish.

    The thicker the gut the more visible the glint.

    (*b*) When fishing in rapid water and casting across the stream, a complete floating cast as in (*a*) is liable to become like a serpent, zig-zagging about on the surface of the current. Accordingly, to make it shew up a little less, it is best not to grease the last 20 inches of the cast near the floating fly, but to rub this last 20 inches with glycerine or a bit of soap, so as to make it sink just below the surface.

    When casting up-stream, it is also best to leave the last 20 inches ungreased; as you are making frequent short casts and using a slightly larger fly which is not so easily drowned or waterlogged if pulled under.

SECTION 11

Oiling or Greasing the Fly

    A simple fly oiler is made by using a small gramo-phone needle box, with a piece of sponge in it. Melt some mucilin and soak the sponge with it.

    To oil the fly just press it on the sponge, turn it over and do the other side, then take off the super-fluous grease by pressing it in the folds of a handker-chief.

36

A fly must be quite dry before you grease it.

If you dip your flies in ordinary paraffin or flotane liquid and hang them up to dry for twenty-four hours before you want to use them, they will float well for some time without further treatment.

Water, grease or oil alters the colour of the silk bodies of flies when tied on a black hook.

Dunne discovered that if the black hook is painted with a white enamel, the colour of the silk is not much affected and the body assumes a delicate translucent colour like the body of a natural fly.

Bodies of flies made of quill or raffia grass when wet or oiled do not alter their colour so much as silk bodies.

Oil or grease causes the wings of winged flies to lose their iridescence, to look sodden and of a darker colour; so try to oil only the hackles of a winged fly.

Hackle flies take oil or grease best, and the hackles shew up the prismatic lights well.

SECTION 12

Drying the Fly

The ordinary method of drying a fly is by casting in the air backwards and forwards, preferably down wind and not over a rising fish.

If very wet press the fly in a handkerchief or in a bit of amadou (*see page* 388).

After catching a fish the fly must be well washed, dried and re-oiled.

Some anglers change a fly after hooking a fish, putting the old one in the hat for the sun and wind to dry it.

Book I: TROUT FISHING

Part III

RISING AND FEEDING FISH

General Conditions which affect Trout

A trout takes a lure because he is hungry and thinks it is something good to eat, *or* he is attracted by it and desires to investigate it.

A trout is a fish of moods, and the following are roughly the weather and other conditions which induce him to feed or not to feed, to rise or not to rise:

1. Barometric conditions
2. The temperature of the water
3. The oxygen content of the water
4. The height of the water
5. The light conditions
6. The wind conditions

It is usually the most pronounced or prevailing condition of the above which decides him.

During the month of August on most waters (except perhaps on chalk streams) fly fishing during the daytime is rather poor; but it usually improves in the evening and after dark.

Barometric Conditions

Trout are very sensitive to atmospheric pressure. They are really good barometers, as they appear to have some sense which enables them to foretell weather twenty-four hours ahead.

With a *high* or *rising* barometer, there is high or rising pressure on the water. The water at the surface absorbs oxygen from the air, becomes well oxygenated, and fish become lively and inclined to feed.

Flies also hatch out well with a high or rising barometer.

With a *low* or *falling* barometer, there is a reduced pressure of air on the water. The water at the surface gives off oxygen to the air, and there is a paucity of oxygen in the surface water. Fish therefore go towards the bottom which is better oxygenated.

Fish do not rise well to surface food, nor do flies hatch out well with a low barometer (*see page* 74).

Worm fishers prefer a low barometer, as fish are near the bottom (*see also Notes on Barometer, page* 297).

SECTION 3

Temperature of Water

Feeding trout are more affected by the temperature of the water, and the amount of oxygen it contains, than by actual hunger.

When water is at a normal temperature, say 50° to 60°, the fish are comfortable, contented, feed well, and breathing, digestion and process of living are normal. In lakes and open water the normal feeding temperature is usually a little higher, say 65°F, no more.

In warm water (say about 70°), trout have a tendency to a rapid process of living: breathing is fast, they require more oxygen (and there is a deficiency in warm water), they easily get out of breath, digestion is slow, they cease to desire food and practically take none.

All animals like heat, but it makes them stupid and languid. (Example, a dog before a hot fire – same with a fish.)

In cold water (say about 44°) trout have a tendency to a slow process of living: they breathe slowly, consume or require less oxygen, digestion is quick, appetite fails, they cease feeding even when ample food is available, they become sluggish and languid, and in a cold winter trout may almost be said to hibernate at the bottom of the deep pools.

Most flies do not hatch out well in cold water.

After a frosty night, fishing is never good until the sun has warmed up the water to about normal temperature.

In a stream the temperature of running water is about the same throughout.

In lakes and ponds the temperature of the water varies in the deeps and shallows.

Deep water heats slowly and retains the heat.

Shallow water heats quickly and cools quickly.

The temperature at the surface is important, and is affected by frost, evaporation, wind and sun's heat. The temperature of the water in a lake varies in a surprising degree between its bed and its surface.

A layer of cold water will sink beneath any layer of water below it which is warmer.

So movements of warm and cold water are con-continually taking place even in an apparently still sheet of water.

When the upper surface is fairly warm, trout tend to come to the surface and rise well.

When the water at the surface is cold, trout keep down towards the bottom.

A rough rule is, in cold weather fish deep and slowly, in warm weather fish your flies near the surface.

In taking the temperature of water in a lake during a spell of hot weather, if the temperature is say 60° at 12 feet, it should be about 70° near the surface: this of course is too hot (*see page* 40).

Trout are very sensitive to a rise or fall of temperature; indeed the rise or fall should be very gradual or it affects their vitality and feeding. Any sudden rise or fall of temperature causes fish great uneasiness, lowers their vitality and is often fatal.

The effect is more serious in still water than in a stream.

In tropical climates, a sudden fall of hail in a pond has been known to kill nearly all the fish in it.

When a good rise of fish stops suddenly, it is often due to a sudden change of temperature and not to any whims of the fish; or perhaps it may be due to the nymphs having suddenly ceased to hatch out and there is little or nothing for the fish to rise to. For a similar reason when a rise of fish commences suddenly it may be that the nymphs have commenced to hatch out and the fish are feeding on them (*see also* Note *on page* 74).

SECTION 4

Oxygen Content of Water

Fish have to depend for their existence on the amount of dissolved oxygen in water, which varies constantly from different causes. They turn sulky and go off their feed when there is a lack of oxygen, and when there is a considerable deficiency they get out of breath, avoid unnecessary movement, become languid and will not feed at all (*see also page* 315).

Some of the causes of an excess or deficiency of oxygen in water are:

1. When water is overheated it gives off much of its oxygen to the air. When water is cooled it takes up oxygen from the air.

2. Warm water can only hold about 6% of oxygen, while cold water will hold about 10%.

3. In strong sunlight green water plants give off oxygen which is absorbed in the water. On the other

hand decomposing vegetable matter absorbs oxygen from the water.

4. With a high barometer the water on the surface takes up oxygen from the air. With a low barometer the water on the surface gives off oxygen to the air.

5. Under a waterfall water is well oxygenated. A good wind causing 'white horses' oxygenates the surface of the water.

6. Pike and perch suffer less from lack of oxygen or sudden changes of temperature than do carp or roach.

(For further notes on oxygen *see page* 420).

(For further notes on oxygen *see page* 420).

SECTION 5
Height of Water

1. In a flood or big spate trout take shelter from the current in the deep holes and sheltered parts of the stream. On the second or third day after a flood (the first day is of little use) they move about again and commence to feed well.

2. When there is a gradual rise of water in a lake, trout feed well round the shores over the newly covered land. When, however, there is a *permanent* rise in the level of water in a lake or pond (say 2 or 3 ft), trout are liable to become mid-water and bottom feeders until such time as they get accustomed to the new conditions and this often takes some time.

I have in mind the permanent rise of 4 ft in Lough Derg owing to the Shannon Electric Scheme.

3. When water is *rapidly* rising or falling in a lake or stream trout seldom feed well.

4. When the water of a stream is high but clear, trout keep down near the bottom. They feed all right, but you have to sink your lure well.

5. When water is at a normal height, fishing is best.

(For further notes on water *see page* 313).

SECTION 6

Light Conditions

1. Light is only an incidental factor in good or bad fishing.

Transparency and illumination of water are two quite different conditions: water can remain clear and transparent for weeks, while illumination may vary from hour to hour with the sunlight.

2. A bright spot in a cloudy sky through which concentrated rays of sunlight pour, causes a sort of reflection in the water.

There is reflection when water assumes an unnatural clearness and every stone in the bottom of a pool is clearly visible, and you can see your line and cast clearly under water.

When water assumes this unnatural clearness I have noticed that overhanging trees and bushes throw little or no reflection in the water.

3. When there is reflection or shadow in the water, fish become shy, come short to the fly, and do not rise freely. There is usually a bright hard glare on the water which is always bad for fishing.

4. Trout dislike continuous strong sunshine, and seek the shade of trees, banks, deep holes. In very bright continuous sunshine they are liable to become partially blind (*see also page* 411). However, on a hot sunny day they like to warm their tummies on a gravelly shallow, but when they do so they become languid and won't feed well.

5. The sun's rays pass through the water and are 'reflected from' and 'heat up' the bottom.

The *light rays* are reflected from the bottom on to
the under surface of the water, and the fish sees your
underwater lure chiefly against the reflection.

The *heat rays* are absorbed into, and heat up, the
bottom, which in turn heats up the water.

A dark coloured bottom absorbs heat better than a
light coloured bottom.

6. A good wind neutralises the effect of a strong
light, as it breaks up the surface of the water and the
rays of light, so the fish are not much dazzled by the
light.

7. The best light for fishing is a diffused light,
i.e. a dull light through clouds, a clouded sun, the
light at dusk.

A clouded sunset is better than a clear sunset.

When, however, there are heavy
black clouds about, or misty clouds
hanging on the hill tops, the
attendant atmospheric conditions
usually put fish down. It is not
the light that does it.

8. The position of the sun is important. A good position is when
the sun is behind and well to the
side of the fisherman, *i.e.* when the angle SBA=40°.

9. Good light conditions are when reflection is
absent and there is no glint from your line or your
cast, and no shadows are thrown on the surface or
down through the water.

You should be unable to see your line and cast
clearly when in the water; this is usually the case in
a good diffused light.

10. When drifting in a boat towards the sun, you
often see 'lanes of light' in the water; these really
don't affect the fishing, as when drifting with your

back to the sun there are no 'lanes of light' to be
seen.

(For further notes on light *see page* 316).

SECTION 7

Wind Conditions

1. Wind (warm or cold) aerates and freshens
water.

In a strong wind the surface of the water becomes
well aerated, absorbs oxygen from the air, and this
helps to make trout lively and inclined to feed.
On a rough windy day, either on a river or a lake you
will usually find the big fish on the move.

2. A steady true wind from any point is all right,
but a gusty, squally, or 'close' wind is not good for
any sort of fishing.

3. A strong light should have a strong wind to
neutralise the light effect. The wind ruffles the
surface of the water, causing flickering lights and
shadows on the bottom which help to hide the falsity
of the lure.

4. Other conditions being equal, a S or W wind,
which is mild and warm, is better than a N or E
wind, which is usually cooler and drier.

5. It is little use fishing on a lake with a wet fly
unless there is a good breeze to ruffle the surface.

6. When drifting with the wind in a boat, and the
sun is directly behind you (*i.e.* the wind is blowing
from the sun), you are rather handicapped as the fish
have their heads up-wind, are facing the sun, and
cannot see your fly distinctly. (A wind blowing
towards the sun would be better).

7. With a dry wind, the wings of freshly hatched
flies dry quickly, and the fly only remains on the

46

surface a very short time, so the fish have not much of a chance.

With a moist wind the wings dry slowly, the fly has to remain on the water longer, and the fish have a much better chance.

(For further notes on wind *see page* 301).

SECTION 8
The Stages of the Rise

A rise of fish may roughly be divided into four stages, thus:

1st Stage. Fish are *bulging*, darting about in the shallows and among the weeds, not quite breaking the water, taking rising nymphs in mid-water.

2nd Stage. Fish are taking duns on the surface (usually a good rise of fish).

3rd Stage. Later they commence taking spinners on the surface.

4th Stage. Eventually they take to grubbing in the bottom among the weeds for larvæ and shrimps, etc.

A *cruiser* makes a wedge-shaped ripple on-the surface.

Smutting fish are taking very minute insects on the surface, making just a dimple of a rise.

SECTION 9
Different Sorts of Rises

1. Nervous and short-rising trout. On certain days trout in a stream appear to be very easily scared. When you approach the bank they rush off at once, cease feeding and remain still as if glued to the bottom. They have become alert and watchful and seem to concentrate their whole attention on you and on their surroundings and not on passing food.

47

On such days the whole underwater population appears to be on the *qui vive*; the weather conditions are usually as follows:

    (*a*) The water is clear and highly illuminated

    (*b*) There is a glassy glare on the surface

    (*c*) The day is dull and heavy with a falling barometer

    (*d*) Your line and cast shew up clearly in the water

These conditions are often the cause of short rises; the fish are nervous, timid and undecided as regards food, and they turn short or rise short at your fly.

A trout feeding in the centre of a stream is usually more suspicious and difficult to catch than one which is feeding close to the bank.

2. Surface rises in a stream.

    (*a*) A *big* rise with a kidney-shaped whorl is made to large spinners and large flies

    (*b*) A *sucking* rise is made to medium sized floating flies

    (*c*) A *sipping* rise is made to small midges and small flies

    (*d*) A *slash* rise is made to moving sedges, etc, blown along the water

    (*e*) A *head and tail* rise is usually made to spinners and duns just on the surface film

Bubbles on the water – when a trout takes a fly on the surface with a suck and also takes in some air; he retains the fly and ejects the air, hence the bubbles.

3. The method of taking *surface food* depends very much on the depth the fish is suspended below the surface.

    (*a*) If he is 3 or more feet down, he rushes up, opening his mouth, extending his gills as he reaches the surface, and making a good 'splash' rise.

(b) If he is only a few inches below the surface, he sucks the fly down quickly, just breaking the water with his tail; he then swings round and takes up his original position.

4. *Underwater food* is taken in one of two ways:

(a) By sucking the fly into his mouth with a current of water and passing the water out through his gills

(b) By rushing at the fly and when about 2 feet away, opening his mouth wide and extending his gills, allowing the water to pass freely into the mouth and out at the gills.

There must be a current of water into a fish's mouth or it is not possible for him to take in food (*see also page* 487).

5. When taking food off the bottom a fish turns over, taking it with the side of his mouth.

6. A trout often takes a nymph just as it gets to the surface. The late Colonel Harding in his book explains this as follows:

'A trout sees the reflection of the ascending nymph on the under-surface of the water and takes it on the surface as it meets its own reflection.' He also points out that the back of an artificial nymph is important as it is the reflection of the back which the trout usually sees.

SECTION 10

Fish following the Lure

1. A 'following fish' is undecided and suspicious about the lure, it is not quite to his liking. The farther a fish follows your lure the less likely he is to take it.

49

On a 'hard' day you are more likely to meet following fish than on a 'soft' day.

2. It is only when fish are near the surface that you can see the wave of a following fish.

The number of fish that follow your lure when fishing deep is very considerable; you do not see or feel them.

3. A following trout will sometimes take a lure if you stop it for a second or so, or slow it down.

If you do this with a following pike, he will not take, but goes off at once.

SECTION II

Short Rising Fish

The following are some of the reasons which may cause a trout to rise short or miss your fly.

1. When fish are nervous or alarmed (*see pages* 47, 48).

2. When the size, colour, or dressing of your fly is not right or when the fly is not properly presented trout become suspicious and turn short of it.

3. When the light is bad and the vision of the fish is blurred by glare or bright light, or the angle of reflected light is wrong, they make a bad shot at the fly.

4. When the temperature of the water is very high or very low, fish become lethargic and lazy and miss the fly through want of effort.

5. When water is low and clear and running slow, fish have a better chance of examining your fly, detecting the deception and changing their mind.

6. With a natural floating fly, a fish often takes it with a 'sip'; with an artificial attached to gut a

harder 'suck' is required to overcome the surface friction, and the fish gets suspicious; or perhaps the volume of water taken into the fish's mouth fails to carry the fly with it.

7. In July, August and September you are more likely to meet short rising fish than in April, May or June.

8. When fish are rising short:

(a) Try sinking your fly well and fishing slow

(b) Try fishing the dropper 6 inches under the surface

(c) Try a fly with no dressing above the dotted line, as A. A sneck bend hook is an advantage

(d) When fish are rising short, jumping over your fly or hitting it with their tail, don't strike or tighten until you *feel* a fish. Give him time.

9. When a trout is alarmed, nervous, watching for enemies and has ceased to feed, and a lure comes in sight, then the trout's voracious appetite overcomes him and he rushes at the lure, but suspicion of danger causes him to turn short, and he rises short and misses the lure.

SECTION 12

Feeding Trout in Streams and Lakes

1. A trout rises to a fly or takes a lure for one of the following reasons:

(a) *Hunger*; because it appears like something good to eat

(b) *Curiosity*; it attracts him and he desires to investigate it (*c*) *Tyranny*; it looks like something alive and in distress

(*d*) *Jealousy*; others in the pool may get it before him.

2. In a rapid stream, trout are quick risers, as they wait for the current to bring them their food, and they must seize it before it has passed by.

In a lake, trout cruise about in search of food. They take the fly more leisurely and then turn to go down, so give them time in the strike.

The larger the trout the more deliberate the rise, and the slower should be the strike.

3. In a lake, trout usually feed and rise better in the shallows along the shore than in the very deep water.

4. A trout hovering in mid water with quivering fins is a feeding fish. He is not very easily scared. His eyes are focused on the surface and on his immediate vicinity on the lookout for food.

5. A *bulging* fish is one that (without breaking the water) is chasing active nymphs before they reach the surface, causing a series of humps on the surface as the fish darts about below.

6. A *tailing* fish is one that is grubbing in the bottom among the weeds for larvæ, shrimps, snails, etc, keeping an almost vertical position by flexions of the body and in shallow water shewing his tail above the surface.

7. All nature rests for a bit in the middle of the day; trout are no exception: they usually rest from say one to three in the afternoon. About 2 p.m. is usually a good time for lunch.

8. For a fish to be properly on the feed, the temperature of the water, the oxygen content, and conditions generally, should be normal and such as to make him feel comfortable and contented.

9. I have noticed that a brown trout in a lake usually comes at a fly from below, thus:

while a rainbow and sea trout come at the fly thus:

Book I: TROUT FISHING

Part IV

ARTIFICIAL FLIES

SECTION I

General Notes on Stream and Lake Flies

In arranging flies for both stream and lake fishing I think it is best to keep them sorted by *colours* in boxes or on strips of paper. You can pick out a March brown or other imitation of the natural fly quite quickly if your flies are arranged by colour as under:

> Clarets and reds, browns, greens and olives, yellows, blacks, blues, nymphs, palmers, various.

There are so many local and fancy names for artificial flies that I find that this method of keeping them arranged by colours is the simplest way in the end.

To protect artificial flies against moths the following sprinkled over the flies in a box will help to keep moth away:

1. Bits of dry cigar ends from a cigar cutter crushed up to powder or even a little snuff will do, or white pepper.

2. Epsom Salts is also effective. Naphthaline and camphor will keep moths away, but they have a tendency to tarnish tinsel-bodied flies.

   If salmon flies are kept in folded paper packets moths seldom attack them.

The qualities of a wet fly in order of importance are:

(*a*) Form and size
(*b*) Movement
(*c*) Colour
(*d*) Transparency.

For the qualities of a dry fly *see page* 30.

Definitions

A *skirting* fly is one which throws off a V-shaped wave when worked on the surface.

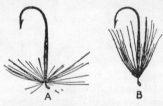

A fly with *kick* when fished downstream or drawn quickly through still water will have what is called a 'bad entry.'

Kick in a fly is usually made by turns of silk behind the hackle to make each fibre stand out (*see diagram* A).

All hackle flies fished upstream should have kick to enable them to keep their shape in the turmoil of the stream and to appear alive and struggling.

A good entry : A wet fly which swims naturally and smoothly when drawn through the water is said to have a good entry. It must offer very little resistance to the water and cause or carry no air bubbles (*see diagram* B).

A fly with soft hackles or sloping penthouse wings (the alder type) fished downstream has a 'good entry.'

A fly with stiff hackles or upright stiff wings when fished downstream causes resistance and has a 'bad entry.'

It is claimed that flies on hooks tied to gut have a better 'entry' when fished underwater than flies tied on eyed hooks, this may be so in a small degree.

A fly tied on a hook with a down-turned eye has really very little effect on the entry, provided the knot is properly made. It is certainly more convenient to use, is easily changed, is more economical and lasts longer.

SECTION 2

STREAM FLIES

Type of Fly

There are two types:

(1) *Deceivers* – imitations of the natural fly. A fly
to excite the fishes' hunger. Usually a fly
the colour of which is in harmony with the
surroundings. Is generally used in slow
streams where fish have lots of time to examine
it.

(2) *Attractors* – a gaudy coloured fly, or tinsel
flies with glitter, to catch the eye of a fish,
usually a fly in contrast with the colour of the
surroundings. Is generally used in rapid
water where fish have little time to examine
it.

In *thick* water or on a very windy day, use a large
dragging gaudy fly. Give plenty of motion to attract.

In *thin* water and little wind use a small sparsely
dressed fly to imitate the natural and to deceive.

The fly should suit the water. In still water it
should not offer resistance or cause or carry bubbles.
It should have a 'good entry.' Example: alder type
with sloping wings *not* the stiff hackle type.

In running water fished *upstream*, a fly should keep
its shape well, should have 'kick' with stiff shiny
cock's hackles.

Fished *downstream* a fly should have a good entry,
offer no resistance and carry no bubbles. Wings
sloping back like an alder or soft hen hackles.

A fly fished in slow water shows better movement
than one fished in running water, as the wings and
hackle open and close better. In running water the
feathers are compressed together by the stream.

SECTION 3

STREAM FLIES

Colour of Fly

A sunk fly is seen by a fish against the reflection of the bottom on to the under surface of the water or against the sunlight from above.

    1. In selecting a fly consider:

      (a) The colour of bottom
      (b) The colour of the water
      (c) The background of light, sky, clouds
      (d) The position of the sun or light

    2. Consider whether you wish the colour of your flies to be in harmony with or in contrast to the colour of the surroundings.

    (a) Example, if '*in harmony*':

Use a red or orange fly	{ In reddish peaty water Red coloured bottom A dark day
Use a blackish or brown fly	{ Brown coloured bottom Water the colour of whey Under shade of trees A dark day
Use a yellowish fly or blue zulu	{ Clear water Sandy bottom Bright day
Use a greenish fly	{ Over green weeds Weedy bottom Bright day

Many anglers use flies in harmony with the light, *viz*:

      Bright weather – bright fly.
      Dull weather – dark fly.

(*b*) Example if '*in contrast*' to colour of sur-roundings.

Use a dark fly
   black, brown,
   claret
{ In bright weather
Clear water
Light coloured bottom
Green weedy bottom

Use a light
   coloured fly,
   yellows, light
   blues, light
   greens
} In dull weather
Coloured water
Dark coloured bottom

The appearance of a fly when being fished varies with the relative position of the sun or light from above.

When the fish is between the fly and the sun the colour of the fly shows up well and is attractive.

When the fly is between the fish and the sun the fly appears indistinct and ghost-like.

In diffused light (*i.e.* in evening or on a cloudy day) a fish can see the colour of your fly much better than in bright sunlight.

Water has a dulling effect on the colour of all artificial sunk flies. So to brighten them up it is an advantage to have a little gold or silver tinsel or wire, a dubbing of seal's fur or pig's wool, a yellow or red tag, etc.

Trout appear to be sensitive to or attracted by a bit of red colour in a fly, under most conditions.

In high, coloured water it often pays to use a large gay coloured fly (a large Wickham or a tinsel-bodied fly) dressed with 'kick' to attract.

In clear, low, water it pays to use a small dark sparsely dressed fly (a black hackle or other dark fly).

See also a trout's sense of colour, *page* 486.

SECTION 4

STREAM FLIES

Size of Fly

The size is very important.

A trout sees the silhouette of the non-transparent parts of a fly against the light in the 'cone of vision' or against the reflection of the bottom on the under-surface of the water, and recognises it by its shape, size, and general outline, more than by its colour or anything else.

The size of a fly to be used depends a great deal on the light, the water and wind conditions. It should be just large enough to attract and *not* too large so as to scare the fish.

Generally speaking:

    You can use a large fly, 12, 14 hook

    (*a*) When fishing upstream

    (*b*) In heavy or coloured water

    (*c*) In a good wind

    (*d*) On a cloudy day

    (*e*) When water is cold.

    You should use a small fly, 15, 16 hook

    (*a*) When fishing downstream

    (*b*) On a bright day

    (*c*) When water is warm or clear

    (*d*) When there is little wind.

The size of an artificial fly should be if anything a little smaller than the natural. I seldom use a hook smaller than No. 16 or 0. (*See* Scale of Hooks, *page* 347).

SECTION 5

STREAM FLIES

Dressings

Trout do not always take a sunk artificial fly for a drowned winged insect. In nine cases out of ten they take your sunk fly for a nymph larva, water insect, or even a small fish.

The majority of wet artificial flies should therefore be dressed to imitate the natural fly before it has assumed the winged stage.

A wet fly should be rather sparsely dressed in wing and hackle so as to show up the body. Most shop flies are too heavily winged and hackled.

The material should be able to take up water.

Dubbed bodies are better than quill bodies.

The hackles of wet flies must not be gummy and stick together, they should separate out in the water and show life and movement. For wet flies fished downstream hen's hackles are better than cock's.

For upstream fishing cock's hackles which are stiff and glisten and shine are preferable to hen's hackles, as they keep their shape in the turmoil of the stream better and give the fly more 'kick' (*see page* 56).

A little gold or silver or coloured ribbing is always an improvement to counteract the dulling effect of the water.

The wing should seldom exceed the bend of the hook. (*See B in diagram, page* 51).

A silk bodied fly loses its colour when oiled or wet. The black hook shows up through the silk (*see page* 37).

SECTION 6

STREAM FLIES

Flies and Trial Casts Recommended

If you know what fly or insect the fish are feeding on of course put up an imitation of it. If not, try the following method:

Make up three or four casts of flies of different colours and see which fly is preferred, *viz*:

March brown (Tail)		Snipe and purple (Tail)	
Greenwell	D	Olive dun	D
Blue dun	D	Red quill	D
Part. and yellow	T	Hare's ear	T
Grannom	D	Blue upright	D
Black gnat	D	March brown	D

A very favourite cast in south of Ireland is:

> T. Orange grouse
> D. Green wren
> D. Hare's ear

If March brown preferred, try March brown, hare's ear, woodcock and hare's ear.

If red quill preferred, try red spinner, red ant, red palmer.

If partridge and yellow preferred, try orange grouse, Wickham, partridge and yellow.

Remember the right fly is:

> (a) The fly you have most faith in
> (b) The one which the trout find is the right size and colour.

A rise of dark olives, try a light olive, and *vice versa*.

A rise of iron blues, try

> Iron blue hackle (red head)
> Black hackle, red body

A rise of March browns, try

> Hare's ear (gold twist)
> Pheasant tail
> Black hackle, silver body
> Sedges

A rise of blue or olive duns, try various shades and sizes.

Some expert fishermen use only four flies of different sizes all the season, *viz :* March brown, red quill, Greenwell, black hackle orange body.

As the size of the artificial fly is so important, the following is worth trying (suppose March browns are about):

Make up a cast of 3 March browns,
> put a small one on the tail
>   ,, a size larger on the 2nd dropper
>   ,, a size still larger on top dropper.

SECTION 7

STREAM FLIES

Droppers and Tail Flies

Tail flies should have a good entry and should be tied on longish hooks. The fly with the heaviest iron should be on the tail, *viz :* Invicta, palmers, alder, small salmon flies.

Droppers should represent active insects which settle or buzz on the surface, should be chunky hackle flies on ordinary short hooks.

Put your best flies on the tail and top dropper and put an experimental fly on the middle dropper.

SECTION 8

STREAM FLIES

Notes on Individual Flies

The names and appearance of imitations of the natural fly, such as March brown, olives, sedges, etc, are of course well known. But the names of many of the fancy flies convey very little to some fishermen. That is why I find it best to sort and keep flies by colours and disregard the various fancy names by which they are known in different localities (*see page 55*).

Many of the fancy flies kill better on certain occasions than the exact imitation of the natural insect.

March brown. In early spring a claret or green body is best.

Later in season a chocolate or orange or purple body is preferred.

Gold ribbing is a useful addition.

There are two flies of similar appearance but of different species both of which are called March brown, *viz*:

> *i.* A fly *Rhithrogena Haarupi*, which appears in March and April in hatches of thousands.
>
> *ii.* A fly *Ecdyurus Venosis*, which appears during the summer months in dribbling hatches.

Pheasant tail – the spinner of the March brown. It also represents some nymphs.

Hare's ear, a good all round fly, useful in spring during a rise of olives.

A little gold twist is necessary.

Greenwell. Very good fly on most waters. Best where fished upstream and on cold days. Represents olives, b.w.o., iron blues.

Coachman. A very good evening fly, best as a tail fly. A dark coachman is a good all round fly.

Nymphs are best as tail flies – sink them well, allow them to swim naturally with the stream, do not jerk the rod top at all. Strike quickly.

Likely places are alongside of or at the tail of a weed bed or where a burn enters the main stream.

In fast water you can use a larger nymph than in an easy stream.

There is a great variety of artificial nymphs, the following are always worth trying, *viz*:

A tup – pheasant tail – Dunn's b.w.o. nymph – half stone – dotterel hackle.

Many hackle flies tied with soft hackles represent nymphs.

Most artificial nymphs have a thick bunch of fine fur to represent the thorax and very spare short-fibred hackles.

A loaded nymph is worth trying when you want to fish very deep, it is made by wrapping a few turns of thin wire round the shank of the hook when dressing the fly.

Wickham. A very good fancy fly. In heavy water on a cold windy day a large Wickham is very useful, fished deep.

If you cut the wings off a large Wickham, it makes a very good palmer. When gold bodied flies are accepted by the fish it is always worth while trying a Wickham on the middle dropper.

Invicta. Best as a tail fly. Ogden's *Invicta* is the best pattern. Ogden's sizes are:

No 2 very small about No 13 hook
No 4   ,,   ,,   about No 9 hook
No 6
No 8
No 10 very large hook.

Snipe and purple. A very good all round York-shire fly. Useful on a cold day.

Hardy's favourite. A useful general fly.

Alder. Useful in May, June and July under bushes. A land fly, best in a breeze. Hackle alder is best, dressed as follows:

Dressing: Body, a few strands from a cock pheasant's tail feather ribbed with well waxed mulberry silk. Hackle, a dark dun cock's with rusty brown tips.

N.B. Put a foundation of the mulberry silk on the hook so as to make a good fat body.

Poole's fancy represents a black water beetle. It is a black fly with a small white tag. Best on a dull day in a full stream.

Pope's nondescript. Useful fished wet upstream to bulging fish.

The Grannom. This fly has a bunch of green floss silk at the end of the body to represent the egg sac of the female.

The natural fly is very numerous on some streams in April and May. It is a species of sedge.

SECTION 9

LAKE FLIES

Type of Fly

Flies for lake fishing can be divided into two types:

1. *Standard* patterns representing natural insects. Usually chunky flies fished as droppers.
   Example : clarets, browns, olives
2. *Tinsel* patterns, tied on long hooks, representing some larva or small fish. Usually fished as a tail fly.
   Example : Invicta, gold and silver bodied flies, dusty miller.

Lake flies can also be divided into *Deceivers* and *Attractors* the same as with stream flies (*see page* 57).

All lake flies fished as tail flies should have a 'good entry' (*see page* 56).

Lake fishing is more of a 'chuck and chance it' style of fishing than stream fishing; indeed many of the standard lake flies may be regarded as nothing more than lures to attract the attention or excite the curiosity of the trout.

SECTION 10

LAKE FLIES

Colour of Fly

The notes on the colour of stream flies apply equally to wet lake flies (*see page* 58).

The volume and open expanse of water, the effect of light, the position of the sun, the strength and direction of the wind, the prevailing tint or colour of nature, all these have much to do with the right colour of an artificial lake fly.

It is always worth considering whether the colour of your fly should be in harmony or contrast with

1. The colour of the water or the bottom
2. The background of light, clouds, etc
3. The prevailing colour or tint of nature, such as the colour of the weeds, flowers, foliage in the water or on the banks.

In many cases I have found that the colour of a lake fly which is in *harmony* with the colour of the surroundings kills better than a fly which is in contrast with that colour.

Here are just three examples (Ireland:)

i. Lough Derg=red peaty water, clarets and reddish flies kill best
ii. In the hill lakes of Connemara where the bottom is dark, with black rocks about, dark coloured flies kill best (Connemara black, butcher and black Pennell)
iii. Lough Carna (near Ballinrobe) the limestone bottom of which is covered with a carpet of light green moss and weeds: I found the killing fly was one with a silver body and a pale green hackle.

SECTION 11

LAKE FLIES

Size of Fly

As with stream flies, the size is very important (*see page* 60).

The normal size is No 10, 12. In rough windy weather or coloured water you can use Nos 6, 7, 8.

On a bright day with a breeze, a No 9 or 10, sombre coloured fly, well sunk, is about right.

On a dull cold 'hard' day it pays to use a vulgar gaudy fly size No 7 or 8 on the tail fished fast as an attractor, or an attractive hackled bob fly, fished on the surface and ignore the others.

As a rule you use a smaller and darker fly about mid-day than you would use in the morning and afternoon.

SECTION 12

LAKE FLIES

Dressings

The dressing of lake flies is similar to stream flies (*see page* 60).

The end of the wing should not extend beyond the bend of the hook, thus:

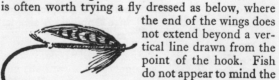

For short rising fish it is often worth trying a fly dressed as below, where

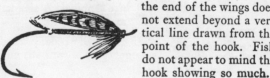

the end of the wings does not extend beyond a vertical line drawn from the point of the hook. Fish do not appear to mind the hook showing so much.

68

Droppers should be hackle flies not too heavily hackled (so as to show up the body).

Tail flies should have a good entry, sloping wings, sparsely dressed on long hooks.

For flies used in evening and night fishing on a lake (see page 95).

Here are three typical lake flies (the dressing of which Mr. Leonard West gave me). I have found them most useful in say May, June, July. They are supposed to represent types of natural insects which frequent lakes in those months.

No 1. Representing the March brown, turkey brown, etc, type of fly.

Body – a warm brown or yellow, always ribbed with gold wire, tinsel or coloured ribbing.

Thorax – fairly large, of peacock herl.

Wings and legs – longish partridge or grouse hackle (speckled).

Tails – pheasant whisks speckled.

Tied on a longish hook this is a good type of tail fly.

No 2. Representing the sedge type of fly, etc.

Body – turkey or green herl, a short thick body, plenty of gold ribbing.

Wings and legs – grouse or cinnamon hackle.

A chunky fly – no whisks.

A good type of dropper.

No 3. Representing various gnats.

Body – of different colours, red, purple, green, etc, with thin gold wire ribbing. A slender body with a big thorax of green herl.

Wings and legs – snipe or partridge hackle.

A good dropper.

SECTION 13

LAKE FLIES

Flies and Trial Casts Recommended

If there is a particular fly on the water, of course put up an imitation of that fly (usually as a dropper), if not use trial casts and find out what flies the fish prefer.

Casts suggested:

Mallard and claret	T	Dusty miller	T
Butcher or Devil dodger	D	Wickham or Peter Ross	D
March brown	D	Golden olive or blue zulu	D
Invicta or Scorcher	T	Thunder & lightning or Lady Caroline	T
Orange grouse	D	Woodcock and green	
Nondescript	D	Teal and red	
		Teal and green	D
		Greenwell	D

When the water is at all coloured, a black fly with gold or silver ribbing on the body is worth trying on any lake.

I presume the ribbing divides the body so that the fly resembles some sort of nymph with the light shewing through the body segments.

If the water is peaty and reddish I think the gold ribbing is preferable.

A hackle fly with a claret or yellow body and a hackle of blended colours (red, blue, yellow, etc) is a useful fly to try as a dropper. On Loughs Mask and Corrib they are called 'Nondescripts.'

Where sticklebacks are plentiful, dusty miller and thunder and lightning are good flies.

When perch fry is about a Lady Caroline is a good imitation.

An imitation of the female Great Red Sedge (*Phryganea grandis*) is a very useful fly, fished dry in the evening during May, June, or July. In Ireland it is called 'the Murrough.'

One fly on a 6-ft cast is best (when there are many weeds about).

Two flies are enough on a 6-ft cast.

Three flies   ,,   ,,   9-ft ,,

When rowing from one place to another on a lake it often pays to trail a large tinsel-bodied fly with a good entry behind the boat – 30 or 40 yards of line out. Fish deep. Row slow.

Favourite flies for May, June, July in various districts are:

Galway – Connemara black

L. Corrib – Golden olive, clarets

Yorkshire – Snipe and purple

Scotland – Peter Ross

L. Derg – Clarets, the murrough

Blagdon – Dusty miller, thunder and lightning

Devonshire – Blue dun and quill

L. Mask – Fiery brown, mallard and claret.

I have noticed that local fishermen in the west of Ireland always prefer an artificial fly to have a little blue jay in the hackle, or even in the wing.

SECTION 14

LAKE FLIES

Droppers and Tail Flies

The notes on stream flies (dropper and tail flies, *page* 63) apply also to wet lake flies.

On an ordinary cast:

The heaviest fly should be on the tail – it should be your best fly – and should have a good entry.

F

The next heaviest fly should be the second or
middle dropper and may be an experimental
fly.

The lightest fly should be on the top dropper –
should be a chunky fly representing some
natural insect on the water.

Roughly speaking:

1. On a 'hard' day (usually a cold N or E wind
   and a hard glassy light) fish the dropper along
   the surface and neglect the others.
2. Fish the tail fly on a 'soft' day (usually
   warmish mild S or W wind – cloudy).

On a bright day or when fish are coming short,
try a small tail fly and a larger fluffy dropper, light
in the iron. The dropper acts as a fish finder or
attractor.

Book I: TROUT FISHING

Part V

NATURAL INSECTS

73

SECTION I

The Process of Insect Development

There are two processes by which nature works in the development of insects to their ultimate form:

(1) The complete metamorphosis
(2) The incomplete   ,,

1. The complete metamorphosis is that adopted by moths, butterflies, etc.

(*a*) The egg
(*b*) The larva or caterpillar, changing to
(*c*) The pupa or chrysalis, changing to
(*d*) The imago or perfect insect.

2. The incomplete metamorphosis is that adopted by Ephemeridæ and other water-born flies:

(*a*) The egg
(*b*) The nymph, which feeds voraciously and grows rapidly (through the larval and pupal stages). There are various sorts of nymphs; some dig, some swim, and some crawl about. The nymph eventually changes to sub-imago and then to
(*c*) The imago or perfect fly.

Note. Hatching nymphs are extremely sensitive to atmospheric and other conditions. Sudden changes of quite a trivial nature will bring on a hatch or cause it to cease with astonishing rapidity.

The following are favourable conditions for a good hatch of fly:

(*a*) A high or rising barometer
(*b*) A sunny day (a good light is important)
(*c*) Soft mild weather
(*d*) Warmish water

The wings of flies hatched out on a dull cold day

are darker in colour than those hatched on a bright, warm, sunny day.

The imagos of *Ephemeridæ* do not feed in the winged state, while the imagos of land flies do.

SECTION 2

Types which interest Trout

There are few insects which settle on the water that a trout will not rise to or anyhow investigate. There are, however, five types of flies in which trout take a special interest, *viz :*

(1) *Ephemeridæ*, flies with cocked wings like a butterfly; the Mayfly type

(2) *Trichoptera*, sedge fly type, with penthouse hairy wings, no setæ, two antennæ, four wings and a small head

(3) *Sialidæ* (alder), penthouse clear wings, no setæ, two antennæ, four wings and a large head

(4) *Perlidæ* (willow fly type), four long narrow wings folded horizontally

(5) *Diptera* (house fly type), two wings folded horizontally; mostly land flies which are blown on to the water. There are, however, water-born species.

SECTION 3

Stages in the Life of Waterside Insects

a. THE EPHEMERIDÆ

1st Stage : Very small eggs are deposited on the water by the imago. They sink to the bottom. Some are deposited singly, some *en bloc*. Some imagos dive to the bottom with an air bubble and deposit the eggs in selected places. Eggs hatch out in about forty days into very small nymphs.

2nd Stage : The nymph eats enormously, grows rapidly, some crawl or swim about, others dig into the bottom. All nymphs have three setæ, some lose one later. They change their skin several times to suit their growth. Finally they go to the surface, the skin splits and the dun emerges.

3rd Stage : The sub-imago or dun. This stage lasts about twenty-four hours, when the dun makes a complete change of its skin, including the skin of the wings, and becomes an imago.

4th Stage : The imago or spinner lives only a few days; after laying its eggs it falls prone on the water and dies from exhaustion.

The period from the 1st to 4th stage is not less than one year. In the case of the Mayfly it is two or even three years.

(i) *The Setæ of the Ephemeridæ*

Family, *Ephemeridæ*
Genus, *Ephemera*
Species, forty in the British Isles
15 have three setæ: 25 have two setæ.

A few of those with three setæ are:

Mayfly and spinner
Blue winged olive ,,
Turkey brown   ,,
Claret dun   ,,
Genus *Cænis*, a very small two-winged fly.

A few of those with two setæ are:

Olive duns and spinners
Pale watery duns   ,,
Iron blues   ,,
March brown and great red spinner
Yellow May dun and spinner
Genus *Cloëon*, a small two-winged fly.

(ii) Duns and Spinners

To distinguish between a dun and a spinner:

A *dun* has dull coloured wings which are hairy on the lower edges, is clumsy in flight, and when on the wing the body hangs down. The flight is usually from the water to the bushes.

A *spinner* has transparent glassy wings, and is active in flight. They are usually on the wing in late afternoon and evening.

When 'dancing' the spinner fills his stomach with air to ascend, and expels it again when dropping. To 'dance' they prefer a warm mild evening (a light breeze is an advantage to blow them off the bushes). In cold or very windy weather they remain on the bushes and do not 'dance.'

The 'dance' of the spinners is caused by the different position of the eye in the male and female.

The eyes of the male are on top of the head with their focus directed upwards.

The eyes of the female are on the sides of the head with their focus directed outwards.

The males are blown into packs by the breeze, and congregate on the leeward side of trees and bushes. They are watchful for a mate. As their eyes are only directed upwards, they rise and subside in the air so as to get below and not miss any passing female. This is what is called 'The dance of the spinners.'

The female, seeing a company of active males, flies just above them knowing they can only see upwards. In this way she finds a mate.

(iii) Male and Female Ephemeridæ

To distinguish a male from a female:
Male duns and spinners have:
   (a) large and coloured eyes
   (b) abdominal forceps

(*c*) Setæ – twice the length of the fly
(*d*) Forelegs twice as long as the others.

Female duns and spinners have:

(*a*) Small eyes at the side of the head
(*b*) No abdominal forceps
(*c*) Setæ – length of fly
(*d*) Forelegs – same length as the others.

(*iv*) *To identify certain Ephemeridæ*

To identify certain Ephemeridæ it helps:

(*a*) To count the setæ (*see page* 76)
(*b*) Is it a dun or a spinner? (*see page* 77)
(*c*) Is it a male or a female? (*see page* 77).

b. TRICHOPTERA

Sedge or Caddis fly type. 130 species in British Isles.

1st Stage : Eggs laid on water or on leaves of water plants and hatch out in about three weeks.

2nd Stage : Larva or Caddis stage. The insect makes a tube of spun silk with pebbles and bits of reed attached. They grow quickly, and when full grown change to a pupa.

3rd Stage : The pupa or chrysalis usually becomes attached to some object, a rock or big stone.

4th Stage : Changing into the imago, which dies soon after depositing the eggs.

Period from 1st to 4th stage one year.

Trout are very interested in the following caddis flies: large red sedge, grouse wing, cinnamon sedge, grannom, Welshman's button.

C. THE SIALIDÆ

Alder or Orle fly. Only 2 species in Great Britain. The egg is laid on reeds or rushes, never in the

water. They hatch out into a small larva in about
10 days.

The larva crawls to the water, eats greedily, grows
quickly, and later crawls to the bank where it digs a
hole about six inches deep in which it passes the
chrysalis or pupal stage and finally emerges as a
perfect fly. The imago soon dies after depositing
its eggs. Period from the egg to the imago is one
year.

To tell a sedge from an alder :

An *alder* when on the water always appears in
trouble as if drowning, and is clumsy in flight.

The *sedge* seems at home on the water, floating
calmly about, and is active in flight, darting about or
dipping when egg laying.

d. THE PERLIDÆ

Willow fly type. There are 31 species in Great
Britain.

1st Stage : Eggs are laid separately on the water;
they sink to the bottom and in a few weeks hatch
out into a small nymph.

2nd Stage : The nymph crawls into deep water,
grows rapidly, and when ready crawls on to a dry
bank or rock and changes into the imago.

3rd Stage : The imago deposits its eggs and
shortly afterwards the fly dies.

Period from 1st to 3rd stage one year.

In the north of England the stone fly is called 'the
Mayfly.'

e. THE DIPTERA

There are 3,000 varieties of which only a few are
water-born flies.

Eggs are often laid on the underside of water
weeds and develop into pear-shaped larvæ with
suckers.

When the larva is full grown it spins a cocoon on the weed.

In the cocoon the larva changes into the pupal stage.

The skin of the pupa bursts and the imago finds its way on to the surface of the water.

Some of the water-born Diptera in which trout are interested: reed smut, fisherman's curse, gravel bed, gnats.

Some of the others in which trout are interested: black gnat, hawthorn fly, oak fly or down-looker, wood fly, cowdung fly.

Book I: TROUT FISHING

Part VI

FISHING WITH NATURAL INSECTS

SECTION I

Fishing an Insect on the Surface

a. NOTES ON DIBBING

Fishing on the surface with natural insects is called dapping, dibbing, bobbing, or shade fishing.

It is usually practised on bush-covered streams where it is difficult to cast an artificial fly.

Quiet shady pools are best, running water is of little use.

You can 'dib' successfully on a bright warm sultry day with almost any insect.

Use a short stiff rod about 8 ft long and a strong gut cast of about 18 inches. The gut cast should be strong, as when you meet a good fish you must hold him hard in the narrow bushy stream.

Put a small bullet or lead at the junction of the reel line and cast, and before passing the rod through the bushes, roll the line and cast round the rod, then unroll it when in position; the weight of the bullet helps to draw off and straighten out the cast when lowering the bait to the surface.

Allow the dib to float on the water unchecked, and with none of the gut cast in the water; the insect should be lively and kept alive as long as possible.

Keep out of sight and remain still.

Strike or lift when the fish has taken down about 1 foot of the gut cast.

You can also dib with any artificial fly (blue upright, alder, sedge, etc) in a similar way. The fly should float 'awash' not entirely dry and floating high.

You should strike at once when dibbing with an artificial fly.

The insects used for dibbing on the surface may be divided into two categories, *viz*:

(1) Winged flies.
(2) Beetles, etc.

b. DIBBING WITH WINGED INSECTS

Here are a few of the winged flies generally used: house fly, wood fly, oak fly, cowdung fly, moths, blue dragon flies and daddy long legs.

Favourite flies are cowdung and wood flies, found on cattle droppings.

Wood flies are black and larger than a house fly.

To *catch* them get a leafy twig and strike down on them; a few will be disabled.

Or, prop a band box over a dropping and suddenly whack it down; make a small hole in the bottom and place a glass carrier bottle over the hole. The flies will make upwards to the light and enter the bottle.

Carry flies in a 6-oz medicine bottle with a grooved cork to admit the air, or in a perforated tin box.

You can also catch a fly in the wet hand with an upward sweep from behind; when you have got him in the closed fist blow hard on him two or three times; this will stupefy him.

To mount a winged fly : Pass the hook (No 12 or 13) through the tough leathery waist at the tail end of the thorax, pass it from underneath with the point of the hook coming out on top and visible;

Or, pass the hook through a bit of the skin on the back between the wings.

The bait should hang cross-wise on the bend of the hook.

c. DIBBING WITH BEETLES AND GRASSHOPPERS

This is done in a similar way to winged insects.

To mount a beetle : Pass the hook No 11 through the edge of one of the hard wing cases of a beetle, or through the back of a grasshopper.

The grasshopper is best in August. When fishing

with it, let it fall on the water with a splash as if it had jumped in.

To raise the wing cases of a beetle, blow under them and they will become extended.

A black cowdung beetle is best; the light coloured ones with a reddish belly are of little use.

d. STONEFLY FISHING

It is best to fish in an open rocky stream.

Use a dry fly rod, greased line, 9-ft cast tapered to oo8. You need only grease the line and the cast, the winged stonefly floats well by itself.[1]

Wade in and cast or swing the bait very carefully upstream with a short line, and let the bait float down towards you unchecked as in dry fly fishing.

To mount a stone fly, use two hooks mounted $\frac{5}{8}$ in apart, top hook size No 13, lower hook size No 14. Pass the lower hook through the abdomen, so that the barb hangs downwards. Pass the upper hook through the head or neck, upwards (*see page* 88).

The fly should be lively; when dead or water-logged it is no use.

Large female flies are best.

You can fish upstream in low clear water. A slightly coloured freshet is, however, a good thing, as the flies are then washed from their hiding places among the stones.

To find stone flies look for the cast-off 'shucks,' and you will find the flies close by.

The stone fly is the imago of the 'creeper' and is called the Mayfly of the North. They appear about the middle of May, and continue for about three weeks.

The male (the Jack) is smaller than the female.

There are several patterns of artificial stonefly but the natural fly is by far the best lure.

[1] For gut sizes *see pages* 334–336.

SECTION 2
Fishing with Sunk Insects
a. NOTES ON UNDERWATER FISHING

Winged flies and caterpillars are a good bait when fished sunk in small streams, in the holes, pools, and dead water under the bushes. (The running water is of little use.)

A sultry still warm day is best.

In a narrow bushy stream a stiff 8-ft rod is usually best; but sometimes a longer rod, say 10 ft is more useful:

(a) To enable you to keep well back from the bank

(b) To extend over bushes

(c) To allow a very short line to be used.

Any ordinary fishing line and reel will do.

Use a 4-ft gut cast tapered to ·008.

Put two No 4 split shot on the cast about 1 foot from the bait, to sink it.

b. FISHING WITH WINGED INSECTS

The usual winged fly baits are: house flies, wood flies, oak flies, cowdung flies.

With these winged flies it is best to use a two hook tackle. The hooks, size No 16, should be close together.

A No 8 shot pinched on the shank of the upper hook helps to sink the bait.

Impale a fly on each hook by passing the hook through the back just between the wings.

There should be some life in the flies; they do not last more than five or six minutes, then you must re-bait.

The method of fishing is as follows:

Let the bait sink down slowly to about mid-water,

hold it still for a little, then move it up and down a few inches to attract. If nothing happens, draw it up slowly and try again.

A fish generally nibbles first at the bait; do not strike until the bait moves away. If, however, he rushes at it and moves off strike at once.

C. FISHING WITH CATERPILLARS

A caterpillar is a good bait about June. You find them on the oak and elm-trees.

It is fished on a windless sultry day in a similar sink and draw method as described for sunk winged flies (*see above*).

To mount a caterpillar, use a single hook No 11. First squash one and smear the bare hook well with the juice; this assists in baiting the hook. Thread the caterpillar on the hook carefully, they are very soft. A No 4 split shot pinched on the cast is necessary to sink the bait.

Carry caterpillars in a perforated tin box with leaves.

Try a black artificial palmer (no ribbing). This is a good bait.

d. FISHING WITH BEETLES

When fishing the sunk beetle the best method is to wade and cast upstream with a short line.

An open stream with few bushes about is an advantage.

Fish the edges of the rapid water, the eddies and pools under the banks.

Keep only enough gut in the water to allow the beetle to sink a few inches under the surface.

You seldom require any lead.

Never mind the splash; it attracts.

Watch the gut. Trout usually take the bait quietly under water. Strike quickly.

The all black cowdung beetle is best; the lighter coloured red bellied beetles found also in cowdroppings are of little use.

To mount a beetle when fishing it *sunk*: First raise the wing covers by blowing under them from behind and they will become extended. Then, holding the beetle in the left hand belly towards you and head uppermost, look over and behind the head and you will see a triangular bit of case (below the head and above the wing cases); pass the point of the hook through this triangle, through the body, and out at the bottom of the belly, transfixing him from head to tail, thus:

If you want to mount *two* beetles, put the second one on in a similar way, the heads of both beetles pointing up the cast thus:

With one beetle use a No 12 hook.

With two beetles use a No 9 hook.

In both cases the barb of the hook is exposed.

Other beetles such as cockroaches, coch-y-bondhu, fern webs, etc, can be mounted and fished in a similar way.

e. FISHING WITH A CREEPER

The creeper is the larva of the stonefly; it is called the 'devil's coach horse,' is formidable looking but is quite harmless. It appears about April and May.

It is about 1 in or $1\frac{1}{4}$ in long and is a very tender bait. The yellowish ones are best.

They are found in the gravel among the stones at the sides of shallow streams.

Keep them in a well ventilated box with damp moss or weeds.

The best method of fishing the creeper is to wade

87

G

and fish upstream, with a 10- or 12-ft rod, short line, 6-ft cast tapered to ·008.

Cast or swing the bait carefully upstream and let it come down towards you with the current, with no drag whatever on the bait.

Try to keep the creeper in mid-water, if it touches the bottom it is liable to be damaged.

There should be a current; still water is of little use. In heavy water use a little lead on the cast about 14 in from the bait.

Strike slowly when the bait stops (allow, say, two seconds).

Weather conditions : You can fish with success in low water and bright warm weather or in a slightly coloured freshet which washes the creepers from their hiding places.

To mount a creeper use a two hook tackle, the upper hook size No 14, the lower hook No 13.

A

The hooks should be $\frac{5}{8}$ in apart, thus:

Pass the lower hook B into the under part of the throat and down through the abdomen so that the barb is below.

B

Pass the upper hook A upwards through the head or neck.

The bait should hang straight on the tackle, the head facing up the cast thus:

A

B

Or, use a single long shanked hook No 7 with a bristle above to prevent the bait slipping. Insert the hook at top of the thorax and thread bait on the hook, bringing the barb out under the belly (*see diagram on page* 105).

Book I: TROUT FISHING

Part VII

EVENING AND NIGHT FISHING

SECTION I

Evening Fishing on a Stream

a. NOTES ON EVENING FISHING

About sunset fish (like all animals) are thinking of an evening meal and under favourable conditions are inclined to feed well.

However bad the day, there is always a chance of an 'evening rise' provided:

(*a*) The wind is not too strong
(*b*) The water is not too cold
(*c*) There is no mist on the water and no fog about.

The evening rise does not begin properly until the sun 'dips' (a screen of hills, trees, a bank of clouds, will accelerate it). It only lasts about half an hour, perhaps a little longer, so don't miss it.

On a very warm mild evening it may last much longer than half an hour.

There are roughly two stages:

The *1st stage* lasts from just before the sun dips (and ceases to warm the water) until the water cools down to a certain temperature, causing the insects and the fish to feel the change; the fish then almost automatically cease rising (*see* Notes on Hatching Nymphs, *pages* 42 *and* 74).

During this stage fish are chiefly interested in the fall of the spinners, the hatches of b.w.o. and pale wateries, etc.

The *2nd stage* is when the fish are gradually getting accustomed to the cooler water, begin to feel more comfortable and contented, and commence to feed on the sedges and moths which, as the light fails, come out and hover about (their natural enemies the birds having gone to roost).

A very gentle breeze is now an advantage to blow these sedges and moths on to the water.

The period between the 1st and 2nd stages depends on how the fish and insect life accommodate themselves to the changed conditions and the temperature of the water.

Fish the pools and where the stream flows gently, running water is not much use.

On a stream dry flies are best; on a lake I have found wet flies are more profitable. In both cases you increase the size of the fly as it gets darker.

When casting try to face the setting sun.

If you must fish when there is a fog or a mist like smoke on the water, your best chance is to fish wet and sink your fly well; try a nymph, a dry fly is no use at all (*see* Notes on Mist, *page* 313).

On a mild windy evening, fish in the calm water under the shelter of trees, banks and bushes, etc.

If you must fish in a strong wind, use big flies, sink them, and fish in sheltered water.

b. WEATHER CONDITIONS

Favourable conditions are: a soft, balmy, mild, warm, calm evening.

Other necessary conditions are: plenty of insect life about, a good diffused light, water of normal temperature, not too cold.

Unfavourable conditions: a hard cold evening, heavy dew, a fog or a mist like smoke on the water, strong wind, a cold wind or cold water, heavy black clouds about, clouds hanging low on hill tops.

c. NIGHT FISHING

Night fishing begins when it is dark and you cannot see your fly on the water.

While it is light you should carefully examine the pools and places you intend to fish in, and note the holes, obstacles, etc, which you must avoid when darkness sets in.

The darker the night the better. The temperature of the water is very important; it must not be too cold.

Fish undoubtedly share with the owl and the cat the power of seeing in the dark.

Use a short line and cast the same length of line each time, a strong cast and usually one fly (especially if there are many weeds about).

Cast in the pools and easy water (rapid water is of little use).

It pays to draw your fly along the surface causing a ripple to attract.

It does not matter if the fly gets water-logged and sinks a little.

A lob worm skimmed along the surface on a dark night is a good lure.

When a fish rises to your fly, you must depend chiefly on the feel or touch before striking.

At night a fish usually makes a good determined rise and means to have it.

An electric torch is very useful.

It is easier to disentangle a cast if you hold it over a white sheet of paper or a handkerchief.

When fishing at night it is a good plan to have a couple of spare casts mounted in your damping box.

Then in case of a bad tangle, don't bother to undo it, but put on a fresh cast. The rise may not last for long and you want to make the most of your time.

d. FLIES FOR EVENING AND NIGHT

On a *stream* I think you have a better chance with a dry fly than with a wet fly.

In the first stage of the evening rise while it is still light—

(*a*) If the evening is warm:

Try a spinner of the natural fly on the water
  ,, a dry olive spinner, size about No 15
  ,, sherry spinner, *ditto*
  ,, Jenny spinner, *ditto*
  ,, small sedges, *ditto*
  ,, Welshman's button, *ditto*
  ,, Coachman, *ditto*

(*b*) If the evening is a little cool:

Try a dry pale watery, about No 15
  ,, b.w.o., *ditto*
  ,, orange quill, *ditto*
  ,, brownish spinner, *ditto*
  ,, wet tup, *ditto*
  ,, wet hackle, dark olive, *ditto*

When the light is failing, try fat-bodied winged flies of a larger size up to No 11, *viz:*

Coachman	
Alder	
Brown moth	Fished dry
Sedges	
Wickham	Fished wet.

When the light is failing and the evening is sultry fish appear to prefer winged flies to hackle flies for some obscure reason.

When it is quite dark try larger fat-bodied woolly flies up to size 8 = $\frac{11}{16}$in:

White moth	Semi-submerged and drawn
Alder	along the surface
Coachman	

A big Wickham fished wet.

SECTION 2

Evening Fishing on a Lake

a. NOTES ON EVENING FISHING

There is generally an evening rise on a lake, provided the weather conditions are favourable.

The conditions are similar to those for stream fishing (*see page* 90).

With a clouded sunset the rise comes on sooner than with a clear sunset.

Trout in a lake leave the deeps and come into the shallows in the evening to feed or to get away from the pressure of the deeps, or possibly to rest.

They commence to move in-shore about an hour before sunset if conditions are favourable.

A trout hooked in the evening is usually well hooked, as he means to have it.

Fish in the shallows and along the shores.

In a lake when fish are rising well try a dry fly, but as a rule wet flies pay best on a lake.

b. NOTES ON NIGHT FISHING

(*See also page* 91)

After the evening rise is over, there is usually a period of an hour or even more before trout 'come on' again. It is then quite dark, the darker the better.

On some lakes it pays to fish a big fly on or near the surface, on others you may do better with comparatively small flies fished deep.

(1) When fishing with a big fly you want a rod about 13 ft long, a gut cast ·014 thick. Cast a short line (say about 30 ft from rod top to fly, no longer).

Cast out the same length of line each time and draw the fly towards you along the surface or just semi-submerged.

One fly is usually enough; if you have a dropper put it well up the cast about 2 ft from the reel line.

(2) When using small flies it is best to fish them deep and draw them slowly.

On a dark night you will find fish quite close to the shore in the shallow water among the rocks and weeds.

Trout move about a lake a good deal, so it is well to note where fish are rising or moving just before sundown, as that is the locality you are likely to find them in at sunset and after dark.

Trout seldom feed in the middle hours of the night, it is not much use fishing between 12 midnight and 4 a.m.

C. FLIES FOR EVENING AND NIGHT

(1) When *the sun dips* try flies of the same pattern but a size larger than those you have been using in the afternoon, fished wet.

(2) When the *light is failing* try flies size about No 7, *viz:* fat bodied patterns of sedges – alders – March browns or a thunder and lightning.

(3) When it is *quite dark* here are two suggestions:

    (a) Try flies same as in (2) but about an inch long, also terrors, woolly bears, caterpillars two inches long; fish them along the surface as described on page 92. Some years ago I was very successful with these big lures on Blagdon lake.

    (b) Try small flies size Nos 8 to 10, fish them deep and work them slowly.

The following patterns are worth trying, *viz :*

    Fiery brown, mallard and claret, teal and red, thunder and lightning and a black fly with broad silver ribbing.

On the Irish lakes I have done very well using
these small flies.

However, I think the large flies referred to in (*a*)
are worth trying on any lake, if they fail you try
the smaller ones.

SECTION 3

Effect of Moonlight

On a moonlight or starlight night I think you have
a better chance on a stream than on a lake.

On a bright moonlight night the larvæ and bottom
food appear to get active and fish are busy feeding on
them: this may be one of the reasons why fish do not
come to the surface much on a moonlight night, so it
is best to fish deep with small flies, size Nos 10-12.

Mind your shadow and that of your rod when
fishing in the moonlight. Even during daytime if
the moon is behind your hand it appears to throw a
shadow.

If there is any shade (under trees, banks, etc) it
pays to cast your flies into the shade and draw them
gently into the moonlit water.

When the moon first comes out the air appears to
get cooler and this does not help to improve the
fishing.

BOOK I: TROUT FISHING

Part VIII

WORM FISHING

General Notes

You can catch trout with a worm in any month of the season.

In the early spring it is a very deadly bait.

The worm is usually tried only when the fly is of little use, *i.e.* in July and August, when the water happens to be very low and clear, and again when the water is too coloured.

You must cast, 'swing out' or 'pitch' a worm very carefully.

If you use an overhead cast, you should make a slow 'continuous motion' cast, with a wide sweep, no jerks of any sort: let the line straighten out well behind you before making the forward cast or you will flick off the worm:

Or, try a gentle side cast or swing. You usually cast upstream, so you don't want to cast a very long line.

The chief points to remember are:

(a) Allow the worm to swim downstream quite naturally, no drag or tension on the cast, no jerking of the rod top

(b) Make the bait dribble along close to the bottom, or even in mid water

(c) Never let the line or cast over-run the bait

(d) A lively worm is much better than a dead one

(e) Try a small ball of sheep's wool (well oiled to float) at the junction of reel line and cast, or on the cast: it floats and acts as an indicator which you can watch

(f) In a backwater or eddy it often pays to try a sink and draw movement of the worm. Draw it up slowly about a foot or so, and then let it sink again slowly.

In running water a trout usually rushes at and
gulps the whole worm.

In still water he often takes it by the tail end and
moves off to a quiet spot to eat it.

In either case it is best to give him time (say 3
seconds) before you strike, and strike downstream if
you can manage it.

Roughly there are two methods:
    (1) Clear water fishing
    (2) Coloured water fishing.

SECTION 2

Fishing in Clear Water

You can catch trout on a bright day in low clear
water by wading and fishing upstream (an upstream
breeze is an advantage).

Your rod should be on the stiff side, and at least
10 ft 6 in long (a light 12-ft rod is better). With a
longish rod you can fish further off and keep most
of your cast out of the water; you can also reach out
well over bushes and obstacles.

Use a 6-ft cast, tapered to ·008.

Reel and line as in fly fishing.

Grease your line to float. Do not grease the cast.

Tread lightly on the banks. When wading move
slowly and deliberately, advance a yard at a time,
cause no ripple, no splash.

Keep behind your fish and out of sight as much as
possible: it is best if you can only see the surface of
the water, because if you can see the bottom clearly
the fish can usually see you.

Mind your shadow.

Cast or 'swing' the worm gently upstream and
slightly to the left or right of you: allow it to come
down with the current unchecked, and let it continue
well past you, taking in line and coiling it in the left

hand as the bait comes down, thus keeping the line taut;

Or, using a short line raise the rod top gently as the bait travels downstream towards you.

The worm must drift down naturally close to the bottom. Never let the line or cast over-run the bait. Watch the gut cast; when it stops give time before you tighten or strike.

Let the worm float down well past you and *draw it to the surface* before making another cast. If you try to cast it while the worm is even 6 in under water, you are liable to flick it off.

First try the gravelly shallows, the eddies behind rocks, in the backwaters and the thin edges of the streams; then try the pools and under the banks, as that is where trout usually go when frightened off the shallows.

SECTION 3

Fishing in Coloured Water

You can fish either up- or downstream.

It is best, if you can, to wade and fish upstream; the method is similar to clear water fishing (*see page* 99).

You can use a thicker gut cast.

When fishing downstream, you can cast a longer line, but mind the belly in the line caused by the current; your worm is not fishing properly until your line is fairly straight in the water, and although you should keep a reasonably tight line there should be no drag on the worm.

If you want to make a long cast down and across, try 'pitching' with a dressed line from loose line coiled at your feet or over the fingers (*see page* 240);

Or try with an Illingworth reel and a very fine line: you can cast a worm a considerable distance in this way.

A favourable time is the first hour of a rising flood before the current gets too strong and dirty. When the current becomes very strong trout go under the banks and into the deep pools, etc;

Or, when the flood is falling and assumes a yellowish tint (usually about the second day of a heavy flood). Try under the banks, in the eddies, in the quiet water, and on the edges of a run.

Swimming the worm is worth trying. This is done using a small float (a bit of cork or a small quill). Put a split shot or a little lead on the cast according to the current.

The worm should swim close to the bottom.

Have no slack line between the float and the rod top.

Let the float swim down unchecked and watch it for a 'bite.'

Fish the pools and easy water, in the eddies, in slack corners and at the edge of a run.

You should have a little breeze in the quiet pools.

SECTION 4

Lead on the Cast

The amount of lead you put on the cast depends a good deal on the strength of the current. A strong current requires more lead than a gentle stream.

1. Pinch two or more split No 4 shot on the cast about 14 in above the worm.

2. Fine lead wire is useful. Lay a pin alongside the gut and wind the lead wire over both, withdraw the pin, then tighten the coils by twisting them until they grip the gut. This is less likely to damage the gut than when using split shot.

3. If a heavier lead is required use a small Jardine lead 2 feet from the worm.

SECTION 5

Weather Conditions

There is always a chance of catching a trout with a worm in almost any conditions of weather or water. Worm fishing is, however, seldom good

    (*a*) When the water is cold
    (*b*) When there is a mist or a fog
    (*c*) On a 'hard' day with a N or E wind.

Favourable conditions for worm fishing would be:

    (*a*) When the temperature of the water is normal or warmish
    (*b*) On a soft mild day with a S or W wind
    (*c*) The first hour or so of a rising flood until the water gets too heavy and dirty
    (*d*) When the water is falling and clearing after a flood
    (*e*) You will usually have better fishing after the fall of a heavy flood than after the fall of a moderate spate.

In Germany 'worm fishers' prefer a low barometer and thundery weather, as they say fish will then be at the bottom.

SECTION 6

Notes on Worms

A well toughened worm is best for baiting. But the fish prefer a fresh dug worm that has not been toughened, kept or scoured. These are, however, soft and must be very carefully handled.

To *toughen* worms keep them for 24 hours in a cool place in a bit of dry flannel.

To *scour* worms keep them in a well ventilated box in damp moss for, say, 24 hours. Rub two bricks together and put some of the fine dust in the moss: this gives a good colour to the worms.

A little finely chopped parsley sprinkled over the moss helps to scour the worms.

To *carry* worms, a bag 3 in square filled with damp moss is useful.

A tin worm box with a compartment for sand or soil is very convenient. Keep the receptacle clean, the smell of the worm is important.

Ghillies sometimes adopt one of the following methods to make the smell or taste of a worm more attractive:

(*a*) Put the foot of a heron in the worm bag
(*b*) Put ivy leaves or ivy gum in the worm bag
(*c*) To the damp moss in the bag add a few drops of oil of rodium or aniseed
(*d*) Dip the worm when mounted in the liquid from a 'tinned salmon' tin
(*e*) Nettles in the worm bag are said to keep the colour in worms.

The *best sorts* of worms are:

Blue heads ⎞
Lob worms ⎬ about 2 in long
Grey worms ⎠ (For trout)

They are found in kitchen gardens and road scrapings, they are the kind that are washed out of the banks of a stream and are appreciated by the trout.

Worms which have got a little bit of yellow at one end (called gilt tails) are a very good bait for a trout.

Dew worms are rather tender and break easily.

Brandlings (with yellow rings) are found in manure heaps and decayed leaf dumps. They do not scour well and emit a pungent odour. Trout don't like the taste or smell of them. They are all right for coarse fish.

Whichever worm you use it should be pinkish in colour, reasonably tough and above all lively.

Worms require air and a moderate amount
moisture, they will die if kept exposed to the sun.

SECTION 7
Mounting a Worm

First of all stun the worm by rolling it in the palm
of the hand or pinching the head.

Then dip it in dry soil or fine sand: this makes it
less slippery and easier to manage.

Here are 3 kinds of worm tackle:

1. Stewart tackle, 3 hooks size No 13 or 14

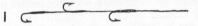

2. Pennell tackle, 2 hooks size No 13, 14

3. A single round bend hook (*see diagram on
page* 105).

1. *On Stewart tackle*, stick the three small hooks,
A, B, and C, through the skin, the top
hook about $\frac{1}{4}$ in from the head, the
middle hook about the middle of the
worm, the bottom hook near the end,
allowing the tail to hang down.

You must hold the shank of the hook
firmly when inserting it each time.

The worm lives long, looks natural,
and the hooks are not very conspicuous.

Some twist the worm once or twice
round the tackle between the hooks.
This is hardly necessary.

2. *On Pennell tackle* it is mounted in
a similar way to that described in No 1.

See that the lower hook is securely
passed through the skin.

For a small worm the Pennell tackle is best.

3. *On a single hook.* Always use a round bend hook.

The size depends on the size of the worm. No 7 hook is a useful size for trout; No $7=\frac{3}{4}$in.

The iron of the hook should be thin.

The McKenzie hook is a good bend to use.

A bristle tied at C helps to keep the worm from slipping down but it is not absolutely necessary.

Single hooks tied to gut are best.

A single hook kills the worm much sooner than a Stewart or Pennell tackle.

To mount the worm put the point of the hook in at the head and thread it on the hook, leaving $\frac{1}{2}$ in to hang down and wriggle.

Be sure not to bring the barb out or break the worm.

The hook must remain quite unseen.

Another way with a single hook: break off say a quarter of the worm, thread it on the hook and pass it up on the gut.

Put on the rest of the worm to cover most of the hook, leaving about $\frac{1}{4}$ in to hang down.

Bring down the top bit to cover the upper part of the shank.

This method kills the worm very soon.

Book I: TROUT FISHING

Part IX

MAYFLY FISHING

SECTION I
Mayfly Fishing from a Boat
a. GENERAL NOTES

Fishing with the natural Mayfly is called 'dapping.' This method is employed a good deal on the Irish lakes from a boat. The Mayfly appears to prefer water which is alkaline; it seldom thrives in the acid water of non-limestone districts.

You must have a wind to make the boat drift and to cause a ripple on the water. The boat should drift evenly and correctly. A good boatman is very necessary. Too much working of the oars causes the fly to float in an unnatural way. A good boatman should be able to manage the boat by using the lee-ward oar only.

A 17 ft rod is very necessary in a light wind, but when the wind is at all strong a 14 ft rod is quite long enough. The rod should be light and not too whippy. You can use almost any reel or line.

On the Irish lakes where you are likely to meet big fish most anglers strike from the reel when dapping (see page 186).

When collecting Mayflies you will usually find them on the sheltered side of bushes, walls and rocks (preferably hazel, hawthorn and gorse bushes).

In a strong wind look for them among the stones and rocks on the windward shore.

A cork split in half and tied to the handle of a dapping rod is very convenient for sticking your hook in when the rod is not in use.

b. BLOW LINE

To your reel line attach a 20- or 30-ft blow line and to that attach the gut cast.

It is an advantage to have two blow lines:

    1 A thin plaited silk line for use in a strong wind
    2 A loose floss silk line for a light breeze.

c. GUT CAST

Under ordinary conditions a 4-ft level gut cast is all right.

In a strong wind you should have a 6- or 7-ft cast. The gut should be as thin as you can use with safety.

On a very bright day rub the last 12 in of gut with heelball or crushed dock leaves. This takes the glitter off the gut (*see also page* 342).

d. HOOK

The hook can be attached to a long strand of gut (say 14 in) and should be whipped on with yellow silk; the whipping should be rough and not varnished, in order to hold the fly better.

Or you can use an eyed hook with a few turns of thin waxed silk whipping on the shank to prevent the fly slipping. I prefer this way.

For one fly use a No $12 = \frac{7}{16}$ inch hook.

For two flies use a No $10 = \frac{9}{16}$ inch hook.

A dapping hook should have a fairly wide gape and be slightly snecked or bent off.

The thickness of the gut cast should not be less than ·010 as on most waters you are likely to meet big fish during the Mayfly season.

e. TO MOUNT A MAYFLY ON A HOOK

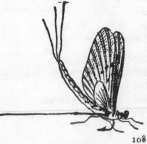

Insert the point of the hook in the lower part of the little chocolate coloured ring to be found at the side of the thorax just below the wings, pass the hook right through the body and push the fly on to the shank of the hook and on to the rough silk binding. Put a second fly on in a similar way, keeping both flies on the shank with the bend and barb of the hook visible.

The flies when impaled should ride on the water with wings properly cocked.

Some anglers put the flies on the bend of the hook, but I think they float and hook better when passed up on the shank, while the few turns of thin waxed silk prevent them from slipping down.

It adds to the attraction of the bait to put a yellow Sally fly between the two Mayflies, or even a bit of yellow gorse blossom will do.

During a squally wind and in certain light conditions it is often difficult to see where your cast is; a tiny bit of white feather attached to the top of the cast by the blow line helps you to locate it.

Fresh gathered greenish coloured flies are best.

Keep them in a well ventilated box, and keep the box in the shade; if left in the sun the flies soon become black.

If your fly gets drowned or water-logged, change it at once.

If there is a very strong wind and your natural fly becomes badly water-logged try a large artificial hackle Mayfly well greased.

f. THE MAYFLY SEASON

The Mayfly season lasts roughly about three weeks:

1st week, the fly commences to come out and rise in patches.

2nd week, there is a good daily rise.

3rd week, the rise dies away and the artificial spent gnat becomes the best lure.

Seasons vary considerably; much depends on the weather conditions, the temperature and height of the water.

Low water and warm weather mean an early season, while high water and cold weather usually mean a late season.

In the boat you drift broadside with the wind. To do this properly the weight must be equally distributed in the boat.

Hold the rod up and allow the blow line to be carried out by the wind at right angles to the boat.

Cause the fly to skim along the surface evenly and naturally; have as little gut cast in the water as possible. With a gusty or changeable wind this is not always easy, but if you can manage to have only 6 in of gut in the water, you are all right.

Short drifts in the boat over likely places are better than long drifts over a large expanse of water.

Watch where the flies are rising, as it is there the fish collect. Watch the gulls, they quickly find where the flies are.

The rise of fly on a lake is very often a local affair; when you find the place, stick to it. On most rivers the rise commences in the lower reaches and gets later in its appearance as one moves upstream.

A soft mild day with a S or W wind and diffused light are favourable conditions.

A hard cold day, N or E wind, are unfavourable conditions.

In very bright weather it is little use fishing in the shallows so try the deeper water.

To fish the shallows the day should be cloudy and dull.

When a fish takes your fly, lower the rod top at once, taking all strain off the line; count six, give him time, allowing him to take down about a yard of the gut cast. Then just lift or 'tighten' and you should have him.

Many fish are lost when they feel a strain on the line before they have the fly properly in their mouth.

So allow him time to turn and go down; he is in no hurry to let go unless he feels a pull on the line.

Coax him round to the windward side of the boat, play him and land him to windward.

g. THE DADDY-LONGLEGS SEASON

In some of the Irish lakes (Loughs Mask and Corrib) when the Mayfly season is over two daddy-longlegs are mounted and fished in a similar way to the Mayfly. Sometimes a green grasshopper is impaled between the two 'daddys'; indeed there is a regular 'Daddy Season' on Lough Corrib.

For this bait you require a hook size No 9 at least, and in striking allow a little more time than with the natural Mayfly.

To mount a daddy pass the hook through the hard part of the body just between the butt of the wings.

To mount a grasshopper turn the insect belly up and put the hook through the body by the butt of the wings.

Pass both daddy and grasshopper well up on the shank of the hook.

The daddy-longlegs=the crane fly.

SECTION 2

Mayfly Fishing from the Shore

a. ARTIFICIAL MAYFLY FISHING

When fishing from the shores of a lake or from the banks of a stream a dry artificial fly is best.

There are various patterns of winged and hackled Mayflies.

Lock's French partridge hackle Mayfly, or Lock's hackle golden bug are both very good flies.

Use them sparsely dressed, in a light breeze, and fully dressed in a wind. I have never done any good in Ireland with a winged Mayfly.

When fish are gorged with the Mayfly, and won't look at your artificial, try an artificial spent gnat fished dry, and see that it lies flat and close on the surface, almost semi-submerged. An alder, Welshman's button, or a Wickham, size No 11 or 12, are also worth trying.

When fish are nymphing, try two flies fished wet, *viz :*

Straddlebug (T)	No 11 Welshman's button (D)
	or artificial spent gnat (D)
Mayfly (T)	No 11 alder (D) or
(sparsely dressed)	No 11 dark sedge (D)

b. SPENT GNAT FISHING

At the end of the Mayfly season, fishing with what is commonly called the spent gnat is usually very good in the evening when the spinners are dancing. Use an artificial spent gnat fished dry; the natural specimen is no use.

Lock's badger hackle spent gnat sparsely dressed is a very good fly.

(For the dance of the spinners *see page* 77.)

The fall of the spinner or spent gnat often only lasts half an hour, so don't miss it.

A mild warm evening with a light breeze is best. A breeze is necessary to blow the spinners off the bushes on to the water.

With an artificial Mayfly or spent gnat, strike slow, give him time.

The type of spent gnat used is very important: it should be dressed so as to lie very close to and quite flat on the surface of the water.

If the spent gnat does not appear to interest the fish, an artificial murrough (*see page* 71) is well worth trying, fished dry.

Indeed, in the evening (when they are usually in flight) a *natural* murrough is a good lure to dap with. They are, however, rather difficult to find. Look for them on the stems of brownish dry reeds by the water side and in the clefts of brown rocks, banks, etc, which blend with their brown colouring.

Never keep the murrough in the same box as Mayflies, the pungent smell of the former sickens the latter.

Book II

SALMON FISHING

Book II: SALMON FISHING

Part I

FLY FISHING

SECTION I

General Notes

Never be in too great a hurry to start fishing the moment you arrive on a new water. It is well worth while spending a little time trying to learn the river, finding out the best pools and where fish are lying, etc. It is a good plan to watch the river before dusk and note where fish are rising.

If possible consult a water bailiff or local fisherman on these points. You will then be fishing with a certain amount of confidence, knowing that you are fishing in the best places, which is an enormous advantage.

Don't follow an angler about when he is fishing; don't ask him what fly he is using, he will tell you if he wants to.

Always try to keep your line straight (with no belly in it).

A crooked cast does not commence to fish until the line is straight.

When you cast a line that is not straight, cast again at once.

In the spring when the weather is cold it pays to fish your fly deep (a foot from the bottom).

In the summer, when the weather is warm, fish your fly shallow (within a foot of the surface).

Hold your rod top low (not high up); when a fish takes your lure, you just lift, or pull, to drive home the hook, using the power of the middle joint and butt (not the power of the rod top as with a trout).

SECTION 2

Fishing a Pool

a. GENERAL NOTES

Commence at the top of the pool.

Cast across and down.

Move on a yard or so, cast across and down, using the same length of line. Search the whole pool with your fly.

When the water is clear you can advance three or four yards after each cast; when it is coloured you should fish the water much more closely.

Keep your rod top low, give a little motion to your fly by working the rod top, or better by pulling line through the rings (*see also pages* 123).

In an *upstream gale* on a pool or easy water, try two flies, using a large heavy tail fly as a drag. As a bob fly use a hackled fluffy fly (the rougher the water the larger the fly).

Fish the bob fly (only) racing upstream, half in and half out of the water, making a good ripple.

Allowing the line to belly out before wind (*see diagram page* 110) let the fish turn to go down before you tighten.

b. BACKING UP A POOL

Best in a pool or sluggish stream.

Begin at lower end of pool or run.

Cast across, and while your fly is coming round, walk back slowly a few yards, keeping the rod low, and so on to the top of the pool, then make another cast. In this way

1. You take belly out of your line.

2. The fly comes over fish from behind.

3. When you walk back you draw the fly along parallel to the bottom: if you lift the rod high up you draw the fly off the bottom towards the surface.

4. Walking back you (so to speak) make current to straighten out your line.

c. FISHING RUNNING WATER

Cast across and down. Let the fly come round with the stream.

You need not work the rod top to give motion to the fly.

As the fly comes round it often pays to pay out a little line so as to cover more ground and to cause the fly to 'hang' over the channel or spot where the fish lie.

Let the rod top follow the line round so that there is no side pull on the fly.

A fish usually follows a fly out of the strong water and takes it when the line is straight and the fly is 'hanging' in calmer water at the side of the run.

Always fish both sides of a run if you can, as light falls on your fly from a different angle.

In a strong stream cast almost downstream, and either walk back or take in line to straighten it out and to cause your fly to hang and commence to fish sooner.

d. FISHING A SALMON FLY NEAR THE SURFACE

When the water is clear enough for the fish to see your fly near the surface and other conditions are favourable, either 'the greased line method' or 'the pulled fly' are always worth trying.

To avoid repetition in describing these two methods I will first mention the equipment and the conditions, etc, which are suitable and apply to both.

(a) A single handed fairly powerful rod about 10 ft long.

(b) A 9-ft gut cast not less than ·012 in thickness.

(c) A light line well greased except the last 12 inches.

(d) The cast or the fly must not be greased at all, and you should see that no grease gets on either of them.

(e) Use only one fly.

(*f*) The fly is fished near the surface and should never be allowed to sink more than 3 or 4 inches. The use of a light hook made of thin wire is a help.

(*g*) The water must be clear enough for a fish to see a fly near the surface.

(*h*) Fishing near the surface is always best when the temperature of the air is warmer than that of the water.

(*i*) Fish the flats and less rapid parts of the stream and avoid the heavy, rapid, and broken water.

GREASED LINE FISHING

The equipment and suitable conditions, etc, have already been referred to.

The following is a rough outline of the greased line method as practised by that expert angler, the late Mr. A. H. Wood, on the Aberdeenshire Dee.

Commence by casting a loose line across and slightly up stream. Drag will soon operate, so to check it you must 'lift over' or 'mend' the line (*see page* 228), then *lead* the fly down and across the current with no drag whatever on it, allowing it to sink just below the surface about 3 inches, no deeper.

While leading the fly keep the top of your rod in advance of (downstream of) the line and keep the curve of your line flattened as much as you can, this enables you to lead the fly down and across at a more or less constant angle to the current, showing the fish *a side view of the fly*.

The more 'lead' you can get the better, consistent with avoiding all drag.

When fishing in very easy water you should hold the rod top low, but when fishing in fast water you must keep the rod top well up especially when the fly gets below you. The belly of your line should be from the rod top to the water, rather than lying on the water.

When fishing with a short line hold the rod top higher up than when using a long line.

Mending the line is very important; you may have to do this several times; an upstream wind is an advantage.

Always keep some slack line in your hand ready to pay out when necessary.

Flies. The ordinary standard patterns of salmon flies will do but they must be thinly dressed on long-shanked sharp hooks.

(*For type of dressing see figure A, page* 134).

As regards colour use a sombre-coloured fly (say a March brown) on a warm bright day and use a more showy coloured fly (say a blue charm) on a cold day.

The size of the fly must suit the weather conditions. When the weather and the water are cold you can use flies size No 1 to No 3 dressed as above. While in low water (usually during the hot summer weather from May onwards) you have to use flies down to size No 10 and very sparsely dressed, sometimes just a hook with a few feathers attached.

Under normal conditions in summer, if in doubt a No 6 fly is a good size to commence with.

The chief points to note are :

1. With greased line fishing there should be a certain amount of current in the river to fish it properly.

2. When fishing watch the floating line. You should have complete control of the fly to enable you to steer or lead it round rocks, eddies and likely places. When necessary you can draw in or let out line through the

rings. The fly should never stop dead; if it
does give a slight movement by pulling the
line through the rings.

3. When a fish takes your fly, lower the rod
and give him slack line, allowing the line to
belly in the current and avoiding any direct
pull on the rod. When he commences to
move upstream and you feel him, then
tighten by a slow horizontal sweep of the rod
downstream and towards your own bank.
With a heavy hook, say No 1 or No 3, you
should tighten a little sooner than when
using smaller hooks.

If everything goes according to plan this is what
happens: The fish takes your fly into his mouth and
is in no hurry to eject it, then the weight of the
current on the belly of slack line causes a downstream pull on it, this makes the fish head upstream
and brings the fly into the back corner of his mouth,
finally the downstream sweep of the rod towards
your own bank drives the hook home.

THE PULLED FLY

The equipment and suitable weather conditions,
etc, for this method have already been referred to
(*see page* 119).

Use the ordinary standard salmon flies, sizes No 5
to No 12 according to the water and light conditions.
(*For type of dressing see figure A, page* 134.)

A black Pennell hackle, size 8 to 12, is a very good
fly on some waters for this sort of fishing, and
should be given a trial.

Cast across and slightly upstream on the flats and
less rapid parts of the water, over likely places or
where you know fish are lying.

Having made the cast, allow the fly to sink below

the surface not more than 3 or 4 inches or to be just
awash near the surface, then by drawing the line
through the rings, drag the fly at a constant speed
across the current, keeping it near the surface.

The movement must be constant. At no time
must the fly stop or travel slowly over where fish are
lying.

Continue until the fly is below you in the stream
and at the next cast shoot the loose line.

Your object should be to bring the fly quickly and
correctly over where a fish is lying; you want to try
and compel him to dash at the fly, allowing him no
time for a slow rise or close inspection.

Strike *only* when you feel the fish.

A detailed description of this method will be
found in Mr. J. E. Hutton's delightful book *Fishing
Ways and Fishing Days*.

e. WORKING THE FLY

You give motion to the fly either by jerking the rod
top or pulling in line through the rings.

With a long line out it is best to pull through the
rings.

With a short line working the rod top will do.

The amount of motion given depends greatly on
weather and water conditions.

Generally speaking:

Give slow motion to flies	When weather is cold When water is coloured When using dull-coloured flies.
Give more motion to flies	In lakes and pools In clear water When using gaudy or tinsel bodied flies.

In a fast stream give no motion at all, let the fly come round with the current.

Always remember that when the rod top is held high up, if you pull at or work the fly, there is a tendency to bring it to the surface.

f. RESTING PLACES

1. Salmon usually lie close to the bottom, in easy water near rocks, in the channel of a stream. When a rock shews above the surface fish will rest in the V-shaped pieces of dead water immediately above and below the rock. When it is submerged there is little or no dead water above; so they usually rest in the dead water below the rock.

2. They like to be near fairly rapid water, on the edge of a backwater or of a run, outside the swirl, in the shade of rocks or trees if any are available.

3. They like places formed by irregularities on the floor of the river which afford shelter from the force of the stream.

They like to lie on a level, gravelly bottom or on a flat slab of rock; they appear to be contented when their bellies are resting on something smooth.

4. When a fence or wall comes down to the water, you often meet a fish there just off the end of it.

5. When the height of the water is about normal, they like resting in the tail of a pool, just above the sill of a weir in the glassy glide before the water breaks and becomes rapid.

In low water you will find them in the deep holes and pools, seldom in the rapid water.

6. In warm water, they prefer the swift runs about 3 ft deep;

In cold water, they prefer the slower deeper parts of the river.

7. When a fish is resting in a pool, and a spate comes down, he feels the pressure of the extra depth and volume of water on him (through the medium of his skin surface and lateral line), and this prompts him to move on, especially if the weather is dull and cloudy.

When the water falls, he feels the reduced pressure, and seeks some convenient pool or place to rest in, to wait for the next rise of water.

8. When you catch a fish in a certain spot it is always worth while trying in the same place a day or so later.

SECTION 3
Rising, 'Taking' and Jumping Fish
a. GENERAL NOTES

Running up a river. When actually engaged in running up a river fish never take well.

On entering a pool and when settled down (after say about 12 hours) fish become active and will take well (other conditions being favourable).

'Lodgers' that have been in a pool some time seldom take well, and never in coloured water.

The longer a salmon has been in fresh water the more critical he becomes of your lure.

Whether a salmon takes a fly or not depends largely on the water, wind, barometer, light and weather conditions at the time.

In comparison with the other salmonidæ, the rise of a salmon is slow, and he is slow to eject anything which takes his fancy. It is the strain or pull on the line which alarms him. The bigger the fish the slower he moves.

The reasons why a salmon takes a fly are quite different from those which influence a trout. A trout is at home in the river and is looking for his daily food. A salmon is a visitor come in from the sea to spawn, and he goes for unusual looking moving objects which attract or annoy him.

b. WATER CONDITIONS

The temperature of the air and that of the water is important, as it usually affects the method of fishing which you should adopt.

> (*i*)   When the temperature of the air is warmer than that of the water, it is best to fish your fly shallow (just below the surface).
>
> (*ii*)   When the temperature of the air is cooler than that of the water fish your fly deep (about a foot from the bottom).

As regards (*i*) perhaps it is that the surface water is well oxygenated, the cold water taking up oxygen from the warmer air.

While as regards (*ii*) the warm surface water is not well oxygenated (*see page* 315).

In most rivers the normal temperature when fish take well is from about 45° to 55°.

A falling or normal height of water is best. When water is rising in a river fish don't take well, as they are thinking of moving on.

Half an hour before a spate comes down, and before the water gets coloured, fish often take well. In this connection it is generally considered that in large salmon rivers, such as the Tweed, Shannon, etc, fish take well when the water is fining down after a flood, while small rivers often give best results on the first day of a spate.

Correct height of the water is very important, as it is the volume and pressure of the water which help salmon to decide whether to run up or remain in the pool.

Each beat has its own height on the local gauge.

If there are rocks on the sides of the centre channel of a stream, fish will take your fly in the rapid stream and won't wait until it comes round among the rocks. They don't appear to fancy taking a lure among a lot of rocks if they can avoid it.

When fishing in high water, fish the cast out well, as fish lie close in to the bank in a flood.

c. WIND CONDITIONS

A moderate, steady, soft wind is best on a river.

A variable or squally wind from any quarter is bad.

A downstream wind is better than an upstream wind (other conditions being equal).

A N or E cold wind is seldom good.

A S or W warmish wind is best.

In a lake start fishing along the shore on to which the wind is blowing.

A good steady wind is a great advantage when fishing from a boat with a wet fly.

d. BAROMETRIC CONDITIONS

A *rising* barometer is *best*.

A *falling* barometer is *bad*.

e. LIGHT CONDITIONS

A diffused light from a clouded sky is best, *viz :* a 'C' or 'D' light (*see page* 316).

The position of the sun as regards your lure is important.

Sun shining directly downstream tends to blind the fish.

Sun shining directly upstream tends to show up your lure.

It often pays to cross over and fish from the opposite bank, thus bringing light on your bait from a different angle.

f. GENERAL WEATHER CONDITIONS

Favourable conditions for salmon fishing are:

1. A warm, steady S or W wind
2. A cloudy sky with glints of sun
3. A falling or normal height of water
4. A downstream wind
5. A rising barometer
6. After a thunder or rain storm has broken and the rain has ceased.

Fish won't take well:

1. When heavy white clouds are about which reflect the light and cause a glare
2. When there is a mist or fog or smoke over the water
3. When there is a mid-day moon
4. Just before or during a thunderstorm
5. When there is much brown acid bog water about
6. When waiting below a weir to get up
7. When there is 'snow brew' in the water. Snow brew is caused by the admixture of freshly fallen snow or hail resulting in a *sudden* lowering of the temperature of the water (this must not be confused with the result of gradual melting snow from the hills).
8. Under certain conditions (especially in thundery weather) salmon become lazy, lethargic, and won't look at anything. You can often wake them up by trying some violent disturbance of the water, such as throwing in rocks and stones or beating the surface of a pool with a branch; any disturbance will help; even the passage of a

motor-boat has been known to make fish move.

When disturbed or driven from their favourite 'lie' in a pool they appear to become irritable and inclined to go for a passing object, so try a fly or lure over them.

9. During August and September when the day is very hot and there is a strong glare on the water, it is seldom much use fishing in the daytime. In the evening after sunset is usually the best time.

g. JUMPING FISH

A fish that throws himself on his side with a splash is not a taking fish.

A fish that makes a quiet rise or roll is usually a taking fish.

Fish don't generally jump or show themselves when the wind is behind them (*i.e.* upstream), or as a ghillie puts it, when the wind is in their tails.

A fish that throws himself with a straight body is usually a 'traveller.'

When fishing down a pool and fish begin to jump behind you, try them again with a lure of a different size (*see also page* 449).

Book II: SALMON FISHING

Part II

FLIES

Size of Salmon Flies

The size of a salmon fly is most important.

The colour is of next importance.

The size of the fly you use depends largely on the height, temperature and colour of the water and on the weather conditions.

When a salmon follows your fly or rises short at it, it usually means that the fly is too big, or the cast is too thick.

It is better to commence fishing with flies as small as conditions will allow than to begin fishing at once with big flies; you can if necessary increase the size later.

A fly on the 'small side' has very good hooking power, but of course does not sink so well as a large one, which has a heavier iron.

The 'size value' of large, medium or small flies varies, and depends on the river. For instance, in a big river like the Tweed or Shannon:

A large fly would be 6° – 5°
A medium   ,,   ,,   2° – 3°
A small   ,,   ,,   No 1, 2 etc.

While in some smaller rivers a 3° would be considered quite a large fly.

Use a *large* fly:

    (*a*) In big or coloured water
    (*b*) In very rough or broken water
    (*c*) In deep holes with a dark bottom.

Use a *medium sized* fly:

    (*a*) In water of a normal height and temperature
    (*b*) With a normal wind and light.

Use a *small sombre* coloured fly:

    (*a*) In low clear water

(*b*) In a light breeze or strong light
(*c*) Over a light coloured shallow bottom.

Use a larger fly in cold water than in warm water, sink it well, and fish it slow. Even when water is low and clear use a larger fly in the spring and autumn than in the summer months.

When fishing for salmon in a lake you seldom require a fly larger than about No 2.

On most lakes flies on hooks Nos 5 to 8 are about right.

SECTION 2

Colour of Salmon Flies

On a bright day use a bright coloured fly.
On a dull day use a sombre coloured fly, *viz :*

On a *bright day* try a
  Dusty miller
  Silver doctor
  Silver grey
  Mar Lodge
  Torrish.

With a *medium light* try a
  Jock Scott
  Gordon
  Durham Ranger.

With a *dull light* try a
  Black doctor
  Thunder and lightning
  Lady Caroline
  Claret and jay

In *coloured water* try a silver bodied fly, *viz*:
  Silver Wilkinson
  Dusty miller
  Silver grey, etc.

132

These are just rough general suggestions as regards the colour of flies; they are usually accepted by fishermen.

Before deciding what colour of fly to use, these two theories are always worth considering:

1. Try a fly the colour of which is in contrast to the colour of the surroundings, *viz*:

   (a) Over a brown or dark bottom use a light coloured fly, *i.e.* a Torrish type

   (b) Over green weeds use a medium coloured fly, *i.e.* a Jock Scott type

   (c) In peaty water use a dark coloured fly, *i.e.* Black doctor type.

The idea being to offer the fish a fly they can see well.

2. Try a fly the colour of which is in harmony with the colour of the surroundings, *viz*:

   (a) Use a brownish fly (say a March brown) over a brown bottom

   (b) Use a greenish fly (say a green Highlander) over weeds and near reeds and rushes

   (c) Use a claret coloured fly (say a claret and mallard) in peaty water

   (d) Use a dark coloured fly (say a black doctor) over a dark rocky bottom.

It is a fact that on some rivers fish will take a certain lure greedily (say a sand eel) during one season, while in the same month the following season they will not look at a sand eel. In this connection, Mr. Hughes Parry, in a very interesting article in the *Salmon and Trout Magazine*, September, 1935, writes, 'I have proved to my own satisfaction that one particular *run of salmon* requires one colour of fly or lure, while *another run* may require lures of a different colour.'

He considers the colour of the acceptable lure depends on the colour of the predominant food available in the sea when the particular run of fish enters fresh water.

For instance, sometimes a red winged fly or a prawn will be preferred, sometimes a sand eel or a blue or yellow fly. When in doubt he suggests try a Jock Scott, if that fails then a dusty miller, then a Torrish, then a black doctor, See what sort of colour is preferred and work out a fly to suit.

(A similar idea of trial casts of flies for trout is referred to on pages 62 and 70.)

SECTION 3
Dressings

The materials of which a fly is made (especially the hackle) should display a good sheen when held up to the light.

A fly should not be too heavily dressed. The wing should be on the skimpy side, the body should not be too much hidden by the hackle. With the smaller sizes of fly these points are important.

Flies built on the principle of having no dressing tailwards of a line drawn perpendicular to the hook point (*see Figure A*), have the advantage of hooking a fish better than if dressed in the usual 'shop' way (*see Figure B*), where the dressing extends up to or a shade beyond the bend of the hook.

134

Figure C is an example of a faultily dressed fly and badly proportioned for hooking purposes.

It is the 'flash' of a salmon fly of suitable size, combined with movement, which usually attracts the fish.

Few salmon flies are copies of anything a fish can ever before have seen in a natural state.

So it is safe to assume that when he goes for or nibbles at a fly he will take hold of the most convenient part, or the part nearest that bit of colour, or what not, which attracts him. He knows nothing about the dangers of the hook and therefore does not try to avoid it.

In most salmon flies the taii at T is of an attractive colour (*see page* 134).

A fish going for the bit of colour at the tail T of a fly dressed as in Figure A, would have the hook point about ¼ in further in his mouth than in the case of a fly dressed as in Figure B.

This is one of the advantages of dressing a fly on the lines indicated in figure A.

SECTION 4

Notes on Salmon Flies

Do not carry about a lot of patterns; several sizes of the following are suggested as enough:

Jock Scott
Thunder and lightning
Silver Wilkinson
Dusty miller
Black doctor
Torrish
Blue charm
Usk grub or prawn fly.

Don't use flies with gut eyes that have been tied some time.

Don't use flies tied on double hooks larger than No 2.

If unsuccessful don't hesitate to change the size or pattern of your fly.

A fly should swim upright, the hook acting as a keel to keep it erect.

An over-dressed fly won't swim upright.

Flies tied on a hog backed hook have a tendency to spin.

In bright weather on a river it often pays to use two flies representing a small fish pursuing a bright object, *i.e.*

Jock Scott (tail)   A yellow fly (dropper)
Dusty miller (tail)   Coachman (dropper)

On most lakes two flies are used when fishing from a boat, the dropper being drawn along the surface, and owing to the clearness of the water the cast should be as thin as you can use with safety.

The following list of flies most commonly used on certain rivers is useful for reference. It is copied from *The Field*, 22nd August, 1931.

River	Spring	Autumn
Tay	Black dog	Jock Scott
	Dusty miller	Benchill
Tweed	Wilkinson	Black ranger
	Silver grey	Wilkinson
Dee	Ackroyd	Ackroyd
	Mar Lodge	Thunder & lightning
Thurso	Childers	Thunder & lightning
	Silver grey	Kate
Spey	Delfur fancy	Thunder & lightning
	Black doctor	Dallas
Forth	Jock Scott	Black doctor
	Green Highlander	Wilkinson

River	*Spring*	*Autumn*
Earn	Wilkinson	Thunder & lightning
	Dusty miller	Turkey claret & yellow
Helms-	Torrish	Black doctor
dale	Black doctor	Joe Brady

SECTION 5
Dry Flies

You can fish for salmon with a dry fly in almost any reasonable conditions of weather and water.

The best conditions, however, are:

(*a*) When the temperature of the atmosphere is warmer than that of the water

(*b*) When the water is clear enough for the fish to see the fly on the surface

(*c*) When the fish are fairly fresh run. A 'stale' fish will seldom rise to a dry fly.

Hackle flies with stiff hackles are best.

The fly must float high in the water, and pass directly over the fish; a salmon will seldom move to one side after it.

Drag on the fly does not alarm the fish, it appears to attract him.

Don't hurry the strike, give him time.

Almost any pattern of large hackle dry fly is worth trying, tied on hook sizes 6 to 8.

A No 6 hackle March brown is useful when March browns are about.

La Branch's flies are always worth trying.

The names of the most suitable are:

Colonel Monel
Lady Pink
Mole
Soldier palmer.

SECTION 6

Gut Casts and Knots

For ordinary fishing use a 9-ft cast made up of $4\frac{1}{2}$ feet twisted gut plus $4\frac{1}{2}$ feet of gut cast, tapered to about ·019.

With small flies use a 9-ft cast, not less than ·014 in thickness, with a short rod.

Salmon are not nearly so gut-shy as trout and sea trout.

Knotting on a fly:

For large flies the best knots are

    (a) Figure of 8 knot
    (b) Turle knot
    (c) Double entry knot.

For flies size No 3 and under use a Figure of 8 jamb knot.

For Knots *see page* 322, *et seq.*

Book II: SALMON FISHING

Part III

SPINNING

SECTION I

General Notes

Spinning for salmon is best in coloured or big water (when the fly is no use).

You must have a wind or a ripple.

A dull light is an advantage.

On a bright day the rapid or broken water is best.

Cast your lure down and across, not directly across (unless you want to sink the bait very deep).

Cast the same length of line each time.

Never throw further than is absolutely necessary.

With salmon the bait should spin fast and be drawn or move slowly; if you draw or reel in fast you draw the bait off the bottom.

An even, straight, slow spin is best. I don't think a 'wobble' is much use, nor is it necessary to work the rod top.

Keep your bait about a foot off the bottom all the time, and try to keep it at the same horizontal level; and especially when reeling or drawing in the last few yards you should go a little slower if anything in order to try to keep the bait horizontal; as if you reel in fast when the line shortens you tend to bring the bait to the surface.

Fish the cast well out, especially in high water, as fish lie close to the bank in a flood.

In rapid water let the bait come round freely with the stream; don't touch the reel until it comes into the easy water at the side, then you can reel in slowly, keeping the bait just off the bottom.

Fish usually follow bait round in the fast water and take it in the easy water at the side of the run.

In very strong water you may have to give out line slowly to keep your bait near the bottom.

In a deep pool you must of course sink the bait; and as there is little or no current you have to reel in very slowly all the time, just enough to make the bait spin. Keep it off the bottom and keep it in a horizontal plane.

A salmon on seeing your bait usually rises slowly and vertically, until he gets on a level with the bait, and then rushes at it (*see also page* 410).

In clear water you must spin or reel in a little faster and use a smaller lure.

When possible cast from the shallow side of the river into the deep side.

When caught in the bottom try one of the methods referred to on page 249.

It is sometimes difficult to tell just by looking at it whether the water of a river is too coloured or not for spinning. Some ghillies use a long stick marked off in feet and inches with a white disc at the end. They know from experience if they cannot see the disc at a certain distance down (say two or three feet) that the water is unfishable.

SECTION 2

Spinning Lures

You should have a better chance of catching a salmon with a natural bait than with an artificial one.

With a natural bait there is the sense of taste or smell in addition to the sense of vision, all of which acting on the nervous system prompt a fish to take a lure; while with an artificial bait it is the eyesight alone which is affected.

Another inducement which is common to all lures is the mysterious sense (of which we know little) possessed by fishes which is affected by:

1. The height and colour of the water
2. The temperature and oxygenation of water.

A sort of general rule is:

In low water use a small dull coloured lure: the
pattern is very important;
In high water use a large gaudy attractive lure:
the pattern does not matter so much.

There is a great variety of baits for salmon, and
one which fish will take well on one river they very
often will not look at on another.

Some lures which I have found successful are:

In *high* or *coloured* water:

Natural sand eel, 3½ in (*see page* 263)
    ,,   silver sprat about 4 in (*see page* 264)
Artificial Devons 2¾ to 3 in, aluminium, wooden
or solid; silver or blue and silver (*see page* 273)
Artificial Phantoms, 3½ in, blue and silver,
brown and silver (*see page* 276)
Artificial spoons, 1 in, 1¾ in (*see page* 271)

In *normal* water:

Natural sand eel (small)
    ,,   golden sprat (*see page* 264)
    ,,   gudgeon (*see page* 263)
    ,,   prawn (fresh) (*see page* 147)
    ,,   minnow (fresh) (*see page* 267)
Artificial Devons, 2 in, 2¼ in
    ,,   Phantoms, 3 in, brown and gold
    ,,   colley, 3½ in
    ,,   golden sprat, 3 in
    ,,   leather eel, 3 in

In *low clear* water:

Natural fresh minnow
Artificial golden sprat, 2½ in
    ,,   Phantoms, 2 in brown and gold
    ,,   colley, 3 in
    ,,   Devons, 1¾ in, 2 in
    ,,   fly spoon (*see page* 272,

In *snow* water:

When water derived from melting snow is in the river it is well worth trying a golden sprat or a large prawn.

In most lakes when spinning for salmon you seldom require a large lure, a 2 in or 2½ in Phantom or natural bait is about right. I have never done any good spinning a prawn on a lake.

For Notes on Casting a Bait *see pages 232 et seq.*

For Notes on Traces *see pages 256 to 258.*

BOOK II: SALMON FISHING

Part IV

PRAWN FISHING

General Notes

The prawn is a lure more suited for normal and low levels of water than for high and coloured water.

Fish usually take a prawn better in warmish than in cold water.

The bait should move slowly, close to the bottom, in a natural way.

The position and amount of lead on the cast in the varying conditions of the current is very important; accordingly it is best to use a number of small leads which can easily be added to or removed as necessary (*see page* 261).

The size of the prawn is important; so if the fish don't fancy the one you are using it is always worth trying a larger or smaller one.

When fishing a prawn pull in the line through the rings (if you can), as you can feel a nibble better thus than when 'reeling' in the line.

The following method is worth trying. Begin with a short line about twice the length of the rod, swing the bait out, pull off from the reel a couple of yards of loose line and pay out line as the prawn noses its way along, keeping in touch all the time with a fairly tight line and keeping the prawn just off the bottom.

In pools try a sink and draw method, *viz*, let prawn sink to the bottom, raise rod top sharply about 2 ft, then lower it again, letting the prawn sink. Do this several times.

Try casting upstream in short casts, causing the prawn to come down slowly towards you and close to the bottom. The weight of added lead must be carefully regulated to avoid getting stuck in the bottom.

Before striking give lots of time, allow the fish to nibble the prawn, or even give him a little line, and when he gives a good tug, strike or rather pull the hook home. At first a salmon usually nibbles at a prawn to kill it; he then makes a gulp at it to get a firmer grip, finally crunching it, the supposition being that the spikes unless crunched up may prick his mouth, or perhaps he only wants to crunch the juices out of it.

SECTION 2

The Prawn

A prawn has a saw-like crest and very prominent eyes. In size they run from $1\frac{1}{2}$ in to 5 in.

A shrimp has no saw-like crest and has very small eyes. In size they run from 1 in to $2\frac{1}{2}$ in. In low water a small shrimp fished slowly is a good lure.

Fresh red boiled prawns are best. Usual size is 2 in or $2\frac{1}{4}$ in measured from the eye to end of fleshy part of tail (not including tail).

In heavy water you can use a larger prawn.

Hen prawns with pea (or berry) are better than cock prawns.

Boiled prawns lose colour if exposed to the sun for long.

Prawns will keep fresh for a week between layers of salt in a tin box.

To produce a red colour, add red ink to some water and warm it slowly over a fire with the prawns in the mixture. Don't spare the red ink.

Prawns preserved in glycerine or by other methods, or artificial prawns, will all catch fish, but I think a fresh prawn is the best. The colour of a prawn should not be too crimson nor should it be too light coloured.

Prawns from some localities, when boiled, produce a much more brilliant colour than those from other localities. Some of the best prawns come from

    a Bantry Bay, Co. Cork
    b The South Coast of England (especially
        round Weymouth)
    c The Channel Islands.

(For the reasons why salmon prefer a *red* prawn, *see page* 443.)

SECTION 3

To Mount a Prawn

All prawn tackles have a needle of some sort to keep the prawn straight.

Before inserting the needle the prawn should be straightened out as much as possible.

Salted prawns are very brittle and should be soaked in water before mounting.

For binding on a prawn, you require at least 2 ft of copper wire, red cotton or red wool.

Whatever the pattern of the tackle, there is a hook or triangle which comes just under the head, hidden away among the legs and feelers; attach the wire or thread to this hook.

Bind the prawn carefully down to the tail and back again, finishing off at the hook under the head.

See that the binding passes over and across the oints of the shell of the prawn's back and does not get in between them.

Bind the tail very securely: this is important.

Do not bind over the legs, allow them to hang down.

Take a turn or two over the horns of the prawn: this helps to prevent it slipping on the tackle.

With a small prawn (2 in long or even less) it is best to mount it on a single hook.

The hook should have a round bend, a thin iron, a shank to suit the size of the prawn, and should be tied to gut.

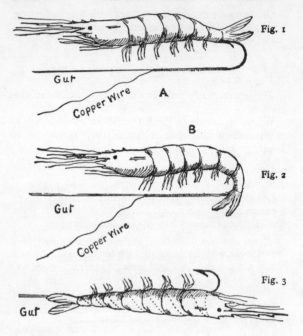

Fig. 1

Gut

Copper Wire

A

B

Fig. 2

Gut

Copper Wire

Fig. 3

Gut

Attach about 2 ft of thin copper wire to the shank
of the hook at A. Straighten out the prawn as
in Figure 1, and insert the hook just under the
tail.

Push the hook in, and as the prawn commences to
bend round it, press with the finger on the back of
the prawn at B Figure 2.

Bring the hook out under the head as in Figure 3.

Bind on the prawn with the copper wire and finish
it off on the hook under the head.

Or, you can mount the prawn with a thin baiting needle, the hook being attached to gut.

SECTION 4

Prawn Tackle

There are many patterns of prawn tackle on the market.

Whatever tackle is used, the hooks should be gilt or painted reddish the colour of the prawn.

There are two sorts of prawn tackle:

(*A*) Where the prawn spins
(*B*) Where the prawn does *not* spin.

(*A*) *The spinning prawn.* I think a salmon takes a prawn that spins much better than one that does not spin, as he sees less of the hooks, etc.

There are two ways of making a prawn spin:

(*i*) By having a spinner on the tackle
(*ii*) By having a spinner on the trace.

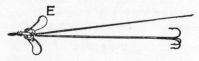

The above diagram shows a celluloid spinner E on the tackle or mount.

A fish is liable to let go altogether when he feels the hard spinner in his mouth.

The second method (*ii*) of having a spinner at the top of the trace is much the best (*see diagram, page 258*).

The trace must be rigid and made of wire so as to convey the turns of the spinner to the bait (gut twists and won't do at all; *see page 258, diagram E, F*).

The diagram below shows a simple tackle. It consists of the hooks or triangles mounted on wire (gut twists) and a needle with a loop of gut attached at D, thus:

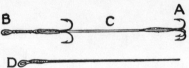

On the Shannon a single triangle is all that is used with the eyed needle to stiffen the prawn.

A little lead wire can, if necessary, be bound to the tackle at C to sink the prawn.

The trace is attached to a loop of wire or a ring at B.

For a large prawn A to B should measure 3 in to 3¼ in.

For a small prawn A to B should measure 2¼ in to 2½ in.

A long shanked single hook can also be mounted in a similar way, but in heavy water a prawn mounted on a single hook in this way is very liable to slip.

Before mounting the prawn:

(*a*) Pass the end of the wire trace through the loop on the needle at D and pass the needle up the trace

(*b*) Attach the wire trace to B

(*c*) Put the needle through the prawn

(*d*) Bind on the prawn (*see page* 147).

A link spring swivel at B, 'stopped' with two turns of copper wire is very useful, especially in strong water. The copper wire keeps the swivel rigid while fishing, and breaks on the first run of a fish; this prevents the severe twisting strain on the wire caused

by the powerful revolving spinner on the trace when
playing a heavy fish in rapid water;

Or, use one of Messrs. Carter's spinners, which
have a device attached that puts a spinner out of
action on the first run of a fish. This obviates the
use of a 'stopped' swivel as you can use a link spring
without any swivel at B.

(B) The non-spinning prawn. Of the many patterns of prawn tackle that shown in the diagram
below is as good as any of them. Some prefer more
hooks but I doubt if
they are necessary.

For a spinning trace
see page 258 *diagram* D.

These tackles are usually attached to gut.

Several small leads on the trace are better than
one large one, as you can easily take off or add one
according to the water, and this has to be done
frequently as a rule.

N.B. – To mount a prawn on a single hook *see*
pages 147, 148.

SECTION 5

Prawning with a Float

Best in slow water of an even depth.

The float should be 'set' carefully to the depth
of the water.

The prawn when cast out should sink slowly and
hang in the water close to the bottom.

The float should swim down quite unchecked. If
necessary pay out line to prevent drag on the float.

If there is any drag the prawn comes up towards
the surface and ceases to function.

A cork with a hole in it and of a neutral brown
colour makes a good float: put a match in the hole
to prevent the line slipping. A *Fishing Gazette*
float is all right for a heavy line.

The float when working properly should swim thus:

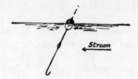

The amount of lead is very important.

The lead should be attached to the trace about $2\frac{1}{2}$ ft from the prawn.

In rapid water you must of course have a heavier lead than in slow water.

Book II: SALMON FISHING

Part V

WORM FISHING

153

SECTION I

Equipment and General Notes

I think a spinning rod is the handiest.

Use a fairly thin line (a thick line is liable to belly over the worm).

Use a 4-ft cast and single hook to gut, size 3°, long shank, round bend.

Cast the worm carefully (no jerk) across and down-stream at an angle of about 30°.

Fish it like a prawn, bobbing along slowly close to the bottom, or when in quiet water let it rest for a little on the bottom.

Keep your line sufficiently tight so that you can feel the slightest touch.

The worm must float down with the current absolutely unchecked, no drag whatever.

Never allow the line or the cast to travel in bellying fashion over the worm.

The amount of lead used and its position on the cast are very important. The lead must suit the current. A strong current requires more lead than a gentle stream.

If the lead is too close to the hook a fish 'senses' the opposing drag and drops the bait.

If the lead is too far from the hook (say 5 or 6 ft) the cast is liable to belly over the worm.

Two feet up the cast from the bait is about the right place for the lead.

Immediately after casting you should draw off about two yards of line, holding the slack in your left hand. The moment you feel a fish, let go some of the slack, and after about half a minute when you feel two distinct pulls or tugs, strike.

A salmon takes a worm in rather a different way from a prawn. He goes about it much more leisurely, investigating it carefully, pushing it with his nose and giving it slight tugs before taking it slowly and gently into his mouth.

It is best to keep your hand on the line. You can then feel a slight touch better. It is also best to strike by pulling the line through the rings.

In easy water, when a salmon takes a worm he usually moves slowly upstream, so try to strike downstream (if you can conveniently do so) as there is then a better chance of hooking him.

Worm fishing is usually best in mild weather and when the water is fairly warm.

When the water is cold or on a hard day with a N or E wind it is seldom of much use.

About half an hour after a rise of water, when it is colouring, and again when the water is falling and clearing after a spate, are both favourable times for worm fishing.

On a pool or in very easy water, you must of course have a breeze of some sort.

SECTION 2

Putting on a Worm

Keep your worm box clean and fresh, the smell and taste of a worm are important.

First 'stun' the worm by rolling it in the palm of your hand: dip it in dry sand or earth to make it less slippery.

Use a round bend hook size 3° tied to gut.

Bait with 2 large lob worms.

1st. Put the hook sideways three times through the worm, making a sort of bunch of it, and push it up the gut.

2nd. Thread a second worm on the hook to cover the iron, leaving a bit hanging down.

3rd. Bring down the first worm, making a sort of bunch of worms.

Another way is:

1st. Impale a lob worm a quarter of its own length and move it up on the gut.

2nd. Impale a large brandling about half its own length to cover the hook, leaving the end hanging down.

3rd. Pull down the lob worm on to the brandling.

Book II: SALMON FISHING

Part VI

HARLING AND TRAILING FROM A BOAT

157

SECTION I

Harling from a Boat

Have two lines out behind the boat, with the rods
parallel to the water and
at right angles to the boat.
The lines should be
of different lengths.

The boatman works
the oars so as to keep the boat almost stationary in
the stream, causing the lures to 'hang' in the current
close to the bottom.

The boat is then allowed to drop downstream
very slowly from side to side, searching the bottom
with the lures.

A skilful boatman is very necessary, so much
depends on him.

When you hook a fish, the boatman must reel up
the other rod at once.

In a big river where there are long, wide pools, if
the fly fails you, try harling, as it suits that sort of
water.

SECTION 2

Trailing in a Lake

For salmon you trail both in the open water of the
lake and along a shore.

When trailing sit on a seat of the boat facing the
stern.

With 3 rods in front of you sitting this way you
can manage your rods better, particularly when you
get a 'pull.'

Your rods should be fairly stiff, whippy ones are
of little use.

Each rod should have a different length of line out.

Keep the rods low and almost parallel with the
water, and at right angles to the boat.

A nail through a cork in the gunwale is useful to support the rods. (A gimlet is useful in a boat.)

You can use a long trace up to say 8 feet.

To check the line use a flat stone (wrapped in a cloth or a reel bag) weighing about $\frac{3}{4}$ lb resting on the bottom of the boat, the line passing under it.

Trailing along a shore your rods should be arranged thus:

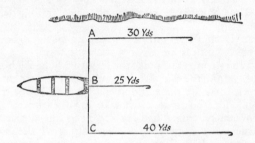

A – a rod of medium length with a medium sized bait.

B – the shortest rod with an experimental bait; a favourite one is a red soldier phantom.

C – the longest rod with a larger bait.

Remember that if your baits or lines touch, the tangle is very bad indeed.

To trail deep have say 50 yards of line out.

To trail shallow have about 20 yards of line out.

With a very long line you must strike or pull fairly hard, as the line stretches.

You don't usually want much lead trailing for salmon; if your bait is about 6 ft below the surface it is generally enough.

With a long line out you want a little lead, as the long line tends to 'sag,' and the bait tends to come to the surface.

When trailing against the wind you want more lead on the trace than when trailing with the wind; as when rowing up-wind the bait has a tendency to come to the surface.

Weather Conditions:

A dull 'soft' day, with a good wind, is best for trailing. You may have to adopt some device to check the drift of the boat (*see page* 16).

Your bait works more evenly when trailing with the wind.

A Loch Ness ghillie does not consider he is 'fishing' unless he is going with the wind.

When you get a 'pull,' the fish usually hooks himself. Hold the rod firmly (parallel to the water at first), then lift the rod and play the fish. Let him run. The boatman must take in other lines.

When playing a fish try and keep him about 20 yards away from you; if necessary, pull the boat away from him. You either play and land him from the boat or, if you happen to be near the shore and can find a suitable place, it is usually best to go ashore and land him as soon as you have him under reasonable control.

a. 'WEAVER' OR 'CORK' FISHING

A cork is used instead of the centre rod.

The cork must be rectangular, 10 in x 5 in x 2 in (the line comes off too easily from a round cork).

Paint the cork yellow and white, or any colour which shows up well in the water.

Attach 50 yards of line firmly to the cork, with 30 yards of it coiled round the cork, then a slip knot, and 20 yards loose behind the boat.

The trace should be sub gut not wire.

Let the cork rest on a seat or on the bottom of the boat with a flat stone on the line.

When you have a fish on:

1. Throw the cork overboard
2. Take in all lines
3. Stow the rods in the bow of the boat
4. Follow the fish, take up the cork, draw in line and coil it carefully in the stern ready to throw overboard again if the fish makes a sudden rush
5. Play him and tire him out in this way.

When the fish is played out:

1. Get in the centre or bow of the boat
2. The ghillie gets in the stern with the gaff or net
3. Draw the fish quietly to the gaff on the windward side.

Book II: SALMON FISHING

Part VII
NOTES

SECTION I

Striking a Salmon

A trout takes a fly as some sort of food, and ejects it as soon as ever he finds out the deception.

A salmon takes a fly or lure roughly for three reasons, *viz*:

(1) It looks a succulent morsel; he is attracted by it and would like to crunch or suck the juice out of it.

(2) From curiosity or jealousy.

(3) From anger and dislike of a strange object which he finds in the river he has chosen to spawn in.

So, having seized your lure, chiefly with a view of investigating it, he is in no great hurry to let it go unless he feels a pull on the line. (It is the pull on the line and not the hold of the hook that arouses his suspicions.)

Accordingly, in striking a salmon give him time, strike slowly (no quick jerk or chuck of the wrist or rod top as in trout fishing). Just drive the hook home by a steady well maintained pull, until you make the rod bend.

Even in running water a salmon moves slowly up and takes your fly, returning with it to his original position, so give him a little time to get there and the chances are the fly will then be further back in his mouth. This is the time to strike when you feel him at the end of the line, and when you do strike, try and arrange to move your rod top parallel with the water and towards your own bank.

W. J. Menzies, in his charming book on salmon fishing, mentions some sound advice on striking a salmon which is well worth making a note of. He says, 'You should have a yard or two of loose line in your hand and let it go when you see or feel a rise and when the line is all out, strike.'

Occasionally a fish may take your fly with a rush or when the line is quite taut as you are drawing it in at the end of a cast; it is now more difficult to make sure of hooking him, as he feels the pull on the line almost at once.

With a very large fly one or two steady pulls are sometimes advisable to drive home the big hook.

A good trout fisherman is usually (at first) a bad salmon fisherman, as he is inclined to strike too quickly.

When spinning you should strike quickly when you feel the fish, as he feels the pull on the line as soon as the bait is in his mouth.

(*See also* Notes on Striking, *page* 185 *et seq.*)

SECTION 2

Playing a Salmon

You should have two main objects in view:

(1) To keep him on the move and make him tire himself.

(2) To try to drown him, by getting his head downstream so that the current will open his gills and limit the amount of water he can force over his gill surfaces.

Hold the rod at an angle of about 70°, not higher; you are then playing the fish on the whole bend of the rod (letting the rod do most of the work).

If you hold the rod low, at say 30°, you are playing him on the butt and middle joint, which is the greatest strain a rod can have.

If you hold a long rod quite upright, you tend to pull the fish to the surface, cause him to bore down and frighten him.

There are two methods of playing a fish:

(1) Hold him hard, if you must and your tackle will stand it

(2) Let him run and tire himself, but mind the obstacles and rocks, they may cut your line.

When a fish makes a rush, let him run (if it is safe to do so). Keep opposite him, and a little below him, by running up or down the bank as necessary.

Keep a tight line, and keep as much line out of the water as you can, *i.e.* don't let the line get drowned, as the fish is then pulling against the weight of the line and force of the stream.

With a short rod (say 10 ft) you should hold the rod as high as possible to avoid the line being drowned and to prevent a fish swimming round rocks or other obstructions.

When a fish takes off a lot of line, get it back on the reel as soon as you can: dispute every inch of line with him.

In warm water a fish usually puts up a better fight than in cold water.

A kelt usually makes his first rush downstream.

A clean fish usually makes his first rush upstream.

When a fish jumps, lower the rod quickly to one side (*i.e.* to the right or left side of you, not towards the fish).

A female fish is more lively and jumps more frequently than the male.

When a fish *splashes* on the surface, lower the rod to one side and give him some line; he will at once settle down in the water. A lightly hooked salmon usually comes to the surface.

A *jigging* fish is usually lightly hooked, and requires careful handling.

A *sulking* fish usually stands on his head with his

nose on the bottom, trying to hit your cast with his tail (*see also page* 195).

Side Strain. To put side strain on a fish (see page 192).

To bring a fish downstream (see page 191, para 7).

To make a fish move upstream. In heavy water it is of little use trying to pull him against the current, so get below him and press hard; he will often rush up (*see also page* 191, *para* 6).

Walking up. In easy water try 'walking up.' Hold the rod low and parallel to the water, hold the line so that the reel does not click, then walk back slowly, drawing the fish upstream. When once you get him moving, keep a steady strain on the line, and he will follow you. Should he become lively or resist, stop at once and wait until he has settled down, then continue walking back.

To stop a fish which is rushing up- or downstream (see page 190, para 5).

When a fish is played out and turns on his side, draw him towards the shore by walking back from the bank, and then advancing, reeling up as you go.

On a fly rod you should be able to play him out at the rate of one minute per pound. When spinning you should land him in half that time.

When wading it is best to get out of the water as soon as you can and play the fish from the bank.

The longer you play a fish the more chance there is of the hook-hold wearing.

Here is a rough description of playing a fish. Suppose the first run of the fish is upstream. Let him run and follow him; when he stops, get opposite to him, and before he has time to look about him, turn his head by holding the rod low and getting a horizontal pull on his head. When you get him broadside to the stream, hustle him downstream, still keeping the rod top low and almost parallel with the water.

When he stops, coax him upstream again by ' walking up' (*see page* 166).

When pulling him down, or drawing him up, hold the line so that the reel does not click.

Do this three times, and he should be ready for the gaff.

Of course, much depends on the fish; all salmon are not so obliging as to be dealt with in this way.

The nearer the sea the wilder the fish when hooked (*see also* Notes on playing *page* 190 *et seq*).

SECTION 3

Landing a Salmon

Before attempting to land a fish, either by gaffing, netting, beaching or tailing, you should hold the line firmly in the fingers of the uppermost hand and pressed against the rod. Then pull about 4 ft of line off the reel, letting it hang slack or holding it in loops in your hand.

The instant the fish is landed, let go the slack, otherwise you are liable to damage your rod top.

Never attempt to land a fish until he is well tired out and turns on his side a few times (*see also page* 199).

Before netting or gaffing a fish be very careful to select a good place to land him. Try and draw him into quiet water of suitable depth, avoid very shallow water or places where there are rocks, etc.

Fishermen sometimes use a light rod and light tackle for salmon. It is a fact that a fish gives up the fight sooner against a light rod than against a heavy one; but with light tackle he is inclined to sulk, and the most *dangerous moment* is when you are about to land him and have to put on strain to draw the fish to the net or gaff; your light cast is then liable to break unless you are very careful.

For Notes on Netting a fish, *see page* 200

,,	,,	,,	Gaffing	,,	,,	201
,,	,,	,,	Beaching	,,	,,	202
,,	,,	,,	Tailing	,,	,,	203

SECTION 4

Summary of the Various Methods to try when Salmon Fishing

1. Fly fishing:
    (*a*) Commence at the top of the pool (*see page* 117)
    (*b*) Try backing up (*see page* 118)
    (*c*) Try the greased line method or 'the pulled fly' (*see pages* 120–122)
    (*d*) Try fishing 2 flies (*see page* 136)
    (*e*) Try a dry fly (*see page* 137).

2. Try spinning with an artificial or a dead bait (*see page* 140).

3. Try prawn fishing (*see page* 145)
    (*a*) With a spinning prawn (*see page* 149)
    (*b*) With a non-spinning prawn (*see page* 151)
    (*c*) Casting from the coil with a dressed line (*see page* 238)
    (*d*) Spinning with an undressed line (*see page* 233 *et seq.*).

4. Try a worm (*see page* 154).

Book III

SEA TROUT FISHING

Book III: SEA TROUT FISHING

Part I

ESTUARY FISHING

SECTION I
General Notes

When fishing in brackish water, watch the tides. There are two tides every 24 hours, one tide=6 hours flow + 6 hours ebb. Tides vary daily.

Example, suppose High Water is at 12 noon (flow)

Low water will be at 6 p.m. (ebb)
High Water will be about 12 midnight (flow)
Low water will be about 6 a.m. (ebb)
High Water will be about 12 noon.

If you want to know the *exact* time of high or low water at any place it is best to consult the local tide tables.

To enter a river sea trout prefer a high tide and a fairly calm sea on the bar.

If it is very rough on the bar they will not enter the river whatever the tide.

When once in the river they drift up and down with the tide in the estuary until there is a good spate, then they run up further.

When there is a sea fog it is little use fishing, either from a boat or from the shore, with a fly or any other lure.

Fresh run fish have very tender mouths, so play them very carefully. Let him run, don't hold him hard.

Care of lines and gear when fishing in brackish water:—

Wash your *undressed* lines in fresh water every third day (at least). Put the line in coils in a basin of tepid water, add a little 'Lux' and leave it to soak for about ½ an hour, then wash it in clean tepid water and hang it up to dry.

Wash your gut casts and flies in fresh water every evening, also your dressed line.

Dry your rod well every evening. Rub over with ceroline, especially the ferrules.

Oil reels, swivels, hooks and all metal parts every evening.

SECTION 2

Harling from a Boat

The best time for harling is from three hours before high tide to three hours after high tide.

The last half hour of the ebb and the first half hour of the flow are, however, not usually good.

Supposing high water is at 12 noon, your best chance would be between:

9 a.m. and 11.30 a.m.=2½ hours
12.30 p.m. and 3 p.m.=2½ hours

Of these two periods I prefer the 2½ hours before high water – 9 to 11.30 a.m.

You must have a good boatman who knows the pools, banks, channels, and the localities which fish frequent at the various stages of the tide. Much depends on him.

Row slowly and carefully, allowing baits to hang over likely places (don't just trail your lures).

About 25 yards of line should be out.

Fish deep and work the baits well, either by jerking the rod top or, better still, by jerking the line through the rings.

When fish are rising put no lead on the trace.

When fish are not rising, put lead on the trace to sink your lure.

LURES

Sand eels. Fresh ones are best; cut a bit off the head if necessary.

In coloured water they should be 4 in long;
In clear water 3 in long.

The end hook should extend ¼ in beyond the tail,

and the hooks should be small and well distributed from head to tail (say 6 hooks, 3 down each side). Brown, Belmont St., Aberdeen, sells a very good spinner (*see page* 263).

You can use preserved eels in rough water or a good wind. Fresh ones are best in clear or calm water.

A strip 4 in long by 1½ in wide from the belly of a fresh run sea trout is a good substitute for a sand eel. From a 7 in fish you can get a strip from each side of the belly.

Terrors, 3¼ in – 2½ in, grey, white or blue, are useful baits: work terrors vigorously by pulling line through the rings.

Spoon, 1½ in gold outside, silver inside.

Pearl spoon, 1 in, is worth trying.

Worm, on Pennell tackle (*see page* 104), fished near the bank is very deadly, as fresh run sea trout keep alongside of the banks.

SECTION 3
Spinning from the Bank

Best with a good current on an ebb tide (going out).

It is little use when the tide is flowing up (coming in).

Cast slightly up and across. Sink the bait well and let it come round in the stream. Give plenty of motion to the bait. Don't strike hard. Play tenderly, let him run.

LURES

Silver Devon, 1½ in.
A fresh sand eel, 4 in (*see pages* 263, 265).
Gurnet skin lure.

Fly Fishing from the Bank

Best time=last of an ebb tide, and first part of a flow tide.

Work the flies well.

Fish the channels and runs.

9-ft trace, ·011 ·012 gut.

Flies, size 10 to 14.

The ordinary flies used in trout fishing are quite suitable; silver bodied flies are usually taken well, but the colour and pattern preferred by sea trout vary on different rivers (*see also page* 177).

SECTION 5

Fishing in Salt Water

When the coastline is broken into deep rocky bays and creeks such as one finds in some parts of the West of Scotland and on the coasts of Connemara, Mayo and West Donegal in Ireland, it is often worth while fishing from a boat in the salt water just out-side the estuary of a river and casting among the beds of seaweed close to the shore in about 10 feet of water; fish frequently congregate here searching for sand eels, etc. Work your flies well and fish along the edge of the seaweed. When you have a fish on, get him away from the weeds as quickly as you can.

The best time is from an hour before to an hour after high tide and again from an hour before to an hour after low tide.

When the weather conditions in the brackish water of the estuary are unsuitable for fishing and the coastal conditions referred to above are favour-able, it often pays to try the salt water.

Book III: SEA TROUT FISHING

Part II

RIVER AND LAKE FISHING

SECTION I

General Notes

Best when the water is falling after a spate.

A dull light and moderate breeze are best conditions.

Fishing during the daytime is not much use in very dry weather; wait for a spate.

In wet weather fish the river.

In dry weather fish the estuary.

When actually 'running up' a river they will not take until they arrive at 'a resting place.'

A sea trout 'runs up' a river in a zig-zag fashion from side to side. A salmon usually runs straight.

In a River :

The usual resting places are:

(1) In channels or long stretches of easy water
(2) They lie practically at the bottom where it is smooth and unbroken
(3) Upstream of a rock or boulder
(4) In the tail of a pool
(5) By day in the faster water of a run
(6) By night in the quieter water above the run
(7) They like to lie on a patch of shingle close to a deep hole into which they can retreat if alarmed. They prefer a stony, gravelly bottom to a sandy bottom.

In a Lake :

They usually rest along the edge or over weed beds, off rocky points, islands, etc, in water 9 to 12 ft deep.

Finnock generally go about in shoals and change their resting places more frequently than the larger fish (say 2 lbs), these latter will remain in the same locality for a day or two, sometimes longer.

There is no doubt that all fish feel the vibration in the water of the passage of a motor-driven boat, and the large number of these boats which are now used on some lakes seriously affects the fishing.

My experience, however, is that salmon and sea trout do not appear to be so easily alarmed or put down as brown trout when a motor boat passes. It is presumed that a brown trout being a resident takes more notice of local happenings of this nature than migratory fish which are just visitors to the water.

SECTION 2

Wet Fly Fishing

In a River. Cast up or downstream as already described for brown trout fishing (*see pages* 4 *to* 11). Play him carefully, do not hold him hard.

In a Lake. In most lakes I think it pays best to fish the dropper along the surface with the tail fly sunk. Anyhow this method is worth trying before you start fishing deep.

When fishing for sea trout in a lake, there should be a larger interval between the flies on the cast than when fishing for brown trout.

Two flies are quite enough on a 9 foot cast. If you want to use 3 flies, a 12 foot cast is advisable.

WET FLIES

The size of the fly is very important and depends chiefly on the weather and water conditions.

Under normal conditions use hooks size No 9 to 11. On windy days you can use hooks Nos 6 to 8.

The colour of killing flies varies considerably on different sea trout waters, for instance, in the lakes of Connemara (Ireland) where the bottom is dark and rocky, with few weeds, I have found that (whatever the weather conditions are) when using a cast of three flies, two of them at least should be dark coloured, a good trial cast for these waters being, *viz*:

Black Pennell or Connemara black (tail)
Butcher or Peter Ross (middle dropper)
Black or Blue Zulu (top dropper).

While on many waters in Scotland and Ireland bright coloured flies are preferred.

It is advisable when fishing a new water to consult a local fisherman before finally deciding. On most waters it pays to have silver or gold ribbing on the body of a sea trout fly.

The following is just a list of the flies which I have found are worth trying, *viz*:

Bright coloured	*Dark coloured*
Teal and silver (Blue hackle)	Butcher
	March brown (silver body)
Peter Ross	Black Zulu
Blue Zulu	Mallard and claret
Wickham	Connemara black
Teal and red	Greenwell
Silver Wilkinson	Black hackle Pennell
	Invicta

The black Pennell hackle is a very good tail fly on most waters; sometimes the fish prefer it with a black, yellow or claret body. In each case there should be broad silver or gold ribbing on the body.

Small double flies similar to above (tied tandem) on hooks No 12 to 14 are also worth trying as tail flies.

SECTION 3

Dry Fly Fishing

Adopt methods similar to those already described for brown trout (*see pages 25 et seq*).

Use a cast tapered to ·009 or ·010. Hackle flies are usually the most successful.

The fly must cock well.

The following flies are worth trying, *viz*:

A large tup, Wickham, black Zulu or sedges.

Night Fishing

In the late afternoon do not disturb pools you intend to fish after dark.

Commence about an hour after sunset.

A warm, still night is best; the darker the night the better. A bright moonlight night is seldom any use.

Fish the pools and easy water, most pools have a gravel bed on one side or the other, this is where fish prefer to lie in the early evening: when it gets dark they congregate at the head or tail of the pool.

Even when water is dead low night fishing is worth while.

Stand motionless in a pool where fish are, cast upstream with a short line (about 8 or 10 yds measured from the rod top to the fly, no more). Cast the same length of line each time.

Make your flies fall lightly, draw them slowly and evenly towards you, do not work or jerk them at all.

Strike at once.

Flies. I think a single fly is best, size No 7 to 12. The lighter the night the smaller the fly.

The following flies are worth trying, *viz*:

Invicta, alder, butcher, March brown, teal and red, teal and silver.

On some waters fat, rough-bodied flies are best, on others silver bodied flies.

It is worth while consulting local fishermen about the type of fly.

SECTION 5
Spinning

Adopt the ordinary spinning methods (*see page 244*).

When fish are not rising sink the bait well, put lead on the trace.

When fish are rising put no lead on the trace.

Lures :

A sand eel (3 in), small hooks well distributed from head to tail (*see page 265*).

A $1\frac{1}{2}$ in india-rubber eel, red, black, or white. This is best in rapid water with a good breeze (a Cumberland bait).

A brown and gold phantom.

A silver Devon, $1\frac{1}{4}$ in, $1\frac{1}{2}$ in $\left.\begin{array}{l} \end{array}\right\rbrace$

Blue and silver phantom $\left.\begin{array}{l} \end{array}\right\rbrace$ In full, dirty water

Wagtail, 3 in

SECTION 6
Worm Fishing

Worm fishing for sea trout is similar to that already described for brown trout (*see pages 98 to 102*).

In coloured water you can use a large blue head worm, it should travel slow and quite close to the bottom. Fish often follow the worm round until it is under your own bank, then if you work it with short jerks the chances are he will take it.

A knowledge of the temporary resting places of the fish is a great advantage. In a flood, or when fish are fresh run, they keep near the banks.

In sluggish water they are usually found in the deep holes.

At Night.

A good lure at night is a piece of worm on the hook of a sparsely dressed fly with a long white wing, tied on a No 6 hook.

Let it travel slowly in mid-water (if in a pool it should sink about 3 feet below the surface).

Don't hurry the strike, let him tug twice before you lift.

BOOK IV

STRIKING, PLAYING, LANDING

Book IV: STRIKING, PLAYING, LANDING

Part I

STRIKING

SECTION I

Methods of Striking

The word 'strike' is unsuitable, and gives a
wrong impression of the operation. To 'lift,' to
'tighten' or 'fasten on' a fish is better.

Striking to a rising fish is a matter of temperament and practice.

The essential precedent to good striking is casting
a straight line and striking on a tight line, also allowing your rod to do most of the work.

An excitable or nervy man will always strike too
hard and too quickly, especially if he has been fishing some time without a rise.

The advice given by a ghillie to a nervous jumpy
man when fishing from a boat appears sound, *viz*:
'After making your cast try to look away, and don't
lift or tighten until you feel a fish.' A very rough
rule is, when you see any sign of a rise on the surface, pause before you strike, and when fishing deep
strike when you feel him.

Never make your strike a snatch, a jerk, or a
chuck, or you are liable to break the cast.

Your strike should always be deliberate, while
on the other hand it may be either quick or
slow.

A fisherman should have that enviable quality
which in connection with horsemanship is known as
'hands.'

He should think before he strikes, and try to control himself at the crucial moment.

If you have a tight line (as you should) it is only
necessary when *trout fishing* to raise the rod top a
few inches (not several feet as one is sometimes
inclined to do in the excitement of the moment), or
just to tighten or draw when you feel the fish.

Some anglers when fishing with a single handed

rod prefer to strike a trout with a sideways down-stream movement of the rod instead of a vertical movement.

Strike a trout with the rod top, not with the whole rod or butt.

With a stiff rod or a stiff top you should be more careful and gentle in the strike than with a whippy rod.

If you are using a very stiff rod and are inclined to be at all nervous, it is best to try striking from the reel (*see below*).

The upward switch of the rod top from the wrist is best for a very quick strike.

A lift of the arm or a draw is more suitable for a slow strike.

When using a single handed rather *whippy* rod and you want to make a quick strike, try this way.

Lift or tighten by raising the rod with the right hand in the usual way and at the same time draw in line through the rings with the left hand. This helps to prevent slack line caused by the dip and rebound of the rod top at the moment of the strike.

Striking from the reel :

1. Set the reel to a light check.
2. It is best to cast a short 'set' length of line each time, say 30 ft from rod top to fly.
3. Keep a tight line, no slack at all.
4. When you 'lift' keep your fingers clear of the line.
5. Do not raise your rod beyond the perpen-dicular.
6. You can strike fairly hard from the reel.
7. With a stiff rod and a thin cast this is a safe way of striking, although it is not the best way of making a very quick strike.
8. When using a large salmon fly never strike from the reel.

Striking down :

The strike is made with a downward motion instead of an upward one. You should have a tight line at the moment of the rise.

A downward twitch of the rod top from the wrist is quite sufficient.

If you do give too hard a strike the result is not so serious as in the up strike.

If you miss a fish, the fly does not move far away, nor is it drawn out of the water, and he may come again.

You do not feel the fish immediately, the reaction of the rod gives just the amount of slack line that a plunging fish requires, so that instead of a sudden tension as with the upward strike, there is nothing but 'slackness.'

The strike is practically instantaneous and quicker than the upward strike.

If the fish jumps it is his own affair, and not caused by being bodily pulled out of the water by an upward pull.

SECTION 2

Timing the Strike

It is difficult to lay down rules as to when to strike at once or quickly, and when to 'give him time' or strike slowly; but the following notes may help:

1. In shallow fast water or with small fish, you should strike very quickly.

2. In slow running water or with big fish, strike slowly – give a fish over 2 lb say 3 seconds before you tighten on him.

3. When you see the glint of a fish turning in the water after taking your fly, tighten on him at once. Never tighten on a fish which is coming up to a fly; always wait until he has turned to go down.

4. When casting upstream, you must strike fairly quickly to the rise.

5. You should strike sooner to a fish which takes your bob fly than to one which takes your tail fly.

6. When fishing downstream just hold him; a trout will hook himself: he will also hook himself when at the end of a straight line, such as when drawing in the fly at the end of a cast.

7. To an under-water rise in deep water, do not 'lift' until you feel the fish.

8. When fishing from the shore of a lake, a hooked fish usually rushes off away from you to deep water and is likely to hook himself.

9. When you are hooking fish on the outside of the mouth, the probability is you have been too quick in the strike.

10. More fish are lost from striking too soon than too late.

11. When dapping with the natural Mayfly, count 4, or allow him to take down about a yard of gut cast before you lift or tighten.

12. In salmon fishing you should strike slow; give him time. A good trout fisherman is usually (at first) a bad salmon fisherman, as he is inclined to strike too quickly (*see also page* 163).

13. When spinning with an artificial bait, you should strike a little sooner than with a natural bait.

14. Trout sometimes have a trick of trying to drown your fly before they take it (especially in the evening). When they do this, give them time before you strike or lift.

For some further notes on *Striking a Salmon* see *page* 163.

Book IV: STRIKING, PLAYING, LANDING

Part II

PLAYING

SECTION I

Playing

When playing a fish either in a stream or a lake: 'Don't let the fish fight you – fight him and fight him hard.'

More fish are lost by timid handling than through reasonable firm treatment. The longer a fish is in the water the more likely he is to escape.

a. PLAYING IN RUNNING WATER

1. If you are above a fish when you hook him, get below him and try to keep below him or opposite to him. When you are below him, he is working against the current and the pressure of your rod. When you are above him, you are pulling against the current and drawing the fly out of his mouth.

2. Under ordinary circumstances when playing a fish hold your rod at an angle of about 60° or 70° so that the rod can do its work.

If, however, you are playing a fish on a *short line* and you hold your rod top too high up, you tend to pull the fish towards the surface; this frightens him and may cause him to sulk on the bottom.

3. Dispute every inch of line with him. Keep him on the move. never let him rest. If he runs up- or downstream follow him at once.

4. When the first run is over, try to draw him downstream and drown him by opening his gills.

5. If you want to stop him when he makes a rush up- or downstream bend the rod over to one side and suddenly give him plenty of slack line; when the pressure of the line is off he very often stops, thinking that he is free.

6. To work a fish upstream:

Get opposite to him,
Wait until he is quiet,
Put on side strain (*see page* 192), and try to
draw his head across the current; the stream
helps you: this usually moves him. Then
walk upstream slowly (do not touch the reel,
it frightens him). He will generally follow
you quietly.

7. To work a fish downstream:

Get opposite to him and wait until he is quiet,
Put on side strain (*see page* 192), try to turn his
head towards you. When once you move his
head a little the current helps you; when he
finally turns, walk him downstream, keeping
opposite or below him. Never let him get
below you.

8. When wading, or fishing from a boat close to
the shore, as soon as the fish is played out it is usually
best to go ashore and land him from the bank;
particularly if the fish is a big one.

9. What is called *pumping a fish* is done in this
way:

Holding the line tight, lower the rod top, then
raise the rod drawing the fish towards you,
reeling up spare line as you lower the rod
again. Continue in this way until you draw
the fish to the net. This is quite a good way
to bring in a large, troublesome fish without
putting undue strain on the rod.

b. PLAYING IN A LAKE

When playing a fish in open water which is clear
of obstacles, let him run, but keep a fairly tight line

on him; encourage him to run as it tires him working against the bend of the rod.

If he runs towards you, take in all slack line at once in readiness for another run.

In a lake, try to keep him to windward of you and play him to windward.

When in a boat, try to keep the boat at right angles to your line.

Try to play him over your same shoulder as you hooked him over, turn the boat but do not turn yourself, *i.e.* move round him and try to keep the fish's same shoulder always towards you. This prevents the hook wearing his jaw.

When you want to stop him while he is making a violent rush, give him slack line suddenly: this often stops him,

Or, if necessary follow him in the boat, paying out line to him.

When you hook a fish in shallow water coax him into deep water to play him.

If he tries to go under the boat, stamp on the bottom of the boat: this often prevents him, or try side strain.

If he gets under the boat, put your rod top deep into the water and work the line clear, either under the bows or stern.

If you can avoid it, never play a fish under the point of the rod, *i.e.* close to the boat; better row away a little distance, putting a side strain on him, and helping to keep him on the move.

C. SIDE STRAIN

Side strain is one of the best methods of drawing or guiding a fish where you want him to go.

Hold the rod horizontally to one side, with the line almost parallel to the water; put on a steady pressure, and you can usually turn his head in the required direction, a fish steadies himself against the current by lateral undulations of the body, so you can nearly always turn him by side strain.

If you hold the rod upright the fish feels he is being lifted towards the surface and won't move, or may even 'bore' down towards the bottom.

d. TO HANDLINE A FISH

Lay your rod down, and take the line in your hand or point the rod at the fish and pull in line through the rings. There is then a direct strain from your hand to the fish.

This method is much harder on the fish, and your gut cast should be strong enough to stand the strain; but you don't frighten him with the click of the reel, and the pull being almost horizontal he does not feel that he is being lifted out of the water.

It is, however, risky, as if the fish rushes off suddenly you have a lot of loose line to get back quickly on the reel, which may be troublesome.

e. GIVING A FISH THE BUTT

The expression 'Giving him the butt' is often misunderstood.

The correct way to 'give the butt' is to lower the rod to about 30°, putting the butt in the region of your stomach; the strain then comes on the stronger portion of the rod, *i.e.* the butt.

In 1934 Mr. E. R. Hewitt, while making some interesting experiments with rods, found that if you hold a 10 foot rod at an angle of 30° the pull exerted on the line is twice as strong as when the rod is held at an angle of 90°, while with a powerful salmon rod the pull is 3 or 4 times stronger if the rod is held at the low angle.

Many have the idea that the proper way is to raise the rod to the vertical, or even beyond, throwing the butt forward. This puts all the strain on the rod top and the middle joint, and is if anything 'middle jointing' a fish.

SECTION 2

Some situations which may arise

A weeding trout.

(a) If a fish bolts downstream and you hold him too hard he becomes frightened, takes cover or bolts into a weed bed; the harder you hold him the deeper he burrows into the weeds. The best plan is to give him line and leave him almost free for a little; try to make him believe himself lightly hooked. He will then commence to flounder about, lashing the weeds aside, and may kick himself free.

(b) If he bolts upstream into weeds, it is easier to manage him. Get well below him and try hand-lining him (see page 193) working him backwards and forwards; he will usually free himself.

(c) When a hooked fish holds on to the weeds with his mouth, or sails round and round a bunch of weeds thus becoming hung up, it requires careful manœuvring and a strong cast to disentangle him.

(d) When playing a fish with a bunch of weeds on the line, you have to hold him hard, as you have the weight of the weeds and also that of the fish to deal with. The mistake is often made of playing him too lightly; this only leads to his becoming further entangled.

A Jumping Fish.

(a) If you have a long line out when he jumps, lower the rod top to the right or left (not to the front towards the fish), and raise it again at once when the fish falls back in the water, but if you allow a very long line (especially a thick one) to become 'drowned' the chances are he will break you, unless you have strong tackle, no matter how much you lower the rod top.

A *line is drowned* when it is sunk and allowed to become slack and when you have really lost control of it.

(*b*) If you have a short line out, raise the whole rod up about two feet into the air and lower it again when the fish falls back in the water. This keeps your short line fairly tight on him all the time.

(*c*) Some anglers believe in lowering the rod top to one side as in (*a*) when a fish jumps away from them and raising it as in (*b*) when a fish jumps towards them.

A fish floundering on the surface.

He is very often lightly or badly hooked, or anyhow he thinks he is.

Give him line by lowering the rod to the right or left for a moment, or paying out some line to him. This seems to make him quiet and he sinks back again in the water.

A Sulking Fish.

Try one of the following, *viz*:

(*a*) Get downstream of him with a long line, get a pull on his head slightly to one side and try to turn him broadside to the stream.

(*b*) Try getting as short a line as possible and putting a strain on him from upstream, then move down below him, still keeping on the strain. The change in the direction of the pull may move him.

(*c*) Try putting a strain on him and then suddenly giving him about two yards of slack line.

(*d*) On a fairly short line, try tapping the rod vigorously about 6 in above the reel.

(*e*) Try a few stones dropped near or on him; he may move.

(*f*) Try to tickle his nose with something, *viz*:

Get upstream and send down on the line

1. a bit of cardboard

2. a circlet of rushes

3. a circular piece of lead

4. a twig attached to a safety pin.

5. I know an Irish ghillie on Lough Derg who is very successful with the following method:

He passes a piece of lead wire through a bit of his strong twist tobacco, makes a circlet of it and lets it down the line to the fish's nose. It appears that the taste or smell of strong tobacco will make most fish move.

(*g*) For the amount of strain which is required to move a sulking fish, *see page* 368.

A Foulhooked Fish.

A fish that is hooked in the back, the fins or the tail, is usually very heavy in play, resenting the restraint on his movements. But when foulhooked in the region of the lateral line, the gills or the sensory nerves (*see page* 415), he is far more lively and excitable. In either case you must be very patient with him; it usually takes some time before you can tire him out and land him.

If hooked in the tail and you can manage to get his head downstream, the current will open his gills, and this limits the amount of water that he can force over his gill surfaces, causing him to become out of breath and helping to drown him (*see page* 422).

A fish hooked in the tongue never plays well.

For some further notes on *playing a salmon* **see** *page* 164.

Book IV: STRIKING, PLAYING, LANDING

Part III

LANDING

SECTION I

Notes on Landing a Fish

1. A rough rule is:

Use a net for a fish under 5 lb.
Use a gaff for a fish over 5 lb.

2. When in a boat, always try to land your fish to windward.

3. Never try to land a fish until he is well played out and turns on his side a third time.

4. When bringing an exhausted fish to the net or gaff, etc, try walking back and drawing the fish after you, then advance towards him, reeling up as you go.

If you can manage to keep his gill covers out of water he usually comes quieter after he has taken a few gasps of fresh air (*see also page* 416).

5. Keep your net, gaff, or other instrument well out of sight until the moment you are about to use it.

If you have a ghillie with a net or gaff, etc, make him keep behind you and out of sight.

If when trying to gaff or net a fish you fail for some reason, it is best to lead him a short distance up or downstream to a fresh place before you try again.

6. Before trying to land a fish, you have him on a short line, and just before you land him put the forefinger of your uppermost hand firmly on the line, then with the lower hand pull a yard or two of line off the reel and let it hang slack.

The instant you land him let go the slack and your rod point will fly up. If you don't do this you run the risk of a broken top.

7. First of all kill your fish and then take out the hook.

8. When weighing a fish pass the hook of the spring balance through his gill cover and not through the gills.

9. It is always worth while to examine the gullet or stomach of the first trout you catch to find out what he has been feeding on.

A narrow spoon is useful for this; wet the spoon, it slips down easier.

a. KILLING A FISH

Use a priest for a fish over 10 in; give him three or four sharp taps with it on the head over the brain.

With a small fish grip the fish in the net, back downwards, and knock his head on the handle of the net.

b. NETTING A FISH

First wet the net well then sink it quietly in the water downstream or below the fish.

Guide the fish over the sunken net; try to keep his eyes out of the water while doing so; then lift the net and draw it towards you with the fish in the bag which is formed by drawing the net towards you.

Do not net a heavy fish by raising the net straight up out of the water if you can avoid it.

With a fish longer than the diameter of the net, it is best to get him in tail first, particularly in running water where you may have to slip the net under him from behind.

With a small fish it does not matter much if you net him head or tail first.

When *wading* and you have the fish in the net, push the butt of your rod into your waders. Grip the handle of your landing net between your knees or with a short handled net tuck the handle under your arm. Both hands are now free to deal with the fish.

In a lake or pool, if you have to net a heavy salmon or pike before he is quite played out, it is best to net him head first: the head and shoulders being heavy he drops into the net easily and he cannot use his tail to jump out, but be careful that the hooks do not catch in the meshes of the net.

Netting two fish. Play the fish until they are quite exhausted.

As to how you get them into the net depends a great deal on the size of the fish and the strength of your cast. If circumstances permit the following is worth trying, *viz*:

First net the fish on the dropper, taking out the hook while he is in the net and keeping it clear. Then net the fish on the tail fly.

C. GAFFING

Never try to gaff a fish that is more than one foot below the surface.

Always try to gaff a fish behind the line, never gaff him *over the line* if you can help it.

Never try to gaff a struggling fish; wait until he is well played out, is quiet, and on an even keel, then manœuvre him into a position at right angles to the stroke you are about to make.

Extend the gaff beyond and over his back, *viz*, over the shoulder half way between the head and the dorsal fin. Draw the iron with a firm stroke towards you and down on his back (not a snatch).

Hold up the gaff handle·perpendicular as soon as the iron is home; this prevents a struggling fish slipping off.

In a strong stream when you gaff a fish, swing him out *against* the stream, as he has a tendency to rush upstream when he feels the gaff.

Some ghillies prefer to gaff a fish with an understroke just by the *anal fin*. (You must have a sharp gaff for this, as the tail end of a fish is more flabby than the shoulder.) A fish has less power to struggle when gaffed near the tail.

If, however, you gaff a large fish with an under-stroke in front of the *ventral fin* the hold is very insecure and liable to tear the belly.

Some prefer to gaff a big pike with an overhand stroke half way between the big back fin and the tail, as this renders him powerless with his tail (*see page* 294).

A big fish gaffed exactly in the middle, *i.e.* behind the dorsal fin, has considerable power to struggle and wriggle while on the gaff.

With a big pike or a salmon, if you are alone, gaff him under the lower jaw, as you can then pull as well as lift, and a big fish rather helps you if he struggles in the water.

Keep the point of your gaff very sharp. It is better to sharpen it with a file than with an arkansas stone, which is more suitable for sharpening a hook.

d. BEACHING

Beach a fish only when he is well played out and practically dead.

Select a suitable shelving bank to beach him on and try one of the following 3 methods:

(1) Get his head out of water and walk back steadily from the bank, drawing the fish to the selected spot (don't touch the reel, it frightens him); increase the speed when nearing the shore, and hustle him ashore. When he touches the beach he usually makes a little jump; this helps you and he almost kicks himself ashore. The ghillie can then put a finger in his gills and carry him to a place of safety or he can grasp the tail (with some grit in his hand) and shove (not lift) him on to the bank.

(2) Manœuvre the fish so that his nose rests on some hard substance such as a stone; then the ghillie can stun him with a sharp tap on his head with a stick and lift him out by the gills. Some ghillies on Tweed are experts at this.

(3) If single handed:

> Tow the fish to a convenient place
> Get him on a short line
> Shift the rod to the left hand

Stop the reel from running by pressure of the fingers of the left hand on the line and draw off some slack line with the right hand (*see page* 199, No 6).

If in running water, turn his head downstream, and the current aids in carrying the exhausted fish towards the bank. When he is quite still, stoop down, keeping a strain on the fish with the left hand, seize the tail with the right hand, and shove the fish up on the shore, half the strain being borne by the line and half by the right hand. Insert a finger in his gills and carry him ashore.

Don't forget to release the slack line when the fish is landed.

e. TAILING

The fish must be well played out and quiet.

Take a handful of grit or put a wet handkerchief round your hand.

Get him in position with his head towards the bank.

Shorten the line, lay the rod over the left shoulder, stop the reel running by pressing the line against the rod with the left hand. Grip the small of the tail firmly with the right hand (thumb and forefingers towards the head, little finger towards the tail), push him on to the shore and while doing so keep a strain on the line; this pull on the line helps to prevent the fish from wriggling.

Then hustle him out.

With a small salmon, get a good grip and you can lift him out by the tail.

When wading, grip the small of the tail firmly (with thumb and forefinger nearest the tail). This gives a firm hold in case of reaction when you lift him out.

It is very difficult to tail a sea trout or a brown trout, as the tail will fold and slip through your hand.

It is dangerous to tail a pike.

A pair of stout cotton gloves are quite useful for tailing a fish as they prevent the hand slipping (*Leather* gloves won't do). They are also a good protection against the very sharp teeth of a kelt when extracting a hook.

When using 'a tailer', (see page 379).

f. WEIGHING HIM IN ON THE CAST

You can only do this with a small fish, unless you have a very strong cast.

The fish must be well played out

Draw him towards you gently

Hold his nose out of the water for about a *minute*

When he is quite still, lift him out steadily by the cast – no jerk – no chuck or he will struggle and break you.

Or draw him to a position parallel and close to you, and when quiet grip him *firmly* with your fingers behind the gills and lift him out quickly.

For some further notes on landing a salmon *see page* 167.

Book V

CASTING AND SPINNING

Book V: CASTING AND SPINNING

Part I

FLY CASTING

ECTION I

Types of Casts

In fly casting there are only two types of cast, *viz*:

1. The two motion cast, *i.e.*
   The overhead cast
   The side cast
   The steeple cast, etc.

2. The continuous motion cast, *i.e.*
   The switch cast
   The double switch cast
   The Spey cast, etc.

Of these two types, a continuous motion cast of some sort is much more used in actual fishing than a two motion cast.

The two motion cast is more suitable when your line is straight in front of you at the commencement of a cast, or in dry fly fishing when after drying your fly in the air you make a cast out in front.

When wet fly fishing in a stream you seldom have an opportunity of making a proper two motion cast, as at the finish of the previous cast your line is downstream to one side of you, and you have to make some sort of continuous motion cast or change of direction to get the fly out to your front.

Whatever type you adopt –

1. Never throw a foot more line than is necessary
2. Try to cast a straight line
3. Try to make your line straighten out in the air about 2 ft above the surface of the water, so that when the line becomes 'spent' the fly will fall lightly
4. Lower the rod top as the fly falls on the water
5. Stand straight up, no leaning forward or stretching out of the arms

6. Allow the body to swing easily with the cast; let the rod do its share of the work

7. The rod should be practically noiseless. If there is any distinct 'swoosh' it shews that the cast is being made with the entire rod instead of with the upper portion

8. When learning, be content at first with 12 or 14 yards of line until master of that amount, then you can lengthen the cast by degrees

9. I find the best way to manage the line when fishing with a single handed rod is:
   Hold the rod in the right hand and with the left hand hold the line so that it runs direct from the bottom ring (the right hand does not touch the line at all). Some anglers prefer to have the line passing under the forefinger of the right hand which is holding the rod, and when necessary drawing it through the rings with the left hand, releasing the pressure of the forefinger to do so.

10. Pay particular attention to the correct timing of the cast.

The *presentation* of the fly is quite as important as the *pattern*.

SECTION 2

General Notes on the two Motion Cast

In the two motion cast there are just two strokes:

(*a*) The backward stroke or cast
(*b*) The forward stroke or cast.

The action of casting a fly is very similar to that of throwing a cricket ball, you throw with an easy swing: the principal movement is in the shoulder, the wrist movement coming in only for the actual speeding up or flip to complete the throw.

Avoid excessive effort in both the back and forward stroke.

Allow the elbow to hang down, but avoid a tendency to hold it close to the side. Let it be free.

a. TIMING THE CAST

The timing of the whole cast is very important.

A two motion cast consists of four separate actions which occupy *equal periods* of time, *viz*:

1. The lift of the line off the water and the back cast with a flip at the finish of it

2. The pause to allow the line to extend behind

3. The forward cast with a flip at the commencement of it

4. The follow on of the rod until it arrives again at the original horizontal position.

N.B. When tired after frequent casting, it often helps to count, 1, 2, 3, 4 while making a cast.

The longer the line out, the slower the count, and *vice versa*.

b. LIFTING THE LINE OFF THE WATER

1. If the line is sunk at all bring it towards the surface before you try to lift it.

2. Lift it gradually, never try to jerk it or use force.

3. Try drawing in some line with the hand before you lift; it is easier to clear the shortened line off the water.

4. Try lifting the rod top to 45° two or three times; this brings the line to the surface when you have a long line out downstream.

5. Try lifting the rod top to 45° and swinging the rod top to the right and then to the left: this helps to bring the line to the surface.

6. When lifting the line off the water, do so by using the entire arm and shoulder muscles, with a slight turn of the body. This helps you to have a narrow entry and a straight following line (*see also page* 213).

If there is any flexing of the wrist or elbow, a circular course is imparted to the rod top, which affects the cast, causing the line to form a broad entry when it goes forward.

C. THE BACK CAST

Throw the line up and behind you and do not bring the rod back beyond the vertical (*i.e.* the position at right angles to the horizontal position assumed at the commencement of the cast), in fact the whole cast must be confined as near as may be within an angle of 90° (*see diagram*).

When casting against the wind it is fatal to come back beyond the vertical A.B; casting with the wind this is not so important.

The finish of the back cast must be gradual, it must not be a dead stop.

To make a long cast, it pays to raise the arm in the back cast until the rod top reaches to C.

The rod top should be at its highest on completion of the back stroke.

The following way of casting is sometimes worth trying, *viz*:

Turn well on the hips and when making the back cast turn the rod so that the reel, rings and the knuckles are uppermost, throwing the line well up behind. In this way you can watch the line extending and at the proper moment make the forward cast.

d. THE FORWARD CAST

If you jerk, hesitate, or creep forward in the forward cast, this causes the line to sag and makes waves in the following line by the rod recoiling backwards, and these waves are reproduced in the forward line thus:

It is important that the cut or flip at the commencement of the forward cast should be short, and gradual. If you make a sharp jerky flip or hesitate at all, this jerks the rod top, causing it to make a backward kick and creating waves in the following line, which are intensified as the rod re-asserts itself.

Every wave or irregularity in the line behind is always reproduced in the forward line.

The secret of good casting is never to come forward until the line is almost fully extended behind (*see diagram*). Sometimes the line may have an upward curl of about a yard (but no more) at the extreme end. Try, so to speak, to 'feel' the fly at the end of the extended line. In practice you acquire this by the feel of the line and by the correct timing of the cast. When once you get the knack of it you don't bother about counting 1, 2, 3, 4 as suggested on *page* 210.

If you come forward too soon or too late, waves occur in the line and it will fall on the water more or less in a heap.

The rod must move in a plane during the back cast and also during the forward cast, the two motions not necessarily in the same plane, *i.e.* straight and not curved.

The line must be kept alive.

The forward cast should be made slightly to one side to avoid the line striking the rod top.

e. A NARROW ENTRY

A narrow entry is when your line in the air appears something like this: The distance AB is a narrow curve.

When casting so as to get this narrow entry in the line, you will find that the smaller the arc made by the rod the narrower the curve made by the line, and the larger the arc the broader the curve.

To illustrate this, wave your rod backwards and forwards in the air (as when drying a fly), first move the rod in a small arc, say between 11 and 1 o'clock, and then in a larger arc, and you will see the difference.

The formation of a narrow entry also depends on the proper timing of the back cast and the forward cast. I think you can cast a narrower entry by casting to one side (say 30° from the perpendicular) than if you make your cast directly overhead.

A broad entry is when your line in the air appears something like this: The distance CD is a broad curve.

With a narrow entry it is easier to cast against the wind, as there is very little resistance offered by the narrow curve in the line. Indeed it is very difficult to cast against the wind when the line presents a broad entry.

With a stiff rod it is easier to cast a line with a narrow entry than it is when using a whippy rod.

SECTION 3
Two Motion Casts
a. OVERHEAD CAST
SINGLE HANDED ROD

Hold the rod in a horizontal position with an easy grip (not tightly). Thumb on the back of the rod (*i.e.* on the side opposite to the reel).

Do not make the cast backwards and forwards in relation to the way the body is facing but make it across the body in four motions occupying equal periods of time, *viz*:

1st motion : Lift the rod (*see page* 210) with an ever increasing speed, terminating with a flip or cut just before reaching the vertical (*see page* 211) and throwing the line up behind.

2nd motion : Pause to allow the line to straighten out behind. The length of pause is exactly the same as that occupied by the lift and the back cast. The longer the line out the longer the pause.

3rd motion : Make the forward cast, with a sharp cut or drive forward at the commencement, aiming fairly high.

4th motion : Allow the rod to follow through until it arrives again at an almost horizontal position.

b. OVERHEAD CAST
TWO HANDED ROD

In many particulars the two handed cast resembles the single handed cast.

The following instructions refer to casting *over the right shoulder*. (The cast over the left shoulder is made in a similar manner except that the rod is held with the left hand uppermost.)

Hold the rod in an almost horizontal position, with

the right hand above the reel and the left hand at the extreme end of the butt, with the rubber button resting on the little finger.

The rod should be held lightly, just resting on the hands. No tight grip anywhere.

The line passing through the fingers of the right hand.

Keep the body upright, do not lean forward.

The cast is made in the direction in which the body faces, and not across the body as with a single handed rod.

The hands should do an equal share of the work.

The cast is made in four motions occupying equal periods of time, *viz*:

1st motion : The lift and back cast; with a smooth upward lift of both arms raise the rod until it is about 45° and the line is ready to be lifted off the water. Without any pause accelerate the back cast, throwing the line up behind, raising the right arm well up (*see diagram* A).

Do not shoot the left arm forward as in diagram B.

Don't forget the flip or cut at the finish of the back cast.

2nd motion : Pause to allow the line to extend out behind. At first try looking back to see when the line is properly extended, keeping the feet firm and turning on the hips. After a little practice timing becomes simple.

3rd motion : The forward cast: at the commencement make a short but gradual cut forward with an upward tendency.

4th motion : The follow on: let the rod follow through until it arrives again at the original horizontal position.

C. THE SIDE CAST

(i) Single handed rod : The principle is exactly the same as the overhead cast, except that it is made to one side.

You make the cast parallel to the water.

Remember the line goes out at right angles to the back position of the rod (*see diagram*).

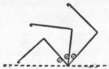

For instance, if you are on the right bank of a stream and wish to cast your fly directly upstream, bring the rod back to a position at right angles to the bank (no further) and in the forward cast from this position your line will go straight upstream parallel to the bank.

It is a matter of choice whether in the forward cast your fly goes out under or over the rod top. The fly falls lighter if your line goes out *over* the rod top.

(ii) Two handed rod : Similar to above.

d. THE WIND CAST

For single and two handed rods.

1. *Against the wind.*

The cast is made similar to the overhead cast (*see page* 214). With an ordinary wind make the cast quietly – no force – forget the wind.

Never come back beyond the vertical (*see page* 211) in whatever plane you are casting.

It is very important to have a narrow entry and a straight following line (*see page* 213).

In the forward cast throw more on the surface than over it. In fact bring the rod top almost to the water with a downward cut.

Against a stong wind cast across it or dodge it as best you can, try casting under the wind with a low side cast.

When casting against the wind it sometimes happens that the line being heavier, it gets beyond or leads the gut cast, to prevent this pull back the line just before the movement of extreme extension, this helps to make the fly fall at the end of a straight gut cast.

It is impossible to cast against a gale of wind.

2. *Across or on the wind.*

Do not use force – forget the wind.

Use a side cast parallel to the water (*see page* 216). The timing is very important.

The back cast is assisted by the wind, while in the forward cast your line goes out at right angles to the back position of the rod and unfolds itself on or across the wind.

e. THE STEEPLE CAST

For single and two handed rods.

The methods are the same as in the overhead cast except that in the back cast you throw the line straight up almost vertically above you, carrying the hands well above the head.

It is useful for a long cast with the wind behind you.

f. THE BACKHAND CAST

SINGLE HANDED ROD

It is a 'two motion' cast made over the left shoulder with a single handed rod.

It is all right when the wind is blowing from the *right* side. The cast is made across the body.

A wind from the *left* side is liable to blow the fly in your face.

g. THE BACKHAND CAST

TWO HANDED ROD

This is a useful cast in salmon fishing when the wind is suitable.

It is usual to make it on the down-wind side of you, so I will describe it in connection with the direction of the wind (*i.e.* when it is blowing from your right side or when it is blowing from your left side).

The cast is made in four motions, which occupy equal periods of time.

The following three examples explain how and when the cast can best be made:

(A) When the wind is blowing from your *right* side and your line is extended downstream to your left, thus:

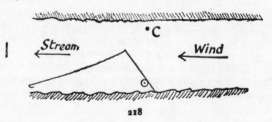

(i) Hold the rod right hand uppermost. Lift the line and continue the back cast up on your left side at an angle of about 45°, throwing the line well back with a vigorous back stroke (if you have a long line out).

(ii) Pause to allow the line to straighten out. The length of the pause depends on the length of line out.

(iii) Make the forward cast with a sweep up and over the left shoulder, causing the rod top to propel the line forward and using pressure with the uppermost hand to do this (especially with a long line).

(iv) The line shoots out over the water in the direction of C.

(B) When the wind is blowing from your *left* side and the line is extended downstream to your right hand side, thus:

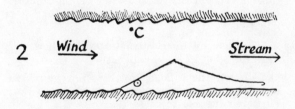

The cast is made in a similar manner, but the rod is held with the left hand uppermost and the forward cast is made over the right shoulder.

(C) When the wind is blowing from your left hand side (i.e. upstream) and your line is extended downstream to your left, thus:

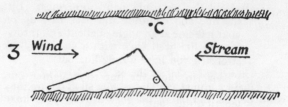

It is very difficult to make this cast except in a very light breeze. If the wind is not too strong try a 'Spey' cast (*see page* 224), or a 'change direction' cast (*see below*).

SECTION 4
Continuous Motion Casts

a. GENERAL NOTES

In all these casts the line must be kept continually in motion and alive, with no pause.

With the switch, double switch and Spey casts, it is difficult to cast against a wind straight from the front, and it is almost impossible if the wind is at all strong.

b. CHANGE OF DIRECTION CAST

1. *Single handed rod.* When you lift a fly from B and want to cast it in the direction of A, it is advisable to cross the courses of the line thus: BX to XA, making a continuous motion cast, maintaining a plane in the courses BX, XA and keeping the line alive.

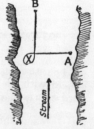

2. *Two handed rod.* Make the cast in a similar way. Hold the rod right hand uppermost when

making the cast over the right shoulder, and *vice versa*.

c. SWITCH CAST

SINGLE HANDED ROD

The line is extended on the water in front of you.

To make a proper switch cast you should have the wind behind you, as in the forward cast your line makes a broad entry and is rather at the mercy of the wind.

This is a useful cast on a lake or pool, where your line is *extended in front of you* after the previous cast.

The cast is made in two motions of equal periods of time.

Stand facing your fly.

Grip and hold the rod in a horizontal position as in the two motion cast (*see page* 214).

1st motion : The lift and back cast are made by drawing the line evenly and smoothly upwards and backwards until it is nearly clear of the water. The extreme back position should be the highest point of the rod's course (don't allow the rod to drop back when once it reaches the highest point).

2nd motion : Without any pause whatever, bring the rod top round and over the right shoulder, increasing the speed and making the forward cast, aiming high and causing the line to extend over the water (no thrash down on the water). It is important that the weight of the line should be brought into play at the right moment in the forward cast.

The fly remains on the water until you make the forward cast.

The fly does not go behind you at all.

Throughout the entire cast the line must be kept alive.

This cast can be made in any plane so long as the backward cast has an upward tendency.

The switch cast may be used in preference to the overhead cast when the wind is from behind.

d. SWITCH CAST

TWO HANDED ROD

It is made in a similar way to that described for the single handed rod.

In the back cast swing the rod upwards and to one side, swinging the body round at the same time, and make the forward cast well over the right or left shoulder, holding the rod right hand uppermost when casting over the right shoulder and *vice versa*.

e. DOUBLE SWITCH CAST

TWO HANDED ROD

Commence with the line downstream B A (*see diagram*).

Face the point C.

The cast is made in four phases of equal periods of time, keeping the line always alive, no pause anywhere.

If the forward cast is to be over the left shoulder, hold the rod left hand uppermost, and *vice versa*.

Example:

Forward cast over left shoulder.

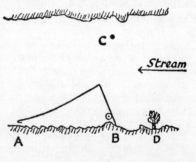

1st phase : Raise the rod top well up, bringing the lower hand to the level of the chin to clear the line almost off the water. If the water is sluggish and you have a long line out you may have to do this twice.

2nd phase : Swing the rod to the right with an easy swing, throwing the belly of the line to the right.

3rd phase : Swing the rod and line to the left, and swing the rod over the left shoulder.

The fly, cast and line are now a little below you in the stream.

4th phase : Make an overhead cast from over the left shoulder, aiming high, and driving the fly over the water towards C.

The fly remains on or near the water until you make the forward cast.

The line does not go behind you.

The whole cast is a free and easy swing; let the rod do the work.

This is a useful cast to avoid an obstruction such as a tree at D.

It is best with a wind from behind or a medium downstream wind.

The chief points to observe are:

   (*a*) an easy swing
   (*b*) correct timing and no pause
   (*c*) let the rod do the work.

f. DOUBLE SWITCH CAST
SINGLE HANDED ROD

In a similar way to that already described for a two handed rod (*see diagram*, *page* 222).

1. Commence with line downstream B A.
Face the point C.
The cast is made in four phases, in one continuous movement, no pause.

1st phase : Lift the line to clear it almost off the water.

2nd phase : Swing the rod to the right, throwing the line to the right.

3rd phase : Swing the rod and line to the left and bring the rod over the left shoulder.

4th phase : Make an overhead cast over the left shoulder, aim high, driving the fly over the water towards C:

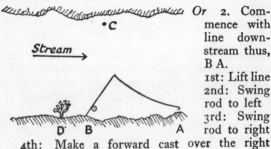

Or 2. Commence with line downstream thus, B A.

1st: Lift line
2nd: Swing rod to left
3rd: Swing rod to right

4th: Make a forward cast over the right shoulder towards C.

g. THE SPEY CAST

1. *Two handed rod.*

Stand firmly at B, facing toward C.

Turn the body on the hips towards A.

Hold the rod almost horizontal.

When the forward cast is to be over the right shoulder hold the rod right hand uppermost, and *vice versa*.

The cast is made in three equal periods of time.
The timing is very important (a sort of valse time).

(i) The lift, count 1, 2, 3
(ii) The swing, count 1, 2, 3
(iii) The cast, count 1, 2, 3

The whole cast is continuous, no pause whatever.

A. When the forward cast is to be over the *right*
shoulder (*see last diagram*).

1st period (count 1, 2, 3): Raise the rod well up
(not too quickly) until the lower hand is at the level
of the chin and the line nearly clear of the water.

2nd period (count 1, 2, 3): Swing rod and body
vigorously to the right, swinging the line in a belly
away from you, carrying the rod top in a rising curve
well behind you; your fly should now be on the water
a trifle above you, say at D (*see last diagram*).

3rd period (count 1, 2, 3): Continue the swing up
and over the right shoulder, making the forward cast
nearly over your head, aiming high, and follow
through until the rod is pointing at C. The line
should shoot out over the water (not *on* the water).

B. When the forward cast is to be over the *left*
shoulder.

Hold the rod left hand uppermost and make the

cast in a similar
way as describ-
ed in A, *viz*:
(i) The lift.
(ii) Swing the
rod, line and
body to the left,
bringing the fly
to D.
(iii) M a k e a
forward stroke over the left shoulder towards C.

N.B. – The line should not go behind you. You can make a good Spey cast with any quick action rod, but I think the best weapon for Spey casting is the Castleconnell type of rod, which has the top joint rather heavier than usual, as its action helps to pick up the line and propel it well forward in the final or third period of the cast.

2. *Single handed rod.* The cast is made in a similar way to that described for a two handed rod (but is not often used).

You need a stiff trout rod and a heavy line.

SECTION 5

Shooting the Line

Commence by drawing off some line from the reel: let it hang down, or fall on the ground if the place is clear of twigs, etc, or gather it in loops on the fingers.

There are three requirements to make a good shoot:

1. To cast a correct forward line

2. To hold the line taut with the fingers until the correct moment when it is well on its way

3. Then release the line and let it run through the fingers as it is travelling forward in the 'follow through' and when the rod top is low. If too much force is used the fly and cast will jump back when the line is fully extended.

If you release the line too soon, or allow it to slacken, the pull on it is lost.

If you release it too late the belly of the line falls on the water and the following line falls in a heap.

It is easier to shoot a line with a stiff rod than with a whippy rod.

For ordinary fishing a greased line will shoot quite well, but much the best for 'shooting purposes' is a clean, well polished line; this, however, may not always be convenient for fishing.

SECTION 6

Casting a Dry Fly

In *wet* fishing the object is to search every yard of the water with the fly.

In *dry* fly fishing the object is how best to cover a fish after you have chosen the best place from which to make your attack.

To cover a fish, make false casts in the air, feeling your way across to the spot where you wish your fly to alight.

Your first cast over a fish is your best chance.

Try to make your fly fall on the water as gently as thistledown.

At the end of the forward cast try advancing the whole rod about 6 inches: this little push helps to make a fly fall lightly.

A side cast of some sort is usually better than an overhead cast.

Drag is one of the chief troubles one has to contend with when dry fly fishing.

Here are four suggested ways of avoiding drag on a fly.

(1) When casting to a fish in quiet water across a belt of rapidly moving water, it pays to cast a a zig-zag line by twitching back the line a few inches with the left hand as it travels forward: this allows the fly to rest a little on the water before the drag comes, thus: (*see also page* 28).

(2) Try to cast a line with an upstream curve in it; thus:

(3) When the current has caused a downstream belly in the line and your fly is about to drag, try 'mending the cast' by swinging the belly upstream and diagonally away from you without seriously disturbing the fly, thus:

Holding the rod low with your hand close to the body, lift the line off the water (well into the curve or belly) with a slightly downstream motion at first, then continue the swing of the rod round and in an upstream direction, at the same time by straightening the arm throw the belly of the line diagonally away from you and upstream.

The whole movement should be carried out slowly, no force is necessary.

(4) Try to make a loose cast rather downstream, checking the line in the air before it falls on the water: this makes the cast fall loose. But when casting a dry fly downstream you can seldom make a second cast over a fish as the recovery of the line usually puts him down.

The two main points in dry fly fishing are:

1. To make your fly fall on the water like a natural insect.
2. To avoid drag by cheating the current, so as to give the fish a chance of having a good look at the fly while at rest or moving naturally with the current.

SECTION 7

The Wind and Casting

The direction of the wind very often decides which sort of cast you should adopt, and you have to try to dodge the wind as best you can.

•C

Stream

Here is just one example, when using a two handed rod casting from B to C.

A   B

i. When the wind is from a point *behind* you

Try: The Spey cast (*page 224*)
      Change direction cast (*page 220*)
      Back hand cast (*page 218*)
      Double switch cast (*page 222*)

ii. When the wind is from your *right hand* side (downstream)

Try: The double switch cast (*page 222*)
      The back hand cast (*page 218*)

iii. When the wind is from your *left* side (upstream)

Try: Side cast on the wind (*page 217*)
      Change direction cast (*page 220*)
      Spey cast (with a light wind) (*page 224*)

iv. When the wind is from your *front*

Try: Overhead wind cast (*page 217*)
      Side cast (*page 216*).

SECTION 8

Tournament Casting

1. The rod should be powerful and have a sufficiency of action. It should combine a reasonable amount of spring (without feeling soft or too whippy).

It should have a touch of spring in the butt giving you a feeling of control right up to the rod top.

2. Use a fairly heavy and well tapered line. The tapering is very important, as if the line is not properly tapered the fly is liable to fall back over the cast at the finish. See that the line does not have any coils in it from being too long on the reel, etc. A well polished line 'shoots' better than a greased line (*see also page* 227).

3. Before commencing draw off a good lot of line and let it lie at your feet.

4. The spot between your feet should be clear of all obstacles; it is best to spread a piece of matting or lay your coat down.

5. Timing is very important. You must give a long line plenty of time to straighten out behind.

6. In the back cast keep the line well up and clear of the ground behind.

7. Raise the arms well up and make the forward cast from vertically over the head.

8. With a long line out you must be very careful to prevent the line striking against the rod in the back and forward stroke.

9. Never let your line sink much in the water: after you complete a cast pick it off at once and cast again.

Try the following method:

Make a cast of medium length, lift at once and

make another cast but longer, and so on until you get out a good line; then finally in the back stroke turn half-right and make a horizontal side stroke thus:

(*a*) When using a single handed rod, turn the right hand over until the little finger is uppermost, and make a powerful horizontal back cast; the line shoots back parallel to the ground, extending fairly quickly. You then make your final forward overhead cast and shoot as much line as you can.

(*b*) When using a two handed rod, try a similar horizontal back cast to one side, keeping the line well up and clear of the ground behind.

SECTION 9

Casting a Fly Spoon

When casting a 'fly spoon' or a very light minnow with a *fly rod*, try the following method; you can throw a longer and straighter line than if you adopt the ordinary method of casting a fly:

In the back cast allow plenty of time for the line to straighten out behind, then make a strong forward cast bringing the rod top down to a horizontal position at the finish and causing the bend of the top joint to drive the bait out straight to the front.

If you use lead on the cast it is better to have two tiny ones about one foot apart than one lead.

Book V: CASTING AND SPINNING

Part II

BAIT CASTING

SECTION I
General Notes

These notes refer only to methods of casting with free running reels such as the Nottingham and Ariel types. They do not refer to mechanically controlled reels which require special instructions for their management. (*See also page* 365.)

When learning to cast, the secret is to begin with a heavy bait (say 2 oz) and at first throw only a short distance, gradually increasing that distance. When you find you can manage a 2 oz bait try with lighter ones.

Correct casting is effortless and easy, no jerk, just swing the bait out.

The use of a finger-stall on the finger that regulates the drum is a great advantage. The finger of a glove is best. A rubber one is unsuitable.

The trajectory of your cast should be like the outside of a William pear.

The heavier the bait, the less effort is required; the bend of the rod will give quite enough power.

For a long cast, a sharp cut or flip at the finish is an advantage. It adds to the distance of the cast if (as the line is running out) you raise the butt of the rod to about the level of the eye. This causes less friction than when the rod is held at the customary angle.

I will now try to describe three methods of casting a bait with a free running reel, *viz*:

  (i) The back swing cast   Section 2
 (ii) The switch cast   ,,   3
(iii) Casting from the coil   ,,   4

The Back Swing Cast

This method is more of a sweep and you require a clear space behind you.

a. TWO HANDED ROD

Holding the rod to one side at an angle of about 45° commence with bait hanging down 4 ft from the rod top.

Hold the rod top with your right hand below the reel, using the forefinger of the right hand to brake the drum. With the left hand hold the rod lightly above the reel (*see diagram page* 241).

Casting from right side :

1. Face III o'clock
2. Left shoulder pointing to XII
3. Swing back to VI with ordinary baits
4. With a light bait you must swing back to IX.

Casting from left side :

1. Face IX o'clock
2. Right shoulder pointing to XII o'clock
3. Swing back to VI with ordinary baits and back to III with a very light bait.

When you swing the bait back 'catch' it at the end of the swing, and swing it forward and upward – no jerk. The whole act is a smooth upward swing of the rod, arms and body (and even a follow-on with the swing of the arms): no excessive effort: make the bend of the rod do most of the work.

When proficient, try to keep your eye on the spot you are aiming at. I think this helps in accurate casting.

Casting from the right side as above described is all right from the bank, but from a boat it is a little awkward to brake the reel, so try as follows:

Hold the rod with your right hand above the reel, brake the reel from behind with the side of the first finger of the left hand, grasping the rod with the thumb and other fingers of the left hand.

b. SINGLE HANDED ROD

Use a short rod about 7 ft long, free reel, and a thin line.

Commence with the bait hanging down about 3 ft from the rod top.

Keep the right arm nearly straight.

Hold the rod with your right hand below the reel. The reel should be near the end of the butt so as to enable you to brake the drum with the forefinger of the right hand.

The stance and the back and forward swing are the same as for a two handed rod (*see page* 234).

When casting from the right side you must come further round in the back swing than when casting from the left side.

I think from the left side the cast is easier and more accurate as the cast is across the body.

The normal weight of a bait is about ¾ oz (line, ·024); with a lighter bait the direction tends to be a little uncertain and requires care.

c. CASTING A VERY LIGHT BAIT

When the bait is very light, you want an easy running reel, a thin line and the sweep of the rod should be at least three quarters of a circle.

Stand with the right or left shoulder pointing to the spot aimed at, XII (*see diagram*) and finish the cast with the rod top pointing to XI or I as the case may be.

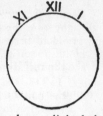

If a longer swing is necessary lengthen it at the beginning of the cast and *not* at the end.

It also pays where you want to drop a light bait at A (*see diagram*) to aim at C when casting from the right side and to aim at B when casting from the left side.[1]

(*See* Regulating the Drum, *page* 240.)

SECTION 3

The Switch Cast

I prefer this method to the Back Swing cast for both a two handed and a single handed rod, because the bait never goes very far behind you.

This method works best with the lead or weight in the bait. When the lead is on the trace it is liable to fall beyond the bait, causing the line sometimes to fall in coils.

a. TWO HANDED ROD

The control of the drum with the forefinger of the right hand and the stance, etc, are similar to that described for the Back Swing cast (*see page* 234).

Commence with the bait at rest, hanging down about 4 ft from the rod top.

---

[1] Very light baits can also be cast from fixed-spool reels (*see page* 365).

Casting from the left side

1. Face IX o'clock
2. Right shoulder pointing to XII
3. Hold the rod at an angle of about 45°, pointing to about VII o'clock
4. Lift the rod top and guide the bait towards you like a pendulum

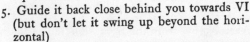

5. Guide it back close behind you towards VI (but don't let it swing up beyond the horizontal)
6. Catch the bait at the end of its swing, and swing it upwards and forwards, making the rod bend.

Casting from the right side :

This is similar to casting from the left side, but you must guide the bait further back close behind you than when casting from the left side.

For a long cast you must guide the bait well back, close behind you, before swinging it forward.

b. SINGLE HANDED ROD

Use a short rod, thin line, free reel.

The method is similar to that described for a two handed rod switch cast (*see page* 236).

The reel must be close to the end of the rod and handy for the first finger of the right hand to brake the drum.

Commence with the bait at rest and hanging down 3 ft from the rod top (with a very light bait you can cast it better if the bait hangs down 5 ft).

Casting from the left side : Similar to that described for a two handed switch cast (*see diagram above*).

The cast is made across the body, and I think it is easier from the left than from the right side.

Let the bait swing back close behind you, catch it, and then just an upward and forward swing.

Casting from the right side : Same as from left side but, of course, not across the body.

You must swing the bait further back than when casting from the left side.

The following 'don'ts' are useful to remember with the switch method:

1. Don't hold the rod tightly
2. Don't start your swing with a jerk
3. In the backward swing don't allow the bait to swing up beyond the horizontal
4. The forward swing must be smooth and even, no jerking.

SECTION 4

Casting from the Coil
(Pitching)

a. TWO HANDED ROD

You should have a fairly thick dressed line (an undressed one won't do at all).

You should have a reel with a click on it, a Hardy Perfect reel is suitable.

You must have a clear spot to coil the line on (no twigs, long grass, rocks, etc). A boat with projecting nails and other things to catch the line on is fatal.

Pull off say 25 yards of line, letting it fall loose in coils on the ground or on the bottom of the boat.

Pitching is suitable when you *must* fish with a heavy line and a light bait. The disadvantage of it is, when you hook a fish you have a lot of loose line which must be got back on the reel as soon as possible. You can, however, 'feel' a fish better when drawing the line in through the rings and letting it fall in coils at your feet than when reeling it in.

'Pitching' is adopted by natives at Castleconnell chiefly when prawning for heavy fish and using a 12½-ft rod, 4½ in Hardy Perfect reel, No 5 Kingfisher line ·064 in thickness. Very strong tackle like this is, of course, not necessary on all waters.

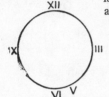

Method from left side :

1. Face XII o'clock.
2. Commence with the rod pointing to IX and the bait hanging down about 5 ft from the rod top.
3. Hold the rod with your right hand uppermost, left holding the butt.
4. Very little back swing of the bait is necessary. The forward cast is more of a pitch than a swing.
5. Press with the upper hand and make the bend of the rod do the work, assisting the cast by turning the body.
6. It is important to let go the line at the right moment at the end of the 'pitch.'

Method from right side :

1. Similar to casting from left side.
2. Hold the rod with your left hand uppermost.
3. From the right side you must start with the rod a little further back.
4. It is best to face III o'clock.
5. Point the left shoulder to XII.
6. Start the forward cast with your rod pointing to about V o'clock.

b. SINGLE HANDED ROD

Use a short rod, fine *dressed* line, and a reel with a click.

The method is similar to that described for 'pitching' with a two handed rod (*see page* 238).

As your line is rather thin the ground must be quite clear of obstacles.

You can cast either from the left side (across the body) or from the right side.

When casting from the right side you must start your forward cast further back than you would from the left side.

Or you can coil the line in your left hand and cast with the right, thus:

5 yards of slack line can be held in 3 coils on fingers of left hand

The first or biggest coil on 1st finger

The second and smaller coil on 2nd finger

The third and smallest coil on 3rd finger

The smallest coil (on the 3rd finger) should be the first to go off when you make the cast.

SECTION 5

Regulating the Drum

The proper control of the drum is very important.

Brake the drum of the reel with the side of the forefinger of the right hand. Keep the tip of the finger on the reel plate and don't allow the finger to wander from the reel plate.

The diagram on page 241 shows the position of the hands.

Always brake the drum gradually, not suddenly.

The general principle is:

The speed of the bait through the air should be such as to take up at once all the line given off by the revolving drum, therefore the speed of the drum

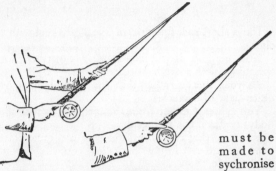

must be
made to
sychronise
or keep pace with the speed of the bait.

So long as the bait can take up all the line given off
by the drum you are all right, but when it can't, you
must brake or slow down the drum, otherwise you
have an over-run.

When casting *with the wind*, the speed of the bait is
accelerated, and you don't have to slow down the
drum very much.

When casting *against the wind*, the speed of the
bait is diminished, so the drum wants to be carefully
controlled, otherwise you will have an over-run.

Using a *heavy bait*, say 1½ oz, and making a long
cast, the heavy bait has good momentum, and goes far
at an even pace, so the drum does not require much
braking until the bait is just falling on the water.

Using a *light bait*, say ¼ oz, and making a long cast,
although it may start fast, the light bait has little
momentum and slows down very soon, so you must
brake the drum when the bait is about half way, or it
will give off more line than the slower moving bait
can take up.

A wet line runs off easier than a dry one, so adjust
your mechanical brake (if you have one) after the
line is wet.

The weight of metal at the rim of the drum is important.

A drum with heavy metal in the rim acts as a sort of fly wheel; although it takes some power to start it, when once started it will continue to revolve for some time.

A large drum is best for a heavy bait, as the heavy bait helps to start the drum.

A small light drum is best for a light bait, as it does not require much weight to start it (but when started requires proper control).

a. SOME CAUSES OF OVER-RUNNING

1. When more line is given off from the drum than the bait in its flight can take up.
2. When you put too much power into a cast and fail to brake the drum properly.
3. When your finger fouls the thumb-pieces of the reel.
4. When the line gets caught in the line guard. A line guard increases the work of undoing an over-run. (I always remove the line guard.)
5. When the line is loosely or unevenly wound.
6. When the line is kinked or sticky.

SECTION 6
The Catapult Cast

With a single handed rod it is sometimes useful to get under trees, etc.

It is best to use a dressed line.

1. Draw off some line, let it fall in coils or hang on the fingers (*see page* 240).
2. Grip the bait in your left hand.
3. Arch the rod horizontally, and aim at the spot where you wish bait to land.
4. Let go the bait and give the rod a short sharp downward cut.

Book V: CASTING AND SPINNING

Part III

SPINNING AND TRAILING

Spinning

a. GENERAL NOTES

Do not 'throw' further than is absolutely necessary.

Try to cast the same length of line each time, so as to search the whole of the water methodically.

Try to keep your line straight in the stream with no belly in it. When spinning in a stream in the ordinary way, you are shewing the fish an end on view of the bait most of the time. I think it pays if you can manage it, to occasionally show him a broadside view. This is not always easy, as it may mean a slack line and a slow moving bait rather out of control.

In heavy or coloured water a bait that wobbles is often better than a straight spin (*see* Baits, *page* 278).

All baits should revolve quickly; loose side hooks tend to retard the spin and should be bound with silk or wire.

It is convenient to have a rubber band on your Spinning Rod below the bottom ring, to which you can attach the hooks of your bait when carrying the rod. Or you can have a small loop made of a thin piece of porpoise hide boot lace whipped on at a convenient place below the bottom ring.

With a very light bait:

1. Try 'pitching,' with a dressed line, if the ground is clean and suitable (*see page* 238).

2. Try casting from coils held in the hand (*see page* 240), or from line drawn off between the 1st and 2nd rings.

3. Try a catapult cast (*see page* 242).

4. Try the back swing cast (sub section c. *page* 235).

With a very light bait, it is all right casting with an Illingworth reel, but you must have plenty of room to play a fish and the water should be clear of obstacles and dangerous spots, as the tackle is not strong. Or you can use a Malloch reel and undressed line of suitable thickness.

b. WEATHER CONDITIONS

When water becomes too coloured for fly fishing, it is usually suitable for spinning.

At the commencement of a spate, when the water is rising and colouring, is a good time.

In clear water there must be a wind to ruffle the surface.

Under any conditions a wind is an advantage.

On a lake you must have a wind.

Good conditions on a lake are: a good wind, a dull light, high water and few weeds about.

A calm bright day on a lake is of little use for spinning.

SECTION 2

Methods in Lakes and Still Water

You can throw far off but make your bait fall lightly and on its side.

Sometimes a bait falls end on and bends the attachment of the tail hooks, or the hooks of the bait double back and get caught in the cast or in the bait itself. Also with a light bait and lead on the trace the lead tends to fall on the water beyond the bait (*see also page* 276 d.).

These troubles can be avoided by checking the line just before the bait falls on the surface.

A bait should commence to spin at once after touching the water, so when it falls, reel in quickly for a couple of yards, unless you wish to spin deep, then of course you must let it sink.

When casting from the bank of a lake you can cover more water if, after making a cast, you walk along the bank about 15 yards, reeling in as you go.

Do not cast directly down-wind, rather cast across it.

With a following wind throw high up and across the wind.

With the wind against you make your cast low and flat.

In deep water when reeling in hold the rod top low, pointing to the incoming bait; you can then feel and strike a fish better.

In clear water reel in fast; you can hardly reel in too fast for a trout.

In coloured water reel in fairly slowly, just fast enough to make your bait spin well.

With a following *trout*, if the bait stops the trout will often take it.

With a following *pike*, if the bait stops the pike generally moves off.

It often pays to vary the speed of your bait, *viz*: wind in very quickly for a yard or two, then slow down for a bit.

SECTION 3

Methods in Running Water

a. SPINNING UPSTREAM

In shallow running water it is best to wade and cast upstream.

Make frequent casts up and across with a short line, drawing the bait quickly across and downstream.

Your bait should commence to spin at once after touching the water.

Use a stiffish rod 8 or 9 ft long. A thin *dressed* line is easier to manage than an undressed one.

It is not necessary to cast from the reel, it is more convenient to cast from coils in the hand or with a fixed short length of line, raising the rod top or drawing in line as the bait comes down towards you.

Fish carefully behind stones, in stickles, currents and eddies.

You can fish in low water and on a bright day, provided the water is well broken. An upstream breeze is an advantage.

b. SPINNING DOWNSTREAM

This is best in water not less than 2 or 3 feet deep, because in shallow water, unless very careful, you are liable to catch in the bottom.

You can cast from the reel, using a short rod, a 4-in ariel reel and a ·020 undressed line; or any other suitable spinning gear.

Fishing from the bank, cast across and down with a fairly long line.

In rapid water let the bait come round with the stream; when the line is straight in the current, reel in, jerking the rod top just a little to give life to the bait.

While fishing hold the rod top low: you can feel and strike a fish better than if held high.

Never cast directly across the current. It is better to cast more down and across. By so doing you avoid too much 'belly' in the line, it straightens out sooner and the bait commences to fish sooner.

Further if the water is shallow, the current helps to keep the bait off the bottom when you cast it well down and across.

When casting in very easy water, you must begin to reel in slowly almost at once, in order to make the bait spin and to give it life and movement.

SECTION 4
Kinking

Some causes:

1. Insufficient effective swivels or a faulty swivel;
2. Uneven or loose winding on the drum;
3. A slight kink is given to the line as the bait flies out;
4. A thin line kinks more easily than a thick one;
5. A heavy bait kinks a line more than a light one.

a. TO PREVENT KINKING

1. Attach a double swivel or a link spring swivel to the end of the reel line. There is a ball-bearing swivel (of French make) which is very effective when used at the end of the reel line.
2. Use an underhung lead, *viz*, a bent Jardine lead; a bullet attached to a swivel; a Geen underhung lead (*see* Baits, *page* 262).
3. Always put lead above the chief swivel.
4. Gut kinks very easily, so always have a swivel about every 2 ft on a gut trace.

b. TO TAKE KINKS OUT OF A LINE

1. Remove the bait and draw 40 or 50 yards of the line through a grass field, or even behind a boat, or let the line out in a strong stream for say five minutes then reel it in slowly.
2. Use a bait with a reversible fin and reverse the fin; *or*, reverse the bend in the tail of a natural bait. *For* how to make a devon or a phantom spin left- or right-handed (*see page* 270).

248

3. Pay out more line than you usually cast, tuck a loop of the line under itself, and wind line on the drum in the reverse way. Continue casting, and this will take out the kinks.

C. TO TEST A LINE FOR KINKS

Hold a portion of the line in each hand, letting a loop of the line fall. If it is kinked it falls twisted, if it is all right it falls in one loop.

SECTION 5

When Caught in the Bottom

1. Get upstream of the bait and use a floating object:

   (*a*) A piece of 1 in board, 12 in x 2 in, suspended at one-third of its length;

   (*b*) A log of wood 3 in in diameter, 12 in long, with a staple at one-third of its length;

   (*c*) A corked bottle (empty);

suspend any of these on a piece of string 4 in to 5 in long.

Use a small 'key ring,' a 'chicken' ring, or a safety pin at A to pass the line through. Pass the floating object down the line as far as it will go, then jerk it up and down by pulling up stream on the line. This jerking and the force of the current may release the bait.

   (*d*) An 'otter board' used in a similar way is very useful for clearing a bait (*see page* 435).

2. Get upstream, lift the rod top and tighten the line, then throw the rod forward, allowing the line to go quite slack. The force of the current may release the bait.

3. Get downstream with a long line out (say 40 yards) and pull gently from different angles.

4. Try a brass ring (a Hardy releaser) with cord attached; pass it down the line to the bait, and get a pull on it from different angles. Let the ring go down with a bump on to the bait; this often releases it.

5. When trailing from a boat and your bait gets stuck in the bottom, turn the boat and row slowly in the direction you came from, this manœuvre often releases the bait.

SECTION 6

WEIGHT OF BAITS, ETC

$$\frac{1}{2}d \text{ weighs } \frac{1}{6} \text{ oz}$$
$$1\frac{1}{2}d \quad ,, \quad \frac{1}{2} \text{ oz}$$
$$3d \quad ,, \quad 1 \text{ oz}$$
$$16 \text{ dms.} = 1 \text{ oz}$$

Weight of Devons (*see page* 275)
   ,,   ,,   Spoons (*see page* 273)
   ,,   ,,   Leads (*see page* 262)

The thickness of the line should suit the weight of the bait.

With baits weighing up to $\frac{1}{2}$ oz use a line thickness ·020 measured with a micrometer.

With baits weighing $\frac{1}{2}$ oz to 1 oz use a line thickness ·024.

With baits weighing 1 oz to 2 oz use a line thickness ·028 or over.

SECTION 7

Trailing

a. BOAT EQUIPMENT

A stiff rod, 10-ft or 11-ft.

A Slater or Ariel reel.

Line should be marked 30, 40, 50 yards.

Let line out slowly and carefully behind the boat, not too fast or you stick in the bottom.

b. ROD RESTS

A thole pin in the gunwale, or a nail through a cork in the gunwale are good rests. (A gimlet is useful in a boat.)

When the rod is resting against a thole pin or nail it is advisable to have the line passing on the opposite side of the nail to that on which the rod is resting. This prevents the line getting jammed between the rod and the nail.

To keep the rods steady, rest the butts against parts of the boat.

c. A CHECK ON THE LINE

1. A flat stone (about 1 lb) rolled in cloth or in a reel bag, resting on the line at the bottom of the boat is a good check.

2. Put a rubber ring on the rod between the reel and first ring; pass the line (making a 3-in loop) under the rubber ring: this makes a useful check.

The rods should be at right angles to the boat and almost parallel to the water (not sticking high up).

You can have a third or middle rod out directly behind the stern seat.

All lines should be of different lengths, the shortest line on the middle rod (*see diagram, page* 159).

Remember if baits or lines touch, the tangle is very bad indeed.

d. LEAD ON THE TRACE

Trailing up-wind you want more lead on the trace than when trailing down-wind.

The normal depth of the bait below the surface should be 3 ft to 6 ft in a lake.

For *pike* you must trail slow and deep, with lead on the trace.

With a very long line out your line sags and the bait tends to come to the surface, so a little lead is wanted.

e. BAITS

You generally use a larger bait when trailing than when spinning.

I think, when trailing, single hooks on a bait are better than triangles.

With a light breeze or in shallow water use a comparatively small bait.

On a windy day or in deep water you can use a larger bait.

On a bright day use a dull coloured bait (say a brown and gold phantom).

On a dull day or in coloured water, use a bright-coloured bait (say a blue and silver phantom).

SECTION 8

Management of Boat

Try rowing a zig-zag course.

Fish appear to take better as the boat changes its direction.

Try rowing nearly up-wind, keeping the bow of the boat three-quarters on wind. Fish lie head to wind, and you cover more fish in this way.

It is best to sit in 'stroke's' seat facing the stern, as you then have your rods in front of you and can manage them better and quicker than if you are facing the bows of the boat.

The speed of the boat is very important. It should move at a steady, even speed. With a natural bait row just fast enough to make the bait spin or wobble properly. With an artificial bait (especially spoons) you should row a little quicker.

If you get a pull and you miss the fish, pay out some line and leave it to him, he will very often come again to the bait.

SECTION 9

Striking

When you get a 'pull' or a 'run' hold the rod firmly, almost parallel with the water at first, and let him run, then lift the rod and play him.

With a stiff rod a fish strikes himself, and the speed of the boat helps.

If you must strike or draw, do so with the rod parallel with the water, not by holding it high up in the air.

With a *natural* bait don't hurry the pull or strike; give a little time before you tighten.

With an *artificial* bait strike at once.

A trout when hooked jumps or bolts off at an angle.

A small pike or a perch when hooked comes to the surface almost at once.

A big pike is heavy on the line at first and dull like a log.

SECTION 10

Weather Conditions

For all fish you must have a wind of some sort, even a ruffle on the water is an advantage.

For *trout*, the best conditions are a soft day, a dull light, a good breeze.

A 'soft' day with a breeze is much better than a hard day with a breeze.

For *pike*, a dull, windy day with a steady barometer is best. Row slowly and fish deep.

For *perch*, a warm sunny day is best. Row slowly and fish near the surface.

253

SECTION II
Trailing Flies

I think trailing flies spoils fly fishing and spoils your dressed line. (The line gets twisted and won't shoot well afterwards.)

With a fly rod, it is best to use it as a middle rod directly over the stern. It is too whippy to use at the side.

If you must trail a fly, add a yard or two of undressed line between your dressed line and gut cast. This will help to take the twist or kinks.

the lengths of gut with loops at each end are handy
for changing, and the loops shew up very little in the
water.

When using sub gut the loops must be whipped.

Put together by passing the gut through the eye of
the swivels, thus:

A BS at C is convenient for easy changing when
necessary.

Attach any lead at E; the gut AB should be rather
stouter than the rest of the cast in order to take the
lead.

2. *To make a trace of sub gut and wire or of wire only
(see diagrams B and C.)*

These are very convenient traces

(*a*) AB should be at least 12 in and fairly stout to
take two Jardine leads at E if necessary.

Have a fairly large swivel at A to take the link
spring swivel at the end of the reel line.

The BS at C is for easy changing of the wire
when required.

The BS at D makes the bait spin better than when
the wire is attached direct to the bait (unless in the

case of a heavy metal bait). It is also convenient for changing baits.

(*b*) Diagram C shows a trace of wire only, using a Geen underhung lead or, if desired, a Jardine or other lead can be put on the reel line.

3. *When using Prawn or Worm tackle* which is usually attached to a long link of gut.

The trace shown in diagram D below is a useful one. Put lead on the gut about E.

D <u>*Reel Line*</u> BS S <u>*3ft Gut*</u> BS <u>*1ft Gut*</u> *Prawn or Worm*
E

4. *When using a wing or spinner* at the top of the trace. (*See diagrams E and F below.*)

E <u>*Reel Line*</u> BS 8   *4 ft wire*   BS

F <u>*Reel Line*</u> BS 8   *4 ft wire*   BS
E

E shows a Geen underhung lead (*see page* 262).
F shows lead on the reel line.

a. WINGS AT THE TOP OF A TRACE

The trace below the wing from A to B must be rigid, *i.e.* made of wire, and there must be no swivel working at the bait B.

In strong water a wing gives a powerful spin.

Use small wings in running water.

Use larger wings in pools and easy water.

In rapid water with big fish it pays to use a link spring swivel at the bait 'stopped with two strands of copper wire. The wire breaks on the first run of the fish.

Messrs. Carter & Co., have a device attached to the wing which puts it out of action on the first run of a fish, so you can use a link spring without any swivel at the bait.

The celluloid wings should only be slightly 'bent off.' You can bend them easily after dipping them in hot water.

b. SWIVELS

Don't put more swivels on your trace than are absolutely necessary.

The size of the swivel depends in a great measure on the thickness of the gut or sub gut used.

With a light bait or a phantom a link spring swivel is very necessary at the bait.

With a heavy bait, such as a solid metal devon, you can attach the trace direct on to the swivel on the bait and it will spin all right.

Keep swivels on safety pins by sizes: they are then easily got at.

Here is a scale of swivels by sizes:—

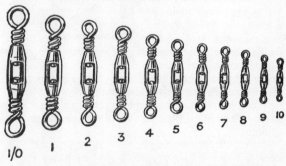

It pays to examine your swivels occasionally as a bit of grit or weed is sufficient to cause a stoppage.

C. WIRE

Black hardened tempered steel wire, **to be** obtained from J. A. Binns, West Mount Works, Halifax, Yorks, in various sizes, is very good for fishing purposes. It is sold by the pound.

No 24 =   774 feet = 1 pound
„ 26 = 1160 „   =   „
„ 28 = 1710 „   =   „
„ 31 = 2780 „   =   „

Useful sizes are:

For Trout   No 31 = ·013 of an inch
For Salmon }   No 28 = ·016   „
  or Pike }   No 26 = ·018   „
Heavy Salmon   No 24 = ·022   „

To attach wire to a swivel, see diagram.

Thread the wire through the swivel and bend the short end so as to make a small loop at A. See that the two ends form rather more than a right angle (a match or a bodkin is useful for making a loop).

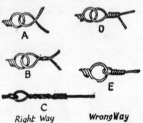

Grasp the two ends firmly where they cross with the thumb and fore-finger of the right hand, and holding the loop and swivel in the left hand, twist the two ends together so that each end is twisted over the other as in B. Three or four complete turns are enough.

Finish off by twisting the short end round the trace 4 times as shown in C. When using thick wire (say ·022) it bends easier if you hold it over a lighted match for about half a minute.

If the short end is merely turned round the trace as in D, there is some danger under a heavy strain of the coils slipping and forming a very small sharp loop at the swivel (as shown in E), which is likely to snap.

A wire trace should be well dried and oiled after use.

Keep wire in, say, 4-ft coils in oiled paper.

d. LEADS

Always put lead above the chief swivel, it acts as a swivel compeller.

In a strong stream you want plenty of lead low down on the trace, as the stream tends to bring the bait to the surface.

In a strong downstream wind you want more lead on the trace than in a breeze.

In a strong stream you want to put your lead on the cast in such a position that the direct strain will be on the lead, thus releasing the upward drag on the bait. According to the strength of the current vary the *weight* and *position* of the lead.

With a thick line you want more lead than with a thin line.

Two $\frac{1}{2}$ oz leads are more effective than one 1 oz lead.

When fishing over a very rocky bottom, tie the lead to about 3 inches of thin gut and attach it to the cast at a knot. The chances are the lead gets hung up before the bait does, and when trying to free it the thin gut will break if the lead is badly stuck. You lose your lead but you save your lure.

Jardine Leads. See the wire ends are not sharp or they will cut the trace: to prevent this wrap a little silk round the trace under where the wire spirals touch.

Measure only the lead portion (excluding the wire
ends).

A 4 in Jardine lead weighs 3 oz
3½ in   ,,   ,,   2½ oz
3 in   ,,   ,,   1½ oz
2 in   ,,   ,,   ½ oz
1¼ in   ,,   ,,   3 dms
¾ in   ,,   ,,   1 dm

Note: 3 pennies weigh one ounce.

To put on a Jardine lead.
Commence in the centre at C and bind the line

outwards, following the grooves.

Bend the lead to make it an underhung lead.
Geen's underhung lead is a convenient lead.

Hardy's bullet lead is useful attached to the eye of
a swivel.

Lead wire (thickness about ·104) makes a useful
lead on a trace and shews up very little in the water.
To mount it, lay a thin match or a big pin on the
trace and bind the wire loosely round both match
and trace. Remove the match and tighten the coils
by pressing them on to the trace.

SECTION 3
Spinners

Sharpe of Aberdeen made for me a good spinner
for baits about 4 in or 5 in long (*see diagram below*).

1. *To mount a sand eel.*

Cut a V out of the eel at B (*see* sketch). Clean out

the inside to make room for the lead. Push the spike
A well into the sand eel, bringing the ends at B up
over the base of the celluloid flanges and bind with
wire. Adjust hook C over this binding and secure
it with wire.

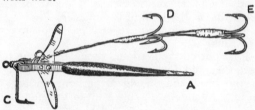

The triangles D and E are then laid alongside and
bound to the bait with a single turn of wire or silk.
See that the binding is not too tight so as to spoil
the shape of the bait.

2. *To mount a gudgeon.*

Do so in a similar way, but cut the sides of the
mouth well back to allow the nose to be bound over
the celuloid flanges with wire as in 1.

3. *To mount a preserved sprat.*

Do so in a similar way. Squeeze out the inside of the stomach to make room for the lead; if necessary pare down the lead for a small golden sprat.

Cut the mouth well back to allow the nose to be bound with wire as in 1.

Mounted on this spinner the bait will never slip off. It will spin on an even keel and if left steady in the water does not dive head or tail downwards but sinks in the same way as a gudgeon or sprat would do naturally.

4. *To mount a small fish or a minnow.*

Use a similar but smaller spinner to that shown in the diagram on *page* 263 but without the hook C. To prevent the bait slipping down secure the fish with thin silver or copper wire, using a baiting needle to pass the wire through the bait just behind the head and fasten the two ends of the wire to the small ring at the head of the spinner.

When the minnows are *very small* you can use two thus:

First put on the head and shoulders of one minnow, then add a whole minnow, pushing it well up to the head and shoulders portion. Fasten the 'whole' minnow with thin wire to the ring at the head of the spinner as described above.

Another very good mount for a minnow is the scarab (*see page* 265).

5. The *Chapman* spinner has the flanges too far forward when mounted. They stand out from the nose instead of from the gills of the bait.

6. The *Archer* spinner is inclined to damage the gills of the bait.

7. The *Crocodile* spinner is best for a thick bait, a gudgeon or a perch.

8. The diagram below shows a good *sand eel spinner* for sea trout when more hooks are necessary. Bind the hooks with silver wire.

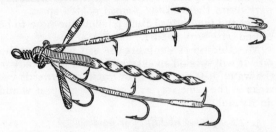

9. *Dee Tackle.* The bore of the lead B C should be large enough to allow the swivel D to pass freely.

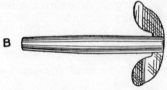

The lead should be pushed well down the mouth until the end B is almost at the vent.

Use a baiting needle to bring the triangle A well up to the vent or point where the needle is inserted in the skin.

For ordinary bait A E = 2 in
   ,,   small   ,,   A E = $1\frac{1}{4}$ in
Dee Tackle works better in rapid water than in slow water.

10. *The Scarab or Celluloid Jacket.*

The scarab tackle is composed of a two hook attachment (similar to above diagram), a celluloid

jacket into which the bait is put and a little lead to
fit into the mouth.

This is a very useful and attractive mounting for
a minnow of any size or even a larger bait.

The celluloid jacket gives a tempting flash to the
bait. It is also economical in baits, as when a fish is
hooked the bait runs up the cast and is not injured.

Most tackle shops supply these scarabs with full
instructions for mounting the bait.

SECTION 4

Flights of Hooks

The *Pennell-Bromley* flight is a very good one (*see
sketch*).

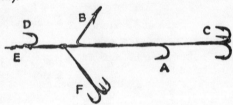

Use it in different sizes, according to length of
bait.

First fix hook A through the back of the bait;

Then fix hook B when you have the desired bend;

Then fix lip hook D through both lips.

With a gudgeon type of bait, pass the lip hook
down through the top of the nose, with the barb
downwards.

With a dace type of bait, pass the hook up through
the chin, barb upwards.

The lip hook should be small: it seldom hooks a
fish.

To shift the lip hook loosen the coils at E and push

the coils through the loops up or down, then tighten
them when the hook is in the desired position.

Twisted wire is better than gimp or gut.

The triangle C can hang down loose.

The triangle F can hang loose, but the bait spins
better if it is bound with thin wire.

This tackle is best for a dead bait, say 6 in and
over, and you can make a bait wobble well if necessary.

SECTION 5

Fresh and Preserved Baits

Fresh baits are always better than preserved ones.

Fresh minnows, gudgeon, dace, sand eels, and
prawns are best.

Always sew up the mouth of a bait or close it with
a lip hook.

Prick the head and shoulders of a fresh bait to let
out the juices, etc: it improves the taste or smell of
the bait.

A bait about 4 in long (under ordinary conditions)
is all right for salmon or a big trout. Baits up to 8 in
long are taken by pike.

A dead bait spins better if you cut off the fins.

A large dead bait (say 6 in and over) sinks well
and does not require very much lead.

a. MINNOWS

Fresh greenish minnows ($1\frac{1}{2}$ in to 2 in long), with
white bellies, are better than reddish ones. Female
fish in spawn do not make good baits.

Minnows will turn reddish if kept any time in a container: some earth put in the bottom will prevent this (*see also page* 384).

To catch minnows. First of all stir up the bottom with a stick to make the water muddy. This collects the minnows. Then use a minnow trap baited with pieces of bread, red worms or lengths of scarlet wool (Farlow sells a very compact trap in a canister), or use a hoop net about 2 ft in diameter, put a bullet in the centre rolled in red cloth, drop it into easy water, leave it about a quarter of an hour: minnows collect to examine the red cloth: raise the net quickly and you have the lot.

Or, get a clear brandy bottle, and with a nail tap round the end of the cavity at the bottom of the bottle; a final hard tap and the ball of glass in the centre will fall out. Make slits in the cork to allow water to pass. Put a little bread in the bottle, tether it by a string, with the neck upstream; place it in a quiet backwater where minnows are. Leave it say half an hour. They enter by the hole at the bottom and cannot get out (*see also page* 384).

b. SAND EELS

A sand eel is a fish (not an eel). They are found at very low tide burrowing in the sand close to the water's edge. When digging them out you require to be very quick with the spade, they are very elusive.

c. YOUNG TROUT

In the Irish lakes a young trout is used as a bait for ferox and pike. Here is an illegal method of catching them, explained to me by an Irish police-man on L. Mask:

Select a pool in a small stream and make it muddy.

Place a landing net with grass in the bottom of it at the lower end of the pool.

Get someone to go upstream, and drive the trout down into the muddy pool. The fish hide in the grass at the bottom of the net and are caught.

d. PRESERVED BAITS

If you use preserved baits salted ones are much better than those preserved in formalin or other mixtures.

To preserve baits in salt, take a wooden box with holes drilled in the bottom and sides, lay the baits in rows covered with salt about $\frac{1}{2}$ inch deep, wet the salt well and leave it for say 10 days allowing the moisture to run off through the holes.

Then fill up with dry salt, nail on the lid, and the baits should keep for quite a year.

If the bait is at all shrunk put wool in the belly: this helps to make it keep its shape.

Formalined baits should be well washed and put in a tin box with layers of salt before use, or soaked for 24 hours in a strong solution of salt and water.

When the eye of a preserved bait becomes white, the bait is of little use.

Never leave *mounted baits* in salt solution or formalin over-night, as it rots the gut and corrodes the steel of the hooks and mount.

Preserved baits are best fished in fast running water. In easy water and pools the fish have too much time to examine and taste or smell them.

Sprats : To obtain a good reddish golden colour, add a little powdered acri flavine to a bottle of sprats in formalin, very little will do, about one-third of what will go on a threepenny bit.

SECTION 6
Flanges on Baits

With a heavy dead bait or when fishing in still water, a fairly large flange is necessary, while in rapid water a smaller one will do.

A flat bait (a preserved sprat) requires a larger flange to spin it properly than a round bait (say an eel).

Flanges should stand out from the gills not from the nose of the bait.

Celluloid flanges are very good, show up very little, but break easily.

The action of revolving flanges is to set up a cone of silvery shiny water all round the bait which helps to attract fish.

To make a devon or phantom spin left handed, the left fin should slope *towards* you when looking at the head of the bait with the tail away from you and should slope *away* from you for a right hand spin.

SECTION 7

Triangles and Single Hooks

Single hooks are suitable for baits under 2 in long. Triangles are better for baits over 2 in.

With single hooks:

(*a*) There is less chance of fouling weeds.
(*b*) It is difficult for a fish to lever it out, as it has good hooking power.
(*c*) It shows up less in the water.

A single hook used with a devon should hang down a trifle more than a triangle would; with a $1\frac{1}{2}$ in devon a single tail hook should hang down at least $\frac{1}{2}$ in.

Tail triangles should never be too small for the bait, they should be nearly as wide as the flanges of the devon or the width of the spoon to which they are attached.

The tail hook or triangle of a phantom or dead bait may be level with the tail of the bait, but never shorter; it is best if it projects $\frac{1}{4}$ in beyond the tail.

The simpler the tackle the better; only have as many hooks or triangles on a bait as are absolutely necessary.

SECTION 8
Artificial Baits

There are roughly two sorts of artificial baits, *viz*:
1. The exact imitation in form and colour of the natural (*i.e.* phantoms, etc). They do best in quick running water.
2. Those that rely on the action of the bait, irrespective of appearance, *i.e.* the flash of the bait to attract the fish. I think the flash should be intermittent rather than continuous, *e.g.*:

A green and silver devon
A reflex devon
A red and gold spoon } Give an intermittent flash
A copper and silver spoon
A wagtail

A round bodied silver
devon or gold devon } Give a continuous flash

One of the chief objects of an artificial bait is to attract, and the best for this purpose is one that gives an intermittent flash of some sort.

Artificial baits are best in full water, and to hide the deception must spin quickly.

a. SPOONS

There are many varieties of spoons; here are some of them:
1. The *egg shaped spoon* fished with the small end uppermost. Spins well in running water. (For shape, *see diagram, page* 273.)
2. The *bar spoon*, fished with the broad end uppermost. Spins well even in easy water. The hooks are on the bar and do not spin.

3. The *broad based spoon*. This shape of spoon
has an **attractive**
s p i n e v e n i f
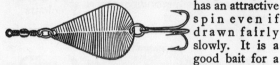
d r a w n f a i r l y
slowly. It is a
good bait for a
pike and is a favourite shape of spoon for mahseer
in India.

4. The *long oval narrow spoon*. Requires rapid
water to make it spin well.

5. The *Colorado spoon*, revolves on a bar, spins
well even when drawn slowly, but is easily thrown
out of gear if the bar is at all bent.

6. The *kidney spoon;* very useful in fast water,
wobbles well.

7. A *pearl spoon*, 1½ in, is useful for trailing for
trout or pike.

8. A *fly spoon*, ¾ in, is useful for trout in coloured
water and for salmon when the water is low, try it
in the evening fished near the surface (*see also page
231*).

Spoons, 2 in and under, spin best with only one
hook or triangle at the bottom.

Spoons over 2 in will spin all right with two triangles, one at the top and one at the bottom.

A big spoon (say 3 in) kinks a line badly unless
you have plenty of swivels.

You can increase the spin of a spoon by using a
spinner at the head of the trace. This is often useful
in very slow water (*see page 258*).

Colour of spoons :

You will do better with a dirty dull coloured spoon
of any shape than with a bright new one (except in
coloured water when you require a bright, highly
coloured spoon to attract the fish).

Dull coloured copper
   ,,   ,,   silver and copper } Are useful
   ,,   brass   colours

The Harlequin spoon is a very good one for

salmon or trout. It is coloured silver and copper, each side of a line drawn from A to B. Both sides of the spoon are coloured in a similar way. It should not be too new and bright.

Pike and perch always prefer a spoon with some red on it or red worsted on the tail triangle.

A 2 in spoon weighs $\frac{1}{3}$ oz (approx)
A 3 in   ,,   ,,   1 oz   ,,

b. DEVONS

There is a great variety of devons of different colours and shapes:

1. The *solid metal devon* is easy to cast, but it soon sinks and must be drawn quickly in shallow water. Hexagonal or fluted devons are best.

2. The *reflex devon* gives a good intermittent flash when revolving. To make it more visible in thick water, paint the flat sides different colours, say one side black and the other side white (with Wadham's 'celire'). One big triangle with a bead is usually best for salmon (*see diagram*).

3. *Wooden devons* are light and lively and good for
shallow water. They can be fished much slower than
metal ones.

4. *Slotted devons* are best in the small sizes, they
usually have a lot of side hooks.

It is an advantage if a devon is able to run up the
cast.

Stiff metal mounts (wire) are better than gut.
They must be well dried and oiled after use.

The mounts should fit the devons. It is convenient to have mounts of different sizes to fit the
various sizes of devon.

The top loop of the swivel in a devon should only
show as at A. If it protrudes too far it is liable to
break off.

A devon with two triangles tied tandem is a useful
bait. The triangles should be mounted on wire,

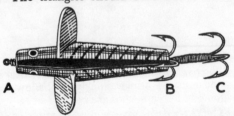

not gut. Triangle B should be a size larger than
triangle C. The length from B to C (*viz* from the
end of the metal part of the devon to the end of the
tail triangle) should not be too long.

For a 1 in Devon BC should be about $\frac{1}{2}$ in

       2 in   „   „   „   „   1 in

       3 in   „   „   „   „   1$\frac{1}{2}$ in

The hole down the centre should be large enough
to allow the swivels to pass freely. The devon should
spin freely without forcing the hooks to rotate as
well.

In the larger sizes side hooks retard the spin. They are generally used in devons about 1 in long only.

Bright or light coloured devons are best in coloured water. A new bright devon fished in clear water is of little use, it must be dulled.

Dull copper colour, dull silver, dull brass, lead or gunmetal colour, are useful colours for ordinary conditions. Aluminium paint gives a good dull, silvery colour.

Whatever colour is used it is best to have the flanges and head dulled.

To dull the colour of a devon, hold it over a match or candle. Rub a silver or copper devon with a bit of indiarubber, or to produce a gunmetal colour smoke it with sulphur.

Under ordinary conditions useful sizes are:

    For streams, 1 in to $1\frac{1}{2}$ in
      ,,   lakes, $1\frac{1}{2}$ in to 2 in
      ,,   salmon, 2 in to 3 in (coloured water)

Weight of solid metal devons :

1 in devon with mount, approx weight					$4\frac{1}{2}$ dms
$1\frac{1}{2}$,,	,,	,,	,,	,,	9 ,,
2 in ,,	,,	,,	,,	,,	14 ,,
$2\frac{1}{2}$,,	,,	,,	,,	,,	$1\frac{1}{4}$ oz

In fastening a devon (or any other bait which can slip up the trace), it is easier to thread the devon on to the trace before fastening the latter to the swivel at the head of the mount.

When you hook a fish on a devon or similar bait which can slip up the trace, you frequently find that the bait has run up some distance. This is caused by the action of the water on flanges of the bait when the fish runs off after being hooked.

Sometimes a fish may be able to eject a bait an inch or so up the trace but no more.

c. PHANTOMS

Phantoms are made in various colours.

A well-worn phantom is better than a new one.

Scratch out the eyes when too prominent.

Black hooks are best.

In shape a phantom should have a sort of hump on its back, just behind the head.

Stuff a phantom with cotton wool through the mouth: it helps it to keep its shape.

Shot is sometimes put in the belly to sink the bait; this makes the phantom rather dull and heavy in the water, and it won't spin well unless it has a large flange or wing.

The side hooks or flying triangles should be bound with silk or thin wire.

The flanges should be unobtrusive and are best when coloured black all over (on the top and underneath).

Celluloid flanges are good, but are easily broken.

d. WAGTAILS

These spin very well, but the rubber gets hard and soon perishes.

Stiffen the tail with a bit of quill if necessary.

Bind the flying hooks loosely with a strand of wire or silk.

This is a very good bait for a pike.

Care is required when spinning, as the tail hooks are very liable to catch in the line, and when the flying hooks are secured with wire the wagtail is liable to get doubled up and out of shape if the wire is too tightly put on. Wagtails are really best for trailing.

SECTION 9

Baits with a Smell

It sometimes makes an artificial bait more attractive to the fish if it is fitted with a chamber into which are put certain essences or 'smells,' such as:

- (*a*) Squashed minnow
- (*b*)   ,,   prawn
- (*c*) Ivy gum
- (*d*) Aniseed
- (*e*) Oil of rodium.

Some devons are fitted with a chamber for this purpose.

In the case of a phantom, the inside can be stuffed with cotton wool soaked in one of these essences.

Some anglers when fishing with a dead bait (minnow, sprat or even a worm) dip the bait into oil of rodium each time before making a cast.

SECTION 10

Measuring a Bait

With *devons* or *spoons* measure the metal part only.

With *wagtails* measure from the nose to the end of the indiarubber at the tail.

With *phantoms* and all *dead* baits measure from the nose to the vertical line cutting the tips of the forks of the tail (*see also page* 401).

When ordering phantoms it is advisable to mention that the measurement of those you require should be taken as above, because some makers have other ways of measuring a phantom.

With a *prawn* measure from the eye to the end of

277

the fleshy part of the tail (excluding the tail fin) after
having straightened out the prawn naturally.

A halfpenny is exactly one inch in diameter.

Wobble or Spin

In heavy or coloured water a wobbling bait is
often better than a straight spin.

As a rule a small bait (4 in and under) mounted on
a spinner is best for a straight spin (*see page* 263).

Any bait can be made to wobble by adjusting the
bend of the body or tail.

Salmon prefer a slow even spin.

Perch prefer a quick even spin.

Trout prefer a quick even spin or a quick wobble.

Pike prefer a slow spin or a slow wobble.

SECTION 12
Weather Conditions and Baits

This is a rough guide:

In bright weather use a dull coloured bait on the
small side. In dull weather you can use a brighter
coloured bait and larger in size.

Dull cloudy day Coloured water Strong wind	Use a light coloured bait, silver devon type, blue phantom type, silver spoon type, a sand eel or silver sprat.
On a bright day or Clear still water	Use a dull coloured smaller bait, dull dirty gold devon, ditto copper spoon, brown and gold phantom, a loach, a minnow, or a golden sprat.

PIKE FISHING

Book VI: PIKE FISHING

General Notes

A pike of 4 lbs and under is usually called a Jack.

In some parts of the country a male pike is called a Jack irrespective of size.

A pike's mouth bristles with teeth; he has long sharp ones in front intended to grab and hold rather than to cut or masticate. He has hundreds of smaller ones on the roof and back parts of his mouth, which are hinged and only bend backwards to facilitate the passage of a fish down the throat and prevent its escape.

A pike may grab a fish sideways, but he turns it and swallows it head first.

A pike will cut any sort of gut with his teeth: it is best to use a wire trace, or the bait should be attached to a few inches of wire anyhow.

Gimp is unreliable stuff.

Pike of three years old and over generally lead a solitary life (except in the spawning season); they live in fear of being devoured by their own kith and kin.

A pike is protected by his colouring; when at rest or when drifting cautiously towards his prey he resembles a mossy log of wood, or a mass of floating weed in the water.

The pike fisher must adapt his methods and tackle to circumstances, *viz*:

   (*a*) Spin when you can, with either a dead or artificial bait; it is certainly the pleasantest method.

   (*b*) In a lake or open water, you can spin or trail from behind a boat, along the side of or over weed beds, keeping as close to them as you can.

   (*c*) In very weedy water, you must use a float tackle, paternoster or ledger, with a live bait, or troll with a dead bait.

The pike fishing season in *England* begins about October when the leaves are off the trees, and lasts until March.

On the *Irish* lakes, September and October are considered the best months for big fish.

Pike caught in the clear water of the Irish lakes, *viz*, Derg, Corrib, Mask, Conn and Cullen, are excellent eating.

When caught in polluted waters, they should be gutted at once after capture to make them at all eatable.

After spawning the flesh of a pike is very unwholesome.

The scale of weight for length given below records only a very rough idea of the weight, as so much depends on a pike's condition.

'MONA'S' LIST OF WEIGHTS OF PIKE FOR LENGTH

Weights of pike for inches of length, based on the supposition that a pike of 40 in weighs 20 lb :

Inches		lb	Inches		lb
20	..	2·500	34	..	12·282
21	..	2·894	35	..	13·398
22	..	3·327	36	..	14·580
23	..	3·802	37	..	15·829
24	..	4·300	38	..	17·147
25	..	4·882	39	..	18·537
26	..	5·492	40	..	20·000
27	..	6·150	41	..	21·537
28	..	6·860	42	..	23·152
29	..	7·621	43	..	24·845
30	..	8·437	44	..	26·620
31	..	9·309	45	..	28·476
32	..	10·240	46	..	30·457
33	..	11·230	47	..	32·444

Inches	lb	Inches	lb
48 ..	34·585	56 ..	54·880
49 ..	36·774	57 ..	57·872
50 ..	39·062	58 ..	60·972
51 ..	41·453	59 ..	64·180
52 ..	43·940	60 ..	67·500
53 ..	46·524		
54 ..	49·207		
55 ..	51·992		

A pike differs from most other fish in that when once he gets a bait well into the back part of his mouth he has considerable difficulty in ejecting it owing to the numerous teeth on the roof of his mouth which are hinged backwards (*see page* 281).

You may catch pike at any hour of the day when they are on the feed and weather conditions are favourable, but your best chance for a *big* one is between sunrise and 10 a.m. and again an hour before dark.

SECTION 2

Food and Haunts

A pike feeds on almost any living thing of suitable and swallowable size which moves in or on the water, *i.e.* fish, waterfowl, rats, mice, etc.

They don't appear to like tench but occasionally eat them.

A pike is a fish of 'moods.' Sometimes they are madly on the feed and will take anything. Sometimes they will not take unless the bait is attractive or brought close to their nose. Sometimes they will not be tempted by any bait.

In the winter pike frequent the deep water. In the summer months they go into the shallows, and on a hot day like to bask in the sun near the surface.

Occasionally a pike (especially a large one) will

feed greedily, and then lie torpid for perhaps two or three days.

Others have regular feeding hours, which vary in different localities. It pays to consult local fishermen about this.

Normally when at rest a pike lies about a foot or so from the bottom, usually at the edge of a bed of reeds, weeds or rushes, in places where small fish are likely to pass or congregate. His colouring helps to make him inconspicuous.

It is often worth while to splash about among the reed beds, drive the fish out into the open water, and then try to catch them by spinning.

Pike thrive best in the alkaline water of limestone soil. They do not do so well in acid peaty water fed from bogs and marshes. In Ireland, pike and perch are seldom found in the acid waters of Kerry, Wicklow, Donegal or Connemara.

SECTION 3

Spawning, Age and Sex

Pike spawn about March and April in the weed beds, ditches and quiet backwaters of streams. In Ireland they spawn earlier.

A female is usually attended by two or three males. She develops a vicious appetite after spawning and will sometimes eat her male attendants when done with, or indeed any unsuspecting female of suitable size which happens to be near.

During the operation of spawning the male fish swims above and parallel with the female; possibly he feels safer in that position.

The fertilised ova stick to the stones or weeds on or near the bottom.

Pike which manage to survive live to a good age. A 30 lb fish would be 16 or 17 years old. In lakes and very open water they may live for 30 years or even longer.

Scale reading is very unreliable in telling the age, etc, of a pike.

Male pike are much smaller fish than the females, and seldom exceed 8 or 9 lbs: perhaps the reason is so few live to grow up.

It is often difficult to tell a male from a female; generally speaking the male fish, although quite deep behind the shoulder, tapers away towards the tail more quickly than the female.

Cases have occurred of pike when opened having alternate layers of milt and roe inside them, or milt on one side and roe on the other.

SECTION 4

Weather

It is difficult to lay down rules in connection with weather and pike fishing, because there are times when pike lie dormant after a bout of heavy feeding and won't take any bait no matter what the weather is.

Here are a few desirable weather conditions (when pike should be on the move):

1. A high and steady barometer is very important.

2. A wind from some quarter is desirable, especially in still water.

3. A full stream is better than low water: when the water is clearing after a flood is a good time.

4. After a spell of hard frost and the weather becomes mild.

5. In winter a sunny day is better than a dull day, provided there is a wind.

Pike fishing is usually *not* good:

1. With an unsteady or falling barometer.

2. When there is a sudden rise or fall of temperature.

3. When the weather is close, damp or muggy, pike appear to become sluggish.

4. When the wind is very squally and changeable.

SECTION 5
Artificial Baits

An artificial pike bait should have a bit of red in it, *i.e.* red paint or red worsted on the triangles, etc.

The bait should revolve quickly when drawn slowly. A pike will not take any bait that is quite still, or not revolving.

Devons, wagtails, phantoms and bar spoons all revolve well when drawn slowly.

Useful colours for a wagtail or phantom are blue and silver or brown and gold.

Size of phantoms for lakes and open water: 6 in and over.

Size for streams: a 4 in bait is long enough.

A spoon is an excellent bait for a pike, but in still water it revolves rather slowly and has to be drawn fairly quickly to make it spin well. (To increase the spin of a spoon *see page* 272.)

The following are useful colours for spoons:

(*a*) A dull copper and red.

(*b*) A brass 'eyed' spoon, with scales on the outside, red inside.

(*c*) A Colorado spoon, red inside or with red worsted on the triangle.

(*d*) A spoon with a broad base: this wobbles and spins well (*see page* 272).

(*e*) A mother o' pearl spoon is very good on some waters.

Size of spoons :

For Lakes 3 in and over
   ,,   Streams, 1 in to 2 in.

A pike will take all sorts of fancy baits mounted on triangles or hooks, *viz*:

The end of a calf's tail
The ear of a hare
A large red prawn
The ear of a rabbit
A frog
A 5/0 gaudy salmon fly.

There is much truth in the saying 'a big bait is needed to tempt a big pike.'

SECTION 6

Dead Baits

A fresh dead bait is better than a preserved one. The order of preference is:

1. A fresh dead bait
2. A salted dead bait
3. A formalined or preserved bait.

Baits built on fine lines, such as dace, bleak, sprats, etc, spin much better than deep bellied fish, such as roach, rudd, perch, bream, etc.

A 6 in or 7 in bait is quite a useful size in a lake.

A medium sized silvery fresh herring is a very good bait for a big pike.

A perch spins better when the spines are cut off.

A dead bait when mounted should be straight, down to the commencement of the curve in the tail.

To make it wobble put plenty of curve or bend near the tail.

A pike prefers a bait wobbling in wide sweeps to one which moves in short quick curves.

287

Flights of hooks :

A Pennell flight is best for a large bait (*see page* 266).

Adjust the tail hook first, putting a proper bend in the tail, and fix the lip hook last.

Spinners :

A spinner is the best mount for a straight spin. A crocodile spinner is as good as any pattern for the smaller baits.

The hooks or triangles should be tied on wire, not on gut.

Use red worsted for binding down the flying hooks; this adds to the attraction of the bait.

SECTION 7
Spinning

For pike spin deep and draw slow, but ensure that the bait revolves well.

A bait with a straight spin may be best for quantity, but a wobbling spin is best for quality (the big ones).

Spin deeper on a cold day than on a warm day.

Never let the bait stop.

Never slow down to a following pike.

Always fish the cast out well.

Try varying the pace of the bait, spin quickly for a yard or so, then spin slowly for a bit.

If you miss a fish throw in again at once; he will often return a second time.

In rivers when the water is coloured spin close to the banks, and try a wobbling bait.

On windy, rough, dark days, use a bright coloured bait and draw it slowly.

On a bright day, low water or little wind, use a small sombre coloured bait, and you must draw it quicker.

When water and weather are normal, a dull coloured

bait is best: *e.g.* an old well-worn copper spoon with a little red on it, or a well-used wagtail or phantom.

It is well worth while to attach a triangle to the lead on your trace as a pike often goes for the lead; he probably takes it for a fish or other object pursued by the bait.

SECTION 8

Trailing from a Boat

You must have a stiff rod for trailing.

Row slowly and evenly in a zig-zag course over sunken weed beds or along the edge of reed beds, keeping as close to them as you can.

With a dead bait row just fast enough to spin or wobble the bait.

With an artificial bait or when there is not much wind, you should row a little quicker.

When trailing you should use baits similar to, but larger than, those used when spinning. A dead bait 8 in or 9 in long, or a spoon up to 5 in, is not too large in a big lake.

When catching pike in a certain part of a lake, do not move away from that spot without giving it a good trial.

SECTION 9

Live Baiting

Live baiting for pike is slow work, but is often productive of big fish.

A live fish is suspended in the water by means of a float tackle, a trimmer, a paternoster tackle, or close to the bottom by means of a leger tackle.

In coloured water a bright coloured bait shews up best, *i.e.* a dace or roach.

In clear water a darker coloured bait is best, *i.e.* a perch or gudgeon.

In a stream you require a strong swimming bait which will keep alive and swim against the current.

289

In a lake or pool you can use a smaller and feebler bait as it will last well in the easy water.

Gold fish are an attractive bait, but they are feeble and die soon.

Whatever bait you use should be lively in the water.

1. *Float Tackle.*

A floating line with a pilot float to buoy up the first few yards is very necessary.

L = the lead; B = the bait. LB = about 24 ins.

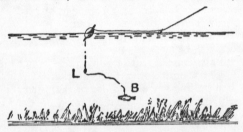

2. *A Trimmer* is a live bait arranged in a manner similar to 1: but attached to a big cork or float or corked bottle. Visit the trimmer about every half-hour. A trimmer set at night will usually attract bigger fish than one set in the day time.

3. *Paternoster Tackle.*

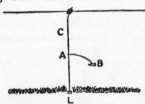

The lead L resting on the bottom.

A to L is composed of medium gut, the trace A to C being made of wire or strong gut.

A to B = about 8 or 10 ins of fine wire.

The bait B should swim about one foot above the weeds.

4. *Ledger Tackle*

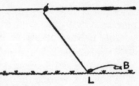

The lead rests on the
bottom and has a hole in
it through which the line
runs freely. A shot or
stop of some sort is fast-
ened to the line about 2 ft above the bait to prevent
the lead L sliding down any further.

A weedy bottom is unsuitable for this tackle as the
bait swims so close to the bottom.

A ledger can be used with or without a float.

In water less than 6 feet deep, that part of a float
which is under water should be coloured white or
light blue. The top half which is above the surface
should be of such a colour as will be easily seen
by the fisherman.

With a long line out use Pilot floats to keep the
line on the top of the water.

There are several tackles for mounting a live bait.
That in the ac-
companying dia-
gram is as good
as any.

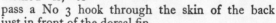

Or, a simple
method is, to
pass a No 3 hook through the skin of the back
just in front of the dorsal fin.

When you get a run and the float disappears,
wind in all slack line, see which way the fish is
moving, and when you strike, do so in the opposite
direction, and parallel with the water. Never strike
upwards.

With a live bait, eight times out of ten a pike
seizes the bait across the middle, sails off to his holt,
stops, turns the bait head in, and tries to swallow it;
so you must give him lots of time before you strike.

SECTION 10

Trolling or Drop Minnow

This is a useful method in very weedy water when spinning is impossible.

The bait is dropped into holes or open spaces among the weeds.

Use a trace about 3 or 4 ft long – no swivels or lead are necessary. The bait must not spin. Tie up the mouth, don't leave it wide open.

The bait is well leaded and when dropped into the water it shoots nearly to the bottom, then work it with a sink-and-draw motion, about a foot at a time.

As a rule a pike takes the bait as it is shooting down in preference to when it is being drawn up.

There are several patterns of snap trolling tackle. The one shown in the diagram is a good one.

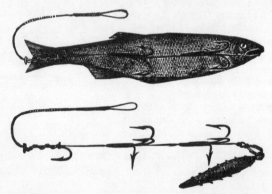

Strike at once and sideways on feeling a fish.

Striking

Always strike a pike sideways, almost parallel with the water. Never strike him upwards.

When spinning with an *artificial* bait, strike at once, as when he closes his jaws upon the bait and feels the hard substance, he is likely to open his mouth wide and shake his head to get rid of the bait. So if you hesitate you may lose him.

When spinning with a *dead* bait, you can allow him more time, as he is less likely to cast the bait off at once.

The bigger and more numerous the hooks or triangles the harder you should strike.

Never try to strike on a slack line.

When live baiting always give the fish lots of time before you strike (*see page* 291), then strike with a steady pull. Try to get a good pull on the fish for two seconds while his mouth is closed, as later when he feels the hooks he will open his mouth wide, shaking his head to try to get rid of the bait.

Playing

The jaws of a pike are like a powerful vice, so the more he keeps his mouth shut the better; it gives the hooks a chance of taking a good hold.

Never help him to open his mouth by pulling vertically upwards.

Keep the rod top low and behind him, putting a horizontal strain on him, and allow him no slack line.

If he sulks strike him again and again, make him fight, and try to keep him moving.

If he comes to the surface open mouthed, give

him slack line; if you hold him at all hard the vicious shake of his head may tear the hold.

SECTION 13

Landing

Gaff a pike close behind the big back fin. It renders him powerless to lash out with his tail.

Or, when you are bringing him in, he usually opens his gills, so try to slip the gaff into his gills,

Or, when you are alone, gaff him under the lower jaw. You can then pull as well as lift him on the gaff; but be careful when he strikes out with his tail.

A small sharp gaff is better than a big one, as a pike is narrower than a salmon and the body is more flabby.

You can land a small pike by placing the fore-finger and thumb in his eye sockets and lifting him out. If this is done it appears to paralyse him, and he does not lash out much with his tail.

If you have only a net, it is best (all things con-sidered) to net him tail first, as if you get his head in first the hooks or his teeth may catch in the mesh.

Book VII

SUNDRIES

Book VII: SUNDRIES

Part I

WEATHER, BAROMETER, WATER, LIGHT

SECTION I

The Barometer

The pressure of the air is about 14½ lbs to the square inch.

A barometer or aneroid only tells the *weight* of the air, *i.e.* it indicates the changes in the weight of the air.

A high or rising barometer :

The barometer rises for: cold, dry, less wind. NE, N, NW.

A high barometer means a high pressure of air on the surface of the water, which causes the water to absorb oxygen.

A rapid rise = unsettled weather.

A slow rise = settled weather.

A steady continued rise for, say, 24 hours = very fine weather.

A steady rise with a falling thermometer = less wind or breezes from N to E.

> Quick *rise after low,*
> *Foretells stronger blow.*

With a rising barometer and a wind which veers or changes clockwise, say S to W, expect fair, cooler weather.

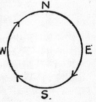

A low or falling barometer :

The barometer falls for warmer, wet, or more wind, SE, S, SW.

A low barometer means low pressure on the surface of the water: this causes the water to give off oxygen to the air.

A rapid fall = more wind or rain.

A sudden fall with a W wind = a storm from NW, N, NE.

A falling barometer and low temperature = snow or sleet or a strong wind from N.

A fall of more than four-tenths of an inch within 12 hours indicates a strong gale with rain.

A falling barometer and a rising temperature = rain and wind from SE, S, SW.

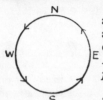

With a falling barometer and a wind which 'backs' or changes anti-clockwise, from say S to SE, expect rain and unsettled weather. A cyclone is approaching (*see page* 300).

The barometer should be studied in connection with the temperature of the air and the direction of the wind.

> *Long foretold, long last,*
> *Short notice, soon past.*

The indications of approaching change are shown more by the rising and falling of the mercury than by the actual height at the time.

SECTION 2

Cyclones and Anticyclones

The direction and force of the wind are influenced by the barometric pressure or readings taken over a given area.

The wind blows nearly parallel to the lines of equal barometric readings or isobars.

a. AN ISOBARIC CHART

If the barometric readings be plotted on a map and lines drawn between those places which have the same values, the result is an Isobaric Chart, and the lines (called isobars) represent equal barometric pressures (*see* the daily weather charts in *The Times*).

An Isobaric Chart shows where pressure is highest and lowest.

When bounded by a line of isobars (usually circular or elliptical) the areas of high pressure are called anticyclones and the areas of low pressure are called cyclones.

In such charts the direction of the wind is nearly parallel with the isobaric lines.

Around areas of low pressure the wind circulates in a direction opposite to the hands of a watch, inclining inwards towards the centre or point of lowest pressure.

Around areas of high pressure the wind moves in the direction of the hands of a watch, inclining outwards on the whole from the centre or point of highest pressure.

These are the directions of the wind in the *northern* hemisphere. In the *southern* hemisphere the directions of the wind round the areas are reversed.

A good deal of the weather in the British Isles is connected with cyclones and anticyclones.

The wind is stronger where the isobaric lines are close together than where they are wide apart on the chart.

B. THE CYCLONE

A cyclone is an atmospheric movement in which the wind blows almost in a circle over a certain region and travels along lines of equal barometric readings of low pressure, converging inwards towards the centre and upwards, and moving in a direction opposite to the hands of a watch, the barometer being lowest in the centre of the movement.

It is characterised by very unsettled weather usually developing into a storm.

If you stand with your back to the wind, the barometric readings in the area on your left hand side will be lower than those in the area on your right.

A cyclone moves rapidly and generally towards the north or NE, and while it continues very unsettled weather and variable winds prevail.

c. THE ANTICYCLONE

An anticyclone is a similar atmospheric movement, in which light winds blow round an area of high pressure outward from the centre, travelling along lines of equal barometric readings of high pressure, and moving in the direction of the hands of a watch. The barometer being highest in the centre of the movement.

It is characterised by clear cold weather in the winter and warm fine weather in the summer.

An anticyclone moves very slowly, and while it continues fair weather prevails, sometimes for several days.

d. THE PASSAGE OF A CYCLONE

The passage of a cyclone is roughly as follows:

In the extreme front there is usually blue sky.

The barometer falls and cirro-stratus clouds begin to form (*see page* 304).

The barometer falls further. The sky becomes overcast, temperature rises, the air is muggy and close.

Centre of cyclone or depression – rain, squalls and low barometer.

In rear of cyclone – heavy rain or clearing showers.

Barometer rises, air becomes cooler, patches of blue sky appear.

The cyclone passes.

There is often a ridge of high barometric pressure between two cyclones, when there is a short spell of fine weather (sometimes only a few hours). The sun is hot and distant objects are very clearly visible.

SECTION 3

Wind

The direction and force of the wind are determined by the distribution of barometric pressure.

When a strong wind springs up from the north you can expect it to die down much sooner than would a strong wind from a southerly direction.

An *east* wind is said to be bad for fishing: it is not entirely the wind, it is the strong light and other atmospheric conditions that prevail with an east wind.

In Ireland they say when the sky is heavy and dark in 'the butt' of the wind, the wind will increase or continue.

When the sky is light and clear in 'the butt' of the wind, the wind will die away.

A strong wind which changes round with the sun E to S to W (clockwise) will die away, and indicates settled weather.

A wind which changes round against the sun W to S to E (anti-clockwise) will increase and indicates unsettled weather.

A fitful, squally and variable wind is not good for any sort of fishing.

If it has been fine and the clouds are moving in a contrary direction to the wind on land, this generally means a change to squally weather.

If it has been wet and windy and the clouds are moving in a contrary direction to the wind on land, this means there will be less wind and rain.

When clouds pass over the sun the breeze usually increases.

When there is a strong wind blowing and sun comes out the wind is likely to become less, or as the ghillies put it, 'The sun kills the wind.'

Wind which changes round *with* the sun (clockwise) is said to 'veer.' Wind which changes round *against* the sun (counter clockwise) is said to 'back.'

a. METHOD OF RECORDING WIND

The force of the wind is measured by an anemometer which registers the velocity according to the Beaufort scale. This scale is sometimes used for making entries in a fishing diary, *viz*:

Beaufort Scale		Approx. velocity of wind M. P. H.
0	*Calm* when smoke is straight, flag on flagpole hangs limp ..	0
1	*Light airs* when smoke slants, flag blows out lightly	2
2	*Light breeze*, wind felt in face, flag flutters briskly	5
3	*Gentle breeze* when leaves, paper, etc are moved and flag on a pole flies out straight	10
4	*Moderate breeze*, bushes sway and an ordinary flag pole staggers a little	15
5	*Fresh breeze*, tree tops sway ..	20
6	*Strong breeze*, trees sway and wind *whistles* through them	30

SECTION 4

Moisture in the Air

The air obtains its moisture from oceans, lakes, rivers, and other moist surfaces.

The quantity of moisture or water vapour which the air will contain is dependent on the temperature. Air at a temperature of 30° contains 2 grs. of moisture per cub.ft

,,   ,,   ,,   50°   ,,   4   ,,   ,,
,,   ,,   ,,   90°   ,,   15   ,,   ,,

So the higher the temperature of the air, the greater the amount of moisture it can contain; when its full capacity is reached the air is said to be 'saturated.' This condition is called the *dew point* or 'point of saturation.'

When warm air is cooled below the temperature of its dew point, it parts with its moisture in the forms of clouds, fog, rain.

When cold air is warmed, it takes up moisture and retains it until it is saturated. Ex: a clear sky and no clouds visible.

It is all a matter of air mixing with air, *viz*: cold air mixing with warmer air, and *vice versa*.

SECTION 5

Clouds

When air is cooled below its point of saturation, the moisture becomes visible in the form of clouds of various shapes.

The following are the recognised nomenclature and altitude of the different forms of clouds:

Name	*Abbreviation*	*Approximate Altitude*
Cirrus (Mare's Tail).	Ci	. 27,000 to 50,000 ft
Cirro-Stratus	. Ci-St	. Average 29,000 ft

Name	Abbreviation	Approximate altitude
Cirro-Cumulus (Mackerel sky) .	Ci-Cu .	10,000 to 23,000 ft
Alto-Cumulus .	A-Cu .	10,000 to 23,000 ft
Alto-Stratus .	A-St .	10,000 to 23,000 ft
Strato-Cumulus .	St-Cu .	About 6,500 ft
Cumulus .	Cu .	4,500 to 6,000 ft
Cumulo-Nimbus (storm cloud) .	Cu-Nb .	4,500 to 24,000 ft
Nimbus (Rain Cloud)	Nb .	3,000 to 6,500 ft
Stratus . .	St .	0 to 3,500 ft

Cirrus clouds, or Mare's tails, are delicate feathery clouds like locks of hair, sometimes appearing in fan-shaped groups. They are composed of very small particles of ice.

The direction in which cirrus clouds are moving is a warning that the wind on the earth's surface will eventually follow the same direction as the clouds.

If the cirrus is moving quickly the wind will be strong and *vice versa*.

If the threads or streaks of Cirrus diverge and form a V-shape, the apex of which points to the N or W, it indicates that wind or rain may be expected from that direction.

The signs of approaching rain are roughly as follows: the cirrus clouds fill up to cirro-stratus, become greyer and darker, and eventually form cumulo-nimbus, from which rain falls.

Again, if the streaks of cirrus appear in a clear blue sky and gradually melt away leaving a deeper blue than before, you may expect a good spell of fine weather.

Cirro-Stratus appear as groups of small clouds, like shoals of fish, or as a thin white sheet of cloud, thicker in the middle than at the edges.

Cirro-Cumulus consists of small round masses of

clouds, like bundles of wool; they are generally in masses, sometimes in lines.

When these masses are close together, it indicates stormy weather and rain.

When they are in detached pieces, it is a sign of fine weather.

Cumulus are like woolpacks, dome-shaped clouds of low altitude, frequently resting on a horizontal base.

They are a typical 'dry weather day cloud.' If, however, they persist in the evening, expect rain.

Cumulo-Nimbus is the storm or shower cloud. They are vast cloud formations rising like mountains in the sky, whitish at the top, copper coloured lower down, and black beneath.

Stratus. Horizontal layers of clouds, sometimes formed of horizontal sheets of lifted fog. They are usually formed in the evening. It is more of a night cloud than a day cloud.

If the sun rises through disappearing stratus, expect a fine day.

Nimbus. The rain cloud: it is a continuous thick layer of dark grey clouds, with rough misty edges and sometimes in the form of long sweeping curtains.

There is often a form of cloud known as 'Flying Scud' moving below Nimbus.

A common indication of coming rain is, scattered patches or a single cloud coming up from the S or W.

> 'When we see a cloud rise out of the west, straightway we say, there cometh a shower, and it is so.'   *St. Luke* xii, 54.

The edges of a cloud are very important. Clouds with rugged broken edges mean rain and wind; with clear cut edges the chances are the clouds will pass without rain.

a. GENERAL NOTES ON CLOUDS

The Sky at Sunrise and Sunset

(*a*) When the sun rises on a clear unclouded horizon expect settled weather for 24 hours

(*b*) A grey sky in the morning expect fine weather

(*c*) A red sky in the morning or when the sun rises above a bank of clouds expect unsettled weather for 24 hours

(*d*) A rosy sunset clouded or clear expect fair settled weather for 24 hours.

(*e*) A grey sky in the evening expect unsettled weather

(*f*) A bright yellow sunset = wind

(*g*) A pale yellow sunset = rain.

Clouds banked together in the west mean coming rain.

Black patches of cloud among woolpacks indicate rain.

Thin clouds hanging low on the hill tops indicate thundery unsettled weather; the air is usually dull and heavy.

Soft delicate clouds in the sky indicate fine weather and moderate breezes.

In forecasting weather by the clouds, it must be remembered that local conditions largely affect weather changes, so we must consider the proximity of chains of hills, the sea coast, the valley, the river beds, etc. The opinions of 'locals' are always worth considering.

SECTION 6

Rain

Rain is produced by the cooling of the air, and in nearly all cases this cooling is produced by the expansion of the air in ascending from lower to higher levels in the atmosphere, forming clouds which are a stage in rain formation.

We know that the temperature of the atmosphere is about one degree cooler for every 300 ft of altitude, and this decrease in temperature is fairly uniform up to an altitude of 6 or 7 miles.

The prevailing wind in the British Isles is SW (warm air charged with moisture). This wind strikes the mountain districts of SW Ireland, Cornwall, Wales and Scotland, and is drawn upwards and cooled. It then parts with its moisture in the shape of rain. After passing over this high ground, it descends to the lower and warmer air on the East Coast, and commences to take up moisture again.

This is one of the reasons why the East Coast of the British Isles is much drier than the West Coast.

'Open rain' usually means ordinary showers of rain.

'Close rain' means a sort of Scotch mist.

a. SNOW

When the temperature of the atmosphere is below freezing point, precipitation takes place in the form of snow.

A foot of loose snow represents about 1 in of rain. It depends, however, upon the density of the snow.

b. HAIL

Hail is frozen rain.

Hailstones are sometimes 2 in and even more in diameter: these larger stones are formed by alternate coatings of opaque and clear ice.

It is very noticeable how frequently a thunderstorm is accompanied by showers of hail.

SECTION 7
Lightning

There are roughly three forms of lightning:

1. Forked or zig-zag, when the storm is close hand.

2. Sheet or diffused lightning, which is the reflection of distant forked lightning.

3. Globular or 'balled' lightning. This is rather rare, and is possibly due to some of the flash coming in the direct line of vision of the observer and so being visible and brighter than the other parts of the flash.

'Balled' lightning is sometimes miscalled a 'thunderbolt.' A thunderbolt is a meteoric stone from the realms of outer space.

To estimate the distance of a thunderstorm, count the number of seconds between the time of seeing the flash and hearing the thunder. An interval of five seconds indicates that the flash is one mile distant. If the interval is increasing it means that the storm is going away. If the interval is decreasing it means that the storm is coming on.

a. THUNDERSTORMS

Thunderstorm formations are usually local atmospheric whirls.

The whirl is confined to the lower stratum of the air, and is only a little distance above the earth's surface.

The lower the altitude of the storm, the more violent the force of the wind.

A whirl may vary from 1 to 10 miles in diameter and travelling at an average rate of about 18 m.p.h.

It is not uncommon to find a number of thunderstorms following one another in a straight line, with calm and dry intervals between.

Thunderstorms usually follow the course of rivers, valleys, a range of hills, etc.

On the approach of a thunderstorm:

The barometer is low or falling,
The air is heavy and dull,
The wind is gusty and changeable.

A clap of thunder is due to a sudden disturbance of the air by a violent discharge of atmospheric electricity through it, causing a vacuum or 'hole' to be made in the air, and the noise is caused by the air closing in again on that hole.

In a similar manner a vacuum is caused by the crack of the flyfisher's line, or the lash of a whip. A 'hole' is made in the air, and the crack is the air closing into the hole again.

b. THUNDERSTORMS AND FISH

During thundery weather the air is heavy and dull, the wind generally gusty and variable.

Fish, like all animals, become depressed, lethargic, and cease to feed well.

The barometer is low, causing the water at the surface to give off oxygen to the air, thus depleting the surface water of oxygen and driving the fish to the lower layers or to the bottom where the water is better oxygenated.

The experience of anglers varies considerably as regards the effect of thunderstorms on rising fish.

1. Some say they get good catches before a storm;
2. Some say they get good catches during a storm;
3. Some say they get good catches after a storm.

As regards 1 and 2 it is difficult to give any reason for the reported success. But as regards 3 the following may be a reason for a rise of fish.

There is usually a heavy downpour of rain towards the end of or just after a thunderstorm, which would cause the water to become re-oxygenated, and the flies to be beaten down on the surface. This may account for a rise of fish after a thunderstorm.

Thundery weather does not appear to affect the rise of fly, as there is often a big rise of fly when thunder is about. The electric discharge appears to bring about a relief from pressure which causes the nymphs, waiting to hatch out, to rise to the surface.

Cases have occurred under certain atmospheric conditions when fish are killed during a severe thunderstorm. They are not what is called 'struck' by lightning. I have seen it suggested that they die from shock or concussion, but I think it is far more likely that the cause of death is the sudden and severe electrification of the water under certain conditions.

Even during an ordinary thunderstorm the air is charged with a certain amount of electricity which affects the water.

But when the centre of the storm happens to be close by and is of very low altitude, the electrification of the water is very sudden and severe, and this is really what kills the fish.

German scientists have proved that if a wire charged with an electric current is drawn through a pool, it will kill or stupefy all the fish in the pool (*see page* 437).

In front of a thunderstorm the atmosphere is very unstable. Small eddies and streams of rising and falling air abound. Such conditions are due to what is called *convection* (which is the process of transmission of heat through gases by means of currents).

These eddies are sometimes of such strength as to lift fairly large pieces of paper and keep them in suspension for quite appreciable periods; even a fisherman's cast has been lifted off the water by one of these up-currents, much to his surprise.

The torrential rains which frequently accompany thunderstorms are often due to the general up-rush of large masses of warm air due to convection.

SECTION 8

Rainbows

A rainbow is caused when the rays of the sun are reflected by rain drops, showing the colours of the solar spectrum, *viz*: red, orange, yellow, green, blue, indigo, violet.

The colour varies with the size of the drops; the smaller the drops the lighter the colour, and *vice versa*.

To get a perfect 'bow,' the sun must be at a rather low altitude (a rainbow cannot be formed when the sun has an altitude of over 42°), and rain must be falling in a close 'curtain' in the opposite direction to the position of the sun.

In situations other than the above a rainbow is imperfect.

A rainbow in the morning is caused by the sun in the east shining on clouds or rain in the west, and as the west is our wet point, this usually means wet weather.

A rainbow in the evening generally means fine weather the following day.

SECTION 9

The Moon

First quarter: ☽   Last quarter: ☾
Full moon: ○   New moon: ●

Effect of moon on clouds :

The moon (especially a full moon) has some power of dispersing or 'eating up' clouds which gather at the time of moonrise.

In Connemara the last two days of an old moon are considered very important for forecasting weather.

The locals say that if the weather is settled during these last two days, it will remain settled for about a week.

If the weather is unsettled, it will continue unsettled for about a week.

A halo round the moon indicates wet weather, the larger the circle the nearer the rain.

Fishing by moonlight :

On a bright moonlight night the larvæ and bottom food in a lake or stream appear to get active, and fish are busy feeding on them. This may be one of the reasons why fish do not come to the surface much on a moonlight night.

From a *fish's* point of view, a bright moonlight night affords him the best chance of obtaining his food.

From a *fisherman's* point of view, therefore, the day following a bright moonlight night is not the best time to expect a full creel.

The moon possesses some power or influence over vegetation and animals concerning which there is still much to learn.

The farmer considers that it affects the time of his seed sowing.

The lumberman considers it is best to fell timber when the moon is in the last quarter, as the sap is then flowing down the tree; and the less sap in newly cut timber the longer it lasts. Indeed the moon is known to affect all plants and vegetation by

causing the sap to flow up the plant when it is in the
1st quarter (waxing), and to flow down the plant
when it is in the last quarter (waning). If the moon
has this powerful effect on plant life it is only reasonable to suppose that it may have some effect on
fish life.

Some fishermen find they catch most fish when
the moon is in the last quarter and during the first
five days of a new moon.

This is also the opinion of anglers on the continent
who have kept careful records over a term of years.
(*See* article by C. B. in *Fishing Gazette,* 21 October,
1933.) So there must be something in this.

SECTION 10

Mist on the Water

Mist over the water occurs when the water is
warmer than the air.   If the air is warmer than the
water there is no mist.

Mist usually occurs in the evening of a hot day,
when the water has been well warmed up by the sun.
The warm water warms the air close to the surface;
this 'warm surface air' takes up moisture, and when
it ascends some feet higher up and mixes with the
cooler air, it parts with that moisture again in the
form of mist.

SECTION 11

Water : its Temperature, Density, etc

In an open stream, the flow of the water in the
middle of the stream is faster than the flow at the
sides.

The flow of the water on the surface is faster than
the flow on the bed of the stream.

The level of the water in a river is highest in midstream (owing to the friction of the banks). In a

very broad river like the Mississippi the difference in level is about 6ft.

On a lake or open sheet of water, the waves made by the wind are much steeper and shorter in the shallows than in the deep water, where they are longer with a gentle slope.

Brown trout thrive best in water of a temperature between 45° and 60°F. Experiments have proved that they cannot live in water at a temperature of over 77°F, while goldfish and the carp species have been kept alive in water at a temperature of 100°F.

Density of water :

Cold water is denser or heavier than warm water, and warm water rises towards the surface; it depends, however, on exactly how cold the water is before it becomes denser than the warm water; the whole question is bound up with the anomalous expansion of water.

As regards the variation of density with the temperature, water has its minimum volume and its maximum density at a temperature of 4°C.

If a volume of water at a temperature of 4°C is cooled or heated it expands.

This irregular expansion of water explains why ponds begin to freeze at the surface.

For thermometer formulæ *see page* 381.

a. HOW WATER FREEZES

First a thin layer of cold water forms on the surface and sinks. When successive layers have formed and sunk and the whole is cooled to a temperature of 4°C, any further cooling diminishes the density, and, being lighter, the colder water ascends to the surface and becomes frozen (when the water at the surface reaches a temperature of 0°C).

Shallow water freezes sooner than deep water. A puddle freezes sooner than a pond.

In fast running water there is practically no difference between the temperature at the surface and on the bottom of the stream.

b. HOW WATER GETS WARM

The sun's rays pass through the water and heat up the bottom, which in turn heats up the water.

A dark coloured bottom absorbs the heat rays better than a light coloured bottom.

Shallow water heats quickly and cools quickly.

Deep water heats slowly and retains its heat well.

To a fisherman the temperature of the upper surface is important. If the upper surface is warm, fish come towards the surface and rise better than when the upper surface water is cold.

c. OXYGEN CONTENT OF WATER

To sustain fish life water must have a certain amount of dissolved oxygen in it.

Cold water is capable of containing more dissolved oxygen than warm water.

Clean river water under normal pressure and at a temperature of 32°F contains 10 cc of oxygen per litre, while at 60°F it only contains 7 cc per litre.

An oxygen content of 6 or 7 cc per litre is about the normal amount required by fish to exist comfortably.

When the barometer is high, water can absorb more oxygen from the air than when it is low.

Green water plants under strong sunlight give off oxygen to the water.

Decomposing water plants use up oxygen from the water.

The formation of ice forces out of the water all gases, including oxygen. Snow is also de-oxygenated in a similar way.

Water under a waterfall is well oxygenated in the 'white water,' as it is well ærated, and free oxygen from the air is mixing with the water.

Peaty or acid water has a lower degree of oxygen content than alkaline water.

Mineral salts :

Water is 'hard' when it has a considerable amount of dissolved salts in it (*e.g.* the sea). Water is called 'soft' when the amount of dissolved salts in it is small (*e.g.* rain water).

SECTION 12

Light

The rays of the sun are composed of heat rays and light rays.

(For the action of heat rays, *see page* 315.)

Light rays are either reflected off the surface or penetrate the water and are reflected from the bottom on to the under surface of the water.

Rays of light striking the surface of the water between an angle of 90° and 48½° penetrate through the water, forming what is known as the fish's window or cone of vision (*see page* 410).

When the surface of the water is broken up by wind or other cause, the rays of light get refracted or broken up on the surface and are unable to penetrate much, causing a subdued light in the water which is favourable for fishing. On a sunny calm day, the light rays penetrate well into the water, lighting up the scales of any fish on an even keel and rendering them more or less invisible or 'ghostlike.'

On a dark day with a breeze, light rays do not penetrate well, and a fish on an even keel loses the power of invisibility. This is the chance for the cannibal, the pike, etc.

It is a scientific fact that the rays from the red end of the spectrum penetrate far more easily into water than those from the violet end.

Most fishermen have noticed that the sun appears red when seen through mist or fog (water vapour). The reason being that the red rays of the spectrum have penetrated the vapour while the rays at the violet end have not.

As a rule, on a fine day the water of a lake looks bluish when you have your back to the sun, and it looks greyish when you face the sun.

From the fish's point of view, one of the chief attractions is the flash or gleam of light on the bright part of a bait or on the feather of a fly, the topping, the tinsel, the eye of the jungle cock feather, etc.

A bright, hard, glassy light on the water is never conducive to good sport.

a. METHOD OF RECORDING LIGHT

The following method of recording light (also used by photographers) is sometimes useful for making entries in a fishing diary.

An A light = bright unobscured sun and a cloudless sky.

A B light = sun through light clouds, strong shadows.

A C light = diffused light, shadows just possible.

A D light = very dull, overcast, gloomy, heavy clouds about.

SECTION 13
Weather and Animals

Many animals undoubtedly have the power of sensing the approach of fair or foul weather. The actions of the following are sometimes worth considering:

Spiders : When rain is coming, spiders make their frames short and are indolent. When, however, they make their frames long and cobwebs float in the air, you can expect fair weather. When a spider commences to strengthen his web you can expect wind.

Slugs come out and move about prior to rain.

Frogs come out on roads and paths on the approach of rain.

Peacocks scream and *geese* cackle on the approach of rain.

Ducks rise on their legs, flap their wings noisily, and quack when rain is coming.

Swallows fly low when rain is coming.

Swallows and *rooks* fly high when more wind is pending.

Cattle and *Sheep :* Cattle raise their noses to the wind and huddle together on the approach of a storm. When cattle lie down in preference to moving about, it is a sign of rain (they want to be sure of having a dry patch to lie on).

Goldfish in a bowl: In fine weather they are lively and usually keep near the surface. In unsettled weather they remain resting on the bottom.

Gulls come inland from the sea on the approach of a storm or high wind.

The following flowers, etc, usually close up before rain: pimpernel, crocus, dandelion, anemone, wood sorrel and fir cones.

SECTION 14

General Notes on Weather

The turning points of the day are roughly 9 a.m., 12 noon, 3 p.m. and sunset. For example:

1. If there is much wind or rain at 9 a.m. it is likely to continue until 12 noon, and if there is no change then, we must look for an improvement

about 3 p.m., etc. These hours are kinds of turning points in the weather.

2. If there is no wind at sunset the evening is likely to continue calm, and *vice versa*.

Definitions :

A hard day – The weather is bright, cool and clear; there is often a glassy glare or light on the water, and usually a wind from the N or E.

A soft day – The weather is mild, warmish, damp, showery, some clouds about, causing a diffused light. There is usually a wind from the S or W.

An open winter means mild weather with some rain.

A close winter means hard cold weather with frost or snow.

A white frost – Hoar frost or rime, composed of ice needles of frozen dew. After three days of hoar frost there is usually rain.

A black frost – Intense frost by which vegetation is blackened.

These old sayings are as true to-day as they were a hundred years ago:

A wet June makes a dry September.

> *Rain before seven,*
> *Fine before eleven.*

The usual explanation given for this is, that the areas of bad weather which cross the country generally consist of a belt of rain about four or five hours in width, and it takes about that time to pass over a given place.

If on a dull grey morning there appears a gap of blue sky, the day is likely to turn out fine.

Unusual clearness of the air by day, or pronounced twinkling of the stars at night, usually means unsettled weather.

Annual Cold and Warm Spells (predicted by Buchan)

(a) Six cold periods each year accompanied by a sharp fall in the barometer, *viz*:

February 7th to 14th
April 11th to 14th
May 9th to 14th
June 29th to July 4th
August 6th to 11th
November 6th to 11th.

(b) Four warm periods:

May 22nd to 26th
July 12th to 15th
August 12th to 15th
December 3rd to 9th.

Book VII: SUNDRIES

Part II

KNOTS AND SPLICING

SECTION I

Knots

A great variety of knots is used by fishermen, and some people are always trying to learn a new knot. It is better to select a few suitable for your purposes and on which you can rely.

Do not change to a new knot until the old one has failed you. The knots in these notes have not failed me; when they do I will try others.

To attach a fly to gut when it is getting dark, push the eye of the fly through a bit of thin white paper; this keeps the feathers clear and the eye shews up well against the paper. Tie the knot above the paper, then tear away the paper.

a. FIGURE OF 8 KNOT

There are two ways of making this knot: both are secure.

1. Pass the end of the line A up through loop B and round the whole loop, then down again through loop B, under line A and under the end of the loop.

Bring the end round and tuck it into the last formed bend. Pull tight.

This knot is useful for attaching a cast to a fly with a gut eye.

2. Pass the end of the line A up through the loop B, and round the whole, then pass it under and round line A and tuck the end into the last formed bend. Pull tight.

This is a useful knot for attaching a line to the loop at the end of a gut cast or when knotting on a fly the eye of which admits of only one thickness of gut.

b. FIGURE OF 8 JAMB KNOT

Hold the hook in the fingers of the left hand, and
with the right hand pass the gut through the eye and
as shown by the arrows (*see diagram*).

Push the eye of the hook through the loop B and
press it against the forefinger of the right hand.

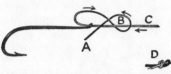

Then holding
the end A pressed
against the hook
shank, pull on the
standing part C,
and the knot
forms round the back of the eye as shown in D. It
will be noticed that when making the knot the wings
and hackle of the fly are not disturbed, which is
important.

This knot is best for trout flies where the size of
the gut suits the eye of the hook.

c. DOUBLE ENTRY KNOT

Pass the gut through
the eye of the hook, then
round the shank and back
through the eye again (*see
diagram*). Make an overhand knot at A.

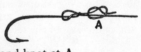

d. FISHERMAN'S BEND

In the following diagram the knot is made round a
piece of wood as it shows up
the details well. It is often
used for attaching a line or
gut to a swivel and is made
as follows:

Pass line or gut through
eye of swivel, bring end up
over forefinger of left hand

323

(which holds swivel) then down through eye
again; repeat this till two loops are formed over
the forefinger and through the ring of the eye.
Bring the end round and back through both loops.
Pull tight, and finish off with two half hitches on the
standing part.

e. TURLE KNOT

Pass gut through eye of fly. Push the fly away up the
gut. Make a running noose as in (1). Pull the knot at

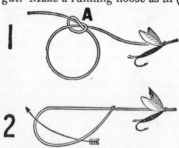

A tight. A loop
is now formed as
in (2). Pass the
fly back through
the loop as shown
by the arrow.
Grip the fly
through the loop
and work the knot
to the back of the
eye. Pull tight.

With salmon flies, a double overhand knot at A is
best. The turle knot is hard to undo.

f. BOWLINE KNOT

Make a loop of the line as at C:
Pass A up through C,
under and round B, and
back through C. Pull tight.

g. OVERHAND KNOT

This is made by holding one end (the 'standing
part') in the left hand, and the other end ('the end')
in the right hand.

Pass the end back
over the standing part,
and then put the end

through the loop thus made. Hence the name overhand knot.

You can have a double or treble overhand knot.

h. BLOOD KNOT

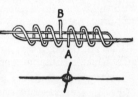

Place the ends parallel. Double one end A back, and twist it three times round the whole, bringing the end A out between the strands as shown opposite.

Reverse and do the same with the other end B, bringing it out between the strands on the opposite side to A. Draw tight.

i. SINGLE FISHERMAN'S KNOT

Lay the two ends parallel: With the end A make a single overhand knot round B: with the end B make a single overhand knot round A, as in diagram.

Pass ends A and B through C in opposite directions.

Draw tight and cut off close.

This is sometimes called the smooth knot.

Some anglers use this knot a good deal. I prefer the double fisherman's knot. It is safer.

j. DOUBLE FISHERMAN'S KNOT

Here are two ways of making it; both are effective. *No* 1 is the neatest for joining two pieces of gut. *No* 2 is the easiest for making a dropper from a part of the cast (*page* 328).

1. Lay the two ends parallel:

Pass the end A twice round B forming two loops. The first loop is gripped by the finger 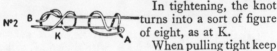 and thumb of the left hand, and the next passed round and gripped in the same way. The end A is then passed up through both loops and pulled tight.

The same process is gone through with the end B.

When both ends are pulled tight, they make a neat knot like a series of rings. It is sometimes called the 'barrel knot.'

2. Lay the two ends parallel: With end A make a double overhand knot round B. With end B make a double overhand knot round A thus. Pull tight.

In tightening, the knot turns into a sort of figure of eight, as at K.

When pulling tight keep the ends A and B parallel with the main parts.

k. A CLOVE HITCH

This hitch is useful when fastening a line to a hook in the wall or to an upright post, etc.

Make two loops at the end of the line as in 1.

Put loop A over loop B as in 2. Pull tight.

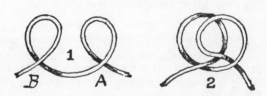

SECTION 2

To Join Two Pieces of Gut

1. Use a double fisherman's knot (*see page* 325).
2. Use a blood knot (*see page* 325).

a. TO ATTACH GUT OR LINE TO A RING

1. Pass the line through the ring and make a double overhand knot on the standing part (*see page* 324), then pull this slip knot tight.

2. A fisherman's bend (*see page* 323), passing the line twice through the ring.

b. TO MAKE A LOOP

1. Double over a portion of line thus:

Make a single overhand knot at A with the doubled line.

2. Bowline knot (*see page* 324).

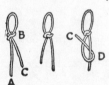

3. Make a loose single overhand knot on the line A, at B. Pass the end C through it. Make the bend at D; this locks the knot. Pull tight and you have a secure loop.

When fastening two loops never pass one end through its own loop if you can avoid it.

c. TO ATTACH A FLY TO GUT

For *salmon flies* use:

1. Figure of 8 knot (*see page* 322 No 1), when the fly has gut loop.
2. Double entry knot (*see page* 323) for hooks with large eyes.
3. The turle knot (*see page* 324).

For *trout flies*:

1. Figure of 8 jamb knot (*see page* 323). The thickness of the gut should suit the size of the eye.

2. The turle knot (*see page* 324). A good knot at any time; is useful with thin gut and a large eye.

d. TO ATTACH A LINE TO THE LOOP OF A CAST

1. Figure of 8 knot (*see page* 322 No 2).
2. Another way is as follows:

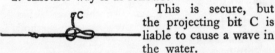

This is secure, but the projecting bit C is liable to cause a wave in the water.

It is easily undone by pushing down the gut loop. No 1 is the better way for general use.

SECTION 3

Droppers and Attachment

1. Cut the cast at a knot. Rejoin with a double fisherman's knot (*see page* 326, No 2), thus:

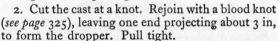

Leave BC about 3 in long, Bring CB round and down through at A and pull tight; *or*

2. Cut the cast at a knot. Rejoin with a blood knot (*see page* 325), leaving one end projecting about 3 in, to form the dropper. Pull tight.

A dropper made as in 1 and 2 stands out well at right angles to the cast. Arrange so that the dropper forms part of the strand which is above and NOT below the knot, the idea being that should the cast break at the knot you only lose the fly or flies below the knot.

3. Make a double overhand knot at A and a single one at B, leaving about 3 inches to hang down. Pull tight, thus:

These three methods of making droppers rather shorten the cast and you may have to add an extra strand or two of gut.

It is sometimes an advantage to have the dropper attachment slightly thicker than the main cast, as the dropper will then stand out better and is less likely to foul the cast.

In this case either of the following methods is good.

1.

Having cut the cast, lay the two ends together and make a double fisherman's knot but do not draw it tight.

2.

(a) Make a loop on the dropper attachment and fix it as in diagram 1. Pull tight.

(b) Make a knot at the end of the dropper attachment and fix it as in diagram 2. Pull tight.

SECTION 4
Splicing

When splicing a line the line must be quite dry.

When splicing gut or gut substitute it must be well soaked.

Scrape off any dressing on the line, then beat and fray out $\frac{1}{4}$ in of the ends B and C.

Wax or varnish the frayed ends well.

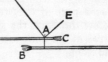

Wax the tying silk well (*see also* Fisherman's wax, *page* 332).

Lay the two ends quite parallel and while binding do not allow them to get twisted.

1. Begin by knotting the tying silk at A.

    Leave A D longer than A E.

    Bind the waxed silk from A to C and from A to B.

    Then come back over all from B to C with A D.

    Finish off at C with whip finish (*see page* 331).

Take a few turns past B and C for about $\frac{1}{8}$ in on the single material to fill up the inequality.

It is always best to have only one whip finish, *viz*, at C.

Wax the splice all over and roll on an ivory or smooth surface to finish it off.

Finally apply two coats of varnish over the splice.

A splice when finished should be pliable, not hard and stiff, so as to pass easily through the rings, neither should it be too long (1 in is about right).

To splice a very thin line or thin gut substitute.

The line must be quite dry. The gut substitute must be well soaked. Lay the two ends together; join with a single fisherman's knot (*see page* 325); do not draw the knots together, but leave about $\frac{1}{4}$ in between them; fill up this space with waxed silk whipping to form a buffer between the knots. Take a few turns of whipping on the single line beyond the knots so as to round off any inequality.

To splice backing to a line :

This is easier done if you can manage to attach the backing to two hooks A and B. Knot the backing to hook A and attach it to the hook B with a clove hitch which can easily be slipped off. Both hands are then free to whip the silk at C. Cut off backing at C when the whipping is finished.

SECTION 5

Whip Finish

Having whipped as far as required, form a loop B as in *figure 1*.

Bring the end E round and up inside the loop 3 or 4 times, as shown in *figure 2*.

Wind B over E, till the spiral turns are exhausted, as in *figure 3*.

Pull loose end E till tight.

Another way :

Take a loop of silk stronger than that used for lapping.

Place this loop along and beyond the whipping.

Wind the last three or four turns over the loop and pass the end of the whipping silk into the loop.

Pull on the loop and draw the end of the whipping silk under the three or four turns referred to above.

Cut off the loose end and the job is completed.

SECTION 6

Splice Whipping

A useful method for attaching a twisted gut cast or a length of twisted gut to a line permanently:

First unlay from 1 in to $1\frac{1}{2}$ in of the twisted gut, soak it well in water, straighten the strands, indent each one slightly at intervals with the teeth.

Next unpick about 1½ in of the line, divide this into as many parts as there are strands in the gut cast, and wax each part well.

Now marry the line and the gut cast, bringing them together so that the forks are closely in touch, and each strand of gut and bit of line comes out at different points. Whip the ends temporarily with a few turns of strong silk.

Then to complete the job whip all over with a piece of well waxed silk.

SECTION 7

Fisherman's Wax

Good hand-made cobbler's wax is the best for general use. Clear wax (which does not darken the silk) is generally used for fly tying.

Whatever wax is used keep it in a bit of chamois leather or sheet rubber.

To wax a piece of silk thread attach one end to a hook (with a clove hitch) and rub the wax *quickly* over the silk, the friction softens the wax; if you rub slowly you break the silk.

Another way is to rub the thread with a bit of tallow or deer's fat and it will pass easily through the wax without breaking.

332

Book VII: SUNDRIES

Part III

GUT, GUT CASTS, GUT SUBSTITUTES

SECTION I
Measuring the Thickness of Gut

A good reliable gut cast of the desired thickness and quality is one of the most important parts of a fisherman's equipment.

There is at present no standard measure for gut; some tackle makers have different names for the various sizes of gut, even x has different values. Some years ago I went to three shops in London and purchased some 2x from each. When I got home I examined them and found they were all of a different thickness or diameter.

So I gave up thinking of gut in values of x, and got a Gut Gauge (or micrometer) capable of measuring the diameter of gut in 1,000ths of an inch. Now when I want to purchase gut, I take my gauge with me, and as regards thickness I get what I require, while as regards quality I always ask for the best procurable and put myself in the hands of a reliable tackle maker.

Some strands of gut taper a little and are slightly thicker at one end than at the other. The size should be the minimum diameter of the strand.

For the same reason the 'size' of a gut cast should be the size of the thinnest strand.

There are several patterns of gut gauge on the market measuring 1,000ths of an inch.

Here are some of the names by which the various thicknesses of gut are known in the market:

1,000*ths of an inch*		
·020	Hebra	0/5
·019	Imperial	1/5
·018		2/5
·017	Marana	3/5
·016		4/5

334

1,000*ths of*
an inch

·015	Padron	5/5	
·014		6/5	
·013	Regular	7/5	
·012		8/5	$\frac{1}{4}$x drawn
·011	Fina	9/5	$\frac{1}{2}$x drawn
·010		ox	$\frac{3}{4}$x drawn
·009	Refina	1x	1x drawn
·008		2x	2x drawn
·007	Refinucha	3x	3x drawn
·006		4x	4x drawn

An effort has lately been made by the leading
tackle makers in consultation to fix a standard scale
for gut sizes.

Fishing Gazette Suggested Scale

In this connection the *Fishing Gazette* suggested
the following scale for general use. It is worth
making a note of, and it differs very little from that
used by many of the leading tackle makers.

Size measurement 1,000*ths of an inch*		Suggested name
·021	.. ..	0/5
·020	.. ..	1/5
·019	.. ..	2/5
·018	.. ..	3/5
·017	.. ..	4/5
·016	.. ..	5/5
·015	.. ..	6/5
·014	.. ..	7/5
·013	.. ..	8/5
·012	.. ..	9/5
·011	.. ..	0/x
·010	.. ..	1/x
·009	.. ..	2/x

Size measurement 1,000ths of an inch	Suggested name
·oo8	3/x
·oo7	4/x

Note : It is much more convenient for fishermen to refer to thickness of gut in 1,000ths of an inch and disregard all names, numbers, letters, etc.

SECTION 2

Notes on Gut

For the fisherman, the gut question is a very important one, and although it may appear extravagant, it pays to use only *fresh* gut and the best procurable.

The gut of commerce is of two sorts:
1. Natural or undrawn
2. Drawn gut.

1. Natural or undrawn gut is about 10 per cent. stronger than drawn gut of equal diameter.

The supply in the very thin sizes is rather limited. ·oo9 is about the thinnest obtainable in any quantity.

Some expert anglers never use anything thinner than the finest undrawn gut obtainable.

2. Drawn gut is natural gut passed through a jewelled plate. It is not easy to draw it straight and level, and unless done very carefully weak spots will occur.

Drawn gut:
   (*a*) Does not remain quite transparent for long, it is liable to become dull and assume a milky colour
   (*b*) It frays easily
   (*c*) It feels softer than natural gut, and has but little spring in it when bent.

a. GOOD AND BAD GUT

Good gut is in appearance round, bright, hard, even in diameter, and colourless.

Inferior gut is in appearance flat, greasy, rough, uneven in size, dull in colour, sometimes spotted and of a greenish tinge.

You can detect a flaw or weak spot in a strand of gut by taking a few inches, holding an end in each hand, and bending it. It will 'give' or bend easily at any weak point or flaw (*see also page* 341).

In the thicker sizes you can test a strand for roundness by rolling it between the thumb and forefinger. If the gut is flat the ends will fly about; if round they will roll evenly.

When you cast a tight knot, cut the cast at once and re-tie.

b. SOAKING GUT

It is best to soak gut in *cold* water.

Thin gut up to ·009 in thickness should be soaked for at least twenty minutes.

The thicker the gut the longer it should be soaked. Gut ·016 in thickness should be soaked for at least forty minutes.

Drawn gut does not require to be soaked quite so long as natural gut.

Salmon gut should be soaked for 60 minutes or more if very thick.

Never leave your cast lying in the sun during lunch time, but lay your rod down with the cast in the water.

If gut becomes frayed, rub it with indiarubber, a piece of cork or a bit of heel-ball; this will clean off the 'frays.'

Never rub gut (drawn or undrawn) when it is damp, as you are liable to take off the outer skin.

Drawn gut will not stand much rubbing at any time.

Some anglers prefer gut treated in one of the following ways:

1. Renforcé or compressed gut
2. A cast made up of strands of different colours is said to show up less in the water
3. Unbleached and unpolished gut is said to be stronger and less visible.

SECTION 3

Making up a Cast

Soak the strands of gut in cold water.

Make the knots, but only partially tighten them. Soak the gut again.

Then pull the knots fairly tight, but do not overdo it. Do not cut the surplus ends off too close.

The gut of the droppers should not be finer than the gut of the main cast, nor should it be too long or it will foul the cast (3 ins is quite long enough).

The flies on a wet fly cast should not be closer to one another than 3 ft.

The flies on a 9-ft cast would be thus:

Note : When the left arm is fully extended, the distance from the chin to the thumbnail of the left hand measures about 3 ft.

The wind usually determines the length of your cast.

Against the wind a 6-ft cast is long enough.

With the wind you can use a 9-ft or 12-ft cast. Nine feet is the usual length. You can cut off or add to it as you think fit.

With a *long* gut cast:

1. You can use thicker gut at the point.

338

2. A 12-ft cast tapered to ·010 will hold its own with a 9-ft cast tapered to ·008 as regards catching fish
3. You can cast easier with the wind
4. Your flies will fall lightly
5. There is less chance of cracking off a fly
6. When drifting in a boat and casting down wind a 12-ft cast is an advantage, especially if you are using a thick cast or a level line.

With a *short* gut cast:
1. Your flies are liable to fall heavier on the water and with more of a splash
2. You can cast easier against the wind.

Generally speaking, for wet fly fishing in a lake or open water a level cast is best.

The taper of a wet fly cast should be from the reel line to about the top dropper; the remainder of the cast can be level.

In dry fly fishing a tapered cast is essential, and the taper should be gradual from the reel line to within 2 ft of the fly.

The length of your cast often depends on the length of your rod. Whatever way the cast is attached to the line, there is always the equivalent of a knot at the join, which may cause trouble by passing through the top ring when landing a fish.

a. TESTING A CAST

Never test a cast when it is wet, as the strain is liable to flatten and weaken the gut at the knots.

In testing a cast, do so with a steady strain; any jerk or sudden pull is very hard on the gut.

Dry gut is about 15 per cent. stronger than when it is wet.

To test the strength of an ordinary trout cast :

1. Hold the cast in the left hand and draw it through the closed palm of the right hand, putting on as much strain as you think its thickness should stand: this also takes the coils out of a cast, *or*

2. Test it on a spring balance:

> *Undrawn natural gut :*
>> Size ·009 should stand 3·75 lbs
>>   ,, ·010   ,,   ,,   4·25 ,,
>>   ,, ·013   ,,   ,,   5·25 ,,
>
> *Drawn gut :*
>> Size ·007 should stand 2 lbs
>>   ,, ·008   ,,   ,, $2\frac{1}{2}$,,
>>   ,, ·009   ,,   ,,   3 ,,

To test a salmon cast :

The gut of course should be quite dry.

1. Attach the loop to a hook, and hold the cast fairly tight in the left hand; with the right hand rub it down with chamois leather until straight. Put on as much pressure with the right hand as you consider the gut should stand. (For thin trout gut this method is rather drastic.)

2. With a spring balance, a salmon cast should stand a strain of at least 8 or 10 lbs.

Although in ordinary play a 40 lb salmon only puts a pressure of 4 or 5 lbs on the cast, still a strong cast is necessary to stand a sudden jerk from a heavy fish.

When a cast breaks at a knot you can retie it; but when it breaks in the middle of a strand destroy it.

Examine the knots carefully. Take the cast and bend it at each knot. If it preserves a position like A it is all right. But if the cast becomes like B, break it at the knot and re-tie it.

Test in a similar way for flat bits, worn places, flaws, etc.

SECTION 4
Colour of Gut

Generally speaking:

1. Use *clear* gut for *surface* fishing.
2. Use *stained* gut for *underwater* fishing.

The background has much to do with the colour of the gut used.

Use clear unstained gut for all surface fishing (dry fly fishing, etc), and for underwater fishing when the water is very clear, or in a river with few bushes, etc, where there is a clear open background.

Use stained gut in underwater fishing, in shaded water, in dark deep water, and when the background or bottom is dark. The fish see a cast against a background of the reflection of the bottom on the undersurface of the water, so try to have the cast the colour of that background.

The following are useful stains for gut when you want to colour it:

1. A *bluish* tint. Put the cast for ten minutes in blue-black ink. If too dark, wash *at once* in clean water until you get the desired tint. (Ink stain wears off with use.)

2. A *brownish* tint. Allow the tea in the teapot or the coffee in the coffeepot to cool until just warm (it must not be too hot), then put the cast in for say five minutes or until you get the desired tint.

⟩ If you want a very dark brown stain, put the cast

in a saucer and cover it with warm tea leaves, leaving it to soak for about six hours.

A brownish stain is useful when fishing in peaty water.

3. A *greenish* tint. Soak in tepid water in which a piece of green baize has been boiled.

Logwood and copperas are sometimes used to give a smoky colour, and nitrate of silver to give a black colour; also Judson's dyes are used. It is open to question whether these injure the gut.

I think Nos 1 and 2 are the best stains to use. No 1 (the ink stain) is very popular.

To dull the glitter of the gut :

The colour of the gut is important, but to prevent the reflection or flash from the sunlight is even more important. The flash of the gut before it hits the water very often scares a fish just as much as the glint of it when on the surface.

Stained gut 'flashes' just as much as unstained gut.

1. Mr. E. R. Hewitt discovered a process whereby the skin of the gut is so treated as almost to eliminate flash. A photographic chemical is used which gives a brownish colour to the cast. These 'Hewitt' casts are sold by Farlow, and give excellent results. They should be well soaked in cold water for about an hour before use or before being knotted as they are rather stiff when dry.

2. Mash up dock or alder leaves into a pulp and rub the cast with it, this will help to prevent glitter.

3. Rub the cast with heel-ball.

a. CARE OF GUT

Where steel goes rusty, gut goes rotten.

Gut should be kept in waxed paper, in an airtight box, away from dust and light.

When gut has been used or soaked it shortens its life, thin gut is more easily affected than that of a thick diameter.

Undrawn gut of good quality which has not been used, will keep quite well for two seasons or even longer.

Drawn gut deteriorates more quickly and should be carefully tested before use if kept until the following season.

I am afraid I am rather extravagant with gut casts, as at the end of the fishing season I discard all casts of a less diameter than ·009 which have been soaked or used.

If you wish to keep gut for use next season the following methods help to preserve it.

1. Steep it in a bath of pure milk for twelve hours, then dry it well and put it away in waxed paper.

2. Soak it in a solution of 10% pure glycerine and 90% of rain water for 12 hours, then hang it up in a draught to dry; this helps to prevent decomposition. The action of glycerine tends to keep gut soft and pliable, whereas if it was left exposed to the air for any time it would rapidly become hard and brittle and unsuitable for the purpose for which it was intended.

If the glycerine solution is too strong, it makes the gut greasy and liable to draw at the knots.

Gut treated with glycerine should be soaked before use in a rubber or oiled silk damper. If put in a metal damping box, chemical action sets up which may injure the gut.

Never keep gut in any receptacle where there are traces of sulphur, chlorine, salts or acids.

Good chamois leather is all right but with inferior chamois leather there is often a trace of acids which injure the gut.

Clean waxed paper is really the best covering to keep gut in.

Celluloid cases let in the dust and light.

Strands of gut are usually tied with red silk or cotton; remove these before soaking or the gut will become coloured in patches.

A cast should always be well dried at night after fishing. Never put it away damp or leave it in the damper overnight.

The twisted gut of a salmon cast should be very carefully dried after use, as it holds the water and will soon rot if put away damp.

SECTION 5

Gut Substitutes

There are many substitutes for gut on the market; they are known by various names, *viz :* Sub gut, Japanese gut, Olympic, Yagut, Surbghut, etc.

In the thinner sizes (*viz* under ·015) they may be rather unreliable.

In the thicker sizes (·019 to ·021) they are frequently used in salmon fishing and some fishermen think highly of them.

The chief complaints against gut substitutes or sub gut are:

1. When wet, sub gut swells and becomes greasy and shows up rather white in the water;

2. When knotted, the gut is liable to slip at the knot (a whipping is safer than a knot);

3. When you 'cast a knot' the gut breaks very easily at the knot;

4. When knotted to a fly, sub gut requires careful attention as it is very liable to wear at the knot, especially after playing a fish.

The safest knots are said to be the 'figure of 8,

344

the turle knot, the blood knot. The loose end should never be cut off too close.

A small drop of Durofix on the knot helps to prevent it slipping and renders it more reliable.

Durofix is waterproof, colourless and dries quickly.

After use when the cast shows the slightest sign of fraying, reject it at once.

Before whipping a loop or making a knot, gut substitute must be well soaked until it is quite soft and pliable and feels slightly sticky when pulled through the hands.

Size ·019 should be soaked for at least half an hour.

Size ·021 should be soaked for at least one hour.

Before making up a cast examine the gut and see that it is not frayed in any part of its length.

Sub gut is stronger than ordinary gut of the same thickness.

The breaking strain of ·015 wet gut is about 6 lbs.

The breaking strain of ·015 wet sub gut is about 8 lbs.

Some fishermen use gut substitute as a running line. When it is used dry it is liable to get tangled round the reel; to prevent this, soak it in a solution of one part glycerine and one part tepid water. This renders the sub gut supple and it should remain so for about two months without further treatment.

See Appendix on Nylon (page 507).

Book VII: SUNDRIES

Part IV

HOOKS

2³/₄"	8/0		
2¹/₂"	7/0		
2¹/₄"	6/0		
2"	5/0		
1⁷/₈"	4/0		
1³/₄"	3/0		
1⁵/₈"	2/0		
1¹/₂"	1/0		
1³/₈"	1¹/₂		
1¹/₄"	1		
1¹/₈"	2		
1"	3		
15/16"	4		
14/16"	5		
13/16"	6		
New Nºⁱ			
9	3/4"	7	
8	11/16"	8	
7	10/16"	9	
6	9/16"	10	
5	1/2"	11	
4	7/16"	12	
3	12/32"	13	
2	11/32"	14	
1	10/32"	15	
0	9/32"	16	
00	1/4"	17	
000	7/32"	18	
New Nºˢ		Old Nºˢ	

No 1 = 1¼"

Measuring Hooks

Most fish hooks are now made to a recognised standard scale.

Scale of Hooks:

Measure a hook from the black line on right, but do not include the gut loop or metal eye (*see* scale diagram opposite).

The size of the hook is governed by the length of the hook shank (excluding the eye).

There are many different bends and shapes of hooks, but the same principle of numbering by length of shank can be applied to nearly all.

The scale shown on p. 347 appeared in my original article on Hooks in the *Fishing Gazette* of 4th April, 1925. The advantage of it is you can describe a hook either by a number or by the length of the shank in fractions of an inch, *viz*: Size No 8 or $\frac{11}{16}$ in.

Dry fly fishermen have adopted (for some reason) a different numbering, *viz*, Nos ooo to 9. It is shown as the 'new Nos' (*see diagram*).

By this scale a No 8 hook would always have the same length of shank whatever the bend, style or make may be, *viz*:

No 8 Limerick bend
No 8 Round bend
No 8 Model Perfect hook
No 8 Smith's patent hook, etc.

When ordering a hook it is best to give the number and also the length of the shank thus: No 8 = $\frac{11}{16}$ in. Anyhow, you make sure of getting the size you want.

SECTION 2
Length of Shank

The length of the shank and the bend or gape of a hook should be considered conjointly when deciding the style of hook one wishes to use.

There are several styles of shank:

1. The long shank
2. The short shank
3. The up-turned shank
4. The hog backed shank, etc, etc.

A Pennell-Limerick hook, which has an upturned shank and a down-turned eye, is a very useful hook for lake trout flies, as it brings the pull of the line in the same plane with the shank of the hook.

If a hook is too 'hog-backed' it has a tendency to spin.

With salmon and lake trout hooks the gape should be about one-third the length of the hook,

viz: C D $= \frac{1}{3}$ A B.

A hook with a reasonably long shank is more effective in its pull and hooking power than a very short shanked hook, because with a short shanked hook the strain of the pull falls on the inside of the barb instead of on the point, and this tends to scratch and not penetrate.

For example, take a hook with a very long shank; tie pieces of gut at three different

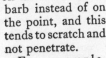

points A, B, C. Pull on each piece and you will at once see the advantage of a hook shank of reasonable length over a very short one.

In trout fishing, a hook with a long shank is generally used for artificial mayflies, and flies representing little fish, larvæ, etc, usually fished as tail flies.

A shorter shanked hook is more suitable for droppers representing natural flies, etc.

SECTION 3
The Bend or Gape of a Hook

There are several bends, the chief ones are:

1. The Limerick bend
2. The round bend
3. The square bend.

The Limerick bend is best for salmon, sea trout and lake trout flies.

A round bend hook is best for the smaller trout flies wet or dry.

The bend of the hook and length of the shank are often governed by the type of fly you wish to tie on it. A sparsely dressed fly sometimes requires to be dressed on a long shanked hook with a narrow gape, so that the narrow gape hook is hidden in the sparse hackle.

SECTION 4
Snecked or 'Bent off' Hooks

Almost any hook can be bent off or snecked. For example, a hook can be 'bent off' from A or B.

A hook bent off at A is much more reliable than one bent off at B, as the point of greatest strain on a hook is at B, and it is more likely to break at that point.

A hook larger than No 3 = 1 in should
not be snecked at all.

A snecked hook has a tendency to
swim or float on its side, and not on an
even keel.

For rapid water snecked hooks are all right.

For still water or for dry fly fishing, un-
snecked hooks are best.

Snecked hooks are used a good deal in
spinning tackle, as they possess more hooking
power than an ordinary hook.

SECTION 5

The Temper of the Iron

With a well-tempered hook the shape of the bend
will not alter under reasonable pressure.

If *over* tempered, the iron will snap or break suddenly.

If *under* tempered, the iron is too pliable: it is like a
bit of wire; the gape will open and remain so. A hook
is then said to be 'sprung' and should be rejected.

The stoutness of the iron should be graduated to
the size and bend of the hook. It also depends on
whether the fly tied on it is required to sink or float.

SECTION 6

The Point of a Hook

The point should be fine, sharp and not too long
from the point to the base of the barb.

Test the point on your thumb nail, if it slips (and
does not stick) it wants sharpening.

To sharpen a hook use a very fine file or a carbor-
undum stone. A few strokes of a file or stone on the
inside of the barb is enough; make the strokes
towards the point. And, if anything, cause the

extreme microscopic point to bend outwards; this helps the hook to take a better hold.

If you file the outside of the barb it shows up bright in the water.

Some fishermen use *barbless* hooks, chiefly when they wish to put fish back without injury. You can make a hook barbless by filing the barb or by pinching it with a flat pliers; the barb either snaps off or bends flush with the iron.

SECTION 7

The Eye of a Hook

The eye is made in various ways, *viz :*

1. The upturned eye
2. The downturned eye
3. The straight eye
4. The gut eye, etc.

The metal must be properly and securely closed, with no rough edges to cut the gut.

There is some difference of opinion as to whether upturned or downturned eyes are best; both have advantages in different kinds of fishing.

For salmon fishing, gut eyes are all right if they are newly tied, but if kept for a season or two the whipping deteriorates, the gut is liable to slip, and the hook becomes unreliable.

I like upturned eyes for salmon flies and for all dry flies.

SECTION 8

The Colour of a Hook

Black is the best all round colour for hooks.

Some fishermen use coloured hooks to suit the colour of the hackle of the fly. I doubt if there is much in this.

With prawn tackle, it pays to use red enamelled hooks.

With a silver sprat or sand eel, silvered hooks are used.

With a golden sprat reddish hooks are used.

SECTION 9

Hooks for Salmon Fishing

The best hooks are those which take the largest hold and keep it.

The hold in a salmon's mouth is mostly a flesh hold, not a bone or gristle hold.

A salmon fly hook should have no sneck or bend-off.

The Limerick bend is about the best.

Dee salmon hooks are longer in the shank than the ordinary hook and the gape is increased a little to suit the long shank:

An ordinary No 4/0 hook $= 1\frac{7}{8}$ in long.

A No 4/0$\frac{1}{4}$ Dee hook $= 1\frac{7}{8}$ in $+ \frac{1}{4}$ in $= 2\frac{1}{8}$ in long.

Double hooks are heavy and swim deep, which is often an advantage. They increase the chances of hooking a fish, but there is also the chance that if one hook has a grip, the other may act as a lever in freeing it.

Never use a double hook larger than No 2 size.

SECTION 10

Hooks for Trout Fishing

For *wet* fly stream fishing an ideal hook would be something like this:

1. A moderate length of well-tapered shank
2. A round bend

3. A downturned metal eye

4. The point of the hook should be sharp and not too long from the tip to the base of the barb.

For *dry* fly fishing:

A round bend, no sneck, an upturned eye.

For *worm* fishing always use a round bend hook, with a wide gape and no sneck.

Book VII: SUNDRIES

Part V

RODS, REELS, LINES, NETS, GAFFS

SECTION I

Fly Rods

A rod for fly fishing should give a firm, even, and gradually increasing bend from the handle to the top. There should be no weak place and no stiff place. The strength should be in proportion all the way down the rod.

In casting, the top begins the movement, which is carried down the rod to the stronger part near the butt.

After making a downward stroke the rod top should come to rest quickly; if it vibrates or dithers much it will not have good hooking power.

The chief thing about a rod is the *action*. A long, short, heavy or light rod should do the work it is designed to do easily and smoothly: if much effort is required in casting, something is wrong.

As regards action, fly rods may be roughly divided into four types, *viz*:

(1) A very stiff rod
(2) A limber rod
(3) A quick action rod
(4) A slow action rod.

Desirable qualities of a rod are:

1. Good casting power, which depends a great deal on the power communicated by the top joint to the line;

2. Good pick up capacity;

3. Good power to control a fish.

In choosing a rod, test it in the hand and see that it suits your requirements, considering two things, *viz*:

(a) The bend of the rod
(b) The balance of the rod.

a. THE BEND OF A ROD

Hold the rod in front of you (without reel or line attached); try it by the *feel*, and wave it up, down, and sideways

- (i) To ascertain that the bend is even and gradual from the top to the butt and that there are no weak or stiff places,
- (ii) To decide whether it is a whippy or a stiff rod. Some find a slow action whippy rod suits their purpose better than a quick action stiff rod.

The points about a *stiff* rod are:

1. It recovers quickly
2. Has good pick up capacity
3. Is good for casting against the wind
4. Kills a fish quickly
5. When casting, the rod top does good work and so saves effort.

A *stiff* rod helps to make a narrow entry in the forward cast; it is therefore useful in casting a line against the wind (*see page* 213).

A stiff rod without action is of course no use.

You can shoot the line better with a stiff rod than with a whippy one.

A fairly heavy line will bend a stiff rod and brings out its action.

It is the steady strain imparted by the bend of the rod that tires out the fish and finally kills him.

The process of the strike is very quick and liable to cause the hook to scrape and not penetrate. If the last 9 in of the rod top is made thin and pliant, this gives the hook more time to take hold, while it does not interfere with the casting qualities of the rod.

A *whippy* rod

1. Recovers itself slowly
2. Is slow in the pick up
3. Is very suitable for casting a thin light line.

A *whippy* rod tends to make a broad entry in the
forward cast, causing the line to offer some resistance
to the air; it is therefore not very effective in casting
against the wind (*see page* 213).

The process of the strike is slow and gives time
for the hook to penetrate.

b. THE BALANCE OF A ROD

To test the *balance* of a rod, put on the reel and
line complete.

Take the rod and make a few casts with a moder-
ately long line out.

(*a*) If you feel a distinct weight in the rod above
the grip, it is top heavy. You can remedy this by
adding a little weight to the reel or by putting on a
heavier reel until the top heavy feeling vanishes; the
main thing is not to pass beyond this point. If you
overdo it, and put on too heavy a reel, the rod
becomes overbalanced with a very lively action (some
call this 'dead' action), and the whole outfit being
heavier you are liable to strain the rod when casting.

(*b*) On the other hand if you feel there is too much
liveliness in the rod, try a lighter reel.

You can always alter the balance of a rod by using
a heavier or lighter reel, or a lighter or heavier line.

If a rod cannot be made to balance with ordinary
reels and lines and has to be balanced with artificial
weights, the man who made it did not know his
business.

As regards the gross weight of a rod, this is much
less important than the actual feeling of balance or
the manner in which the weight is placed.

When a single handed rod is put together with reel and line complete, it should balance on the finger at a point about 4 inches above the uppermost end of the hand as it grasps the rod to make a cast.

C. NOTES ON RODS

If you carry a rod over your shoulder, the closer you hold it to where it rests on your shoulder the less the top will wag about behind.

It is best to carry a rod 'at the trail' – butt foremost.

When not in use a rod should be hung up on a nail or hook in a dry place and not put leaning against a wall.

When in the rod bag the tapes should not be tightly fastened.

When *putting a rod together* first fit the top into the second joint and then join up with the butt joint.

With a spliced rod keep the ribbon in a roll or spool. Bind the splice very firmly to ensure that there is no wobble whatever. Bind the ribbon direct off the spool. This is a two-man job.

A broken, or a 'sprung' rod can be repaired (as a temporary measure) by placing a split goose quill or large tooth pick over the fractured part and firmly securing it with adhesive tape or whipping it with waxed silk. The quill should first be soaked in warm water to make it pliable.

When the varnish of a rod is at all cracked, it lets the water in and it should be re-varnished. Most rods require to be re-varnished every five or six years.

It is extraordinary what a small strain a good rod puts on a fish during play, judged by the bend of the rod.

Fix a spring balance to a post, attach your line to the balance and using, say a 9-ft 6-in rod, pull on it while someone else reads the balance, you will find that when your rod is almost bent double the pull is really small and can be measured in ounces (while most good gut casts will stand a steady pull of 2 or 3 lbs).

If you attach a dead weight (say a soda-water bottle) to the line, you will find a remarkable difference in the strength of the pull required even to move the bottle.

Here is proof that a good rod is a powerful weapon in playing and tiring out a fish.

The following test was made at Aberdeen in May 1931:

A powerful swimmer weighing 147 lbs had to endeavour to swim 50 yards against the holding power of a 11-ft 8-in split cane rod weighing 11¾ oz. The swimmer was completely stopped at 40 yards and held there.

For a fly rod metal snake rings are better than bridge rings, although the latter *look* neater.

If the rings of the top joint are too far apart the line is liable to sag and cause friction.

A 9-ft 6-in rod usually has four rings on the top joint. With a whippy top five or even six are better for shooting. 8 in or 10 in apart is about right in this case.

Length of Rods

For wet fly fishing the length of the rod you use should suit the water, *viz*:

1. In a stream up to say 15 yds across, use a trout rod 9 or 10 ft long (no more)

2. In a lake or in a river 30 yds or more across, you want a 12 or 14 ft rod (when fishing for trout) because,

    (*a*) You can get out a long line

    (*b*) You can keep less line in the water than with a shorter rod (*c*) When sitting in a boat you have more command over your flies (*see page* 16).

3. For salmon fishing a 14 to 16 ft rod is quite long enough for most rivers.

For dry fly fishing the rod may be from 8 to 10 ft long according to your requirements.

Present day ideas favour short and light rods when possible.

d. STUCK JOINTS

1. Hold a lighted match below the female ferrule: when the match is burnt out you can often draw the joints apart.

2. Try using two wet handkerchiefs or two pieces of crêpe sheet rubber, or two bunches of wet grass to get a grip on the male and female ferrules, and twist in opposite directions.

3. Make two loops of string about 3 in long, wet them, wind one loop round the male ferrule and one round the female in opposite directions; put a bit of stick in each loop and twist in opposite directions.

4. Try a few drops of paraffin; allow a few minutes for it to soak in.

5. Try holding the metal of the male joint with the fingers of the left hand at A. Clasp the metal of the female joint with the right hand at C. Gripping hard with the left hand at A press the thumb of the right hand firmly against the left hand. You can often push the joints apart.

6. If you keep the ferrules clean and occasionally apply a little oil or grease this helps to prevent them from sticking.

SECTION 2

Spinning Rods

The whole rod should have swish or 'dither' and should bend from the top down to the hand. Hold it in front of you and move it up and down; a good spinning rod should spring back to 'the straight' without a lot of vibration.

The chief play should be in the butt and middle joint with a relatively stiff top joint.

The top should never be swishy like a fly rod.

The *suppleness* of the rod you use depends to a great extent on the *weight of the bait* you wish to throw with it.

For baits under 1 oz you want a fair amount of bend or play in the whole rod.

For baits over 1 oz you want a more powerful rod, stiffer throughout. The heavy bait will bend the stiff rod.

The *rings* of a spinning rod are as a rule on the large side, this is all right with an ordinary spinning line; but when you are using a very thin undressed line smaller rings are an advantage, as the thin line is liable to buckle and catch in the large rings.

Mr. Andersen (*F.G.*,18.7.31) made some very interesting experiments to determine the material which would ensure the easiest running and the least friction on the line. He tried rings made of porcelain, brass, steel, agate and german silver, testing them with both wet and dry lines, and found that rings made of good *german silver* are by far the *best* in every way for a *spinning* rod. (Most fishermen have always sworn by agate or porcelain rings.)

Whatever ring is used the inside surface must be true and circular in section: there must be no ridge or unevenness to wear the line.

When carrying a spinning rod complete with trace

and lead, the lead swings about and is liable to
damage the varnish of the rod; it pays to tie the lead
to the rod with a loop of string.

SECTION 3

Trailing Rods

You must have a *stiff* rod for trailing, as you have
a lot of line out and the fish is some way off when
struck.

The rods must also be fairly long, 12-ft to 13-ft, so
as to keep the baits well apart and away from the
wash of the boat.

If your baits touch, the tangle caused in the lines
is usually very bad indeed.

A fly rod or a whippy rod of any sort is very little
used for trailing when fished at right angles to the
boat. If you must use a whippy rod put it as a
centre rod pointing straight behind the boat.

SECTION 4

Notes on Reels

Care of Reels.

Keep a reel dry, well oiled, and entirely free from
rust, grit, dust, etc.

'3 in 1' oil is the best for a reel.

Never use vaseline or similar stuff, as it gets mixed
with grit, etc, and if used when sea fishing collects
the salt.

To measure a reel.

Measure the diameter on the side where the
thumbpiece is: Take the measurement over all,
including the rim.

The *weight* of a reel should be such as to suit the
balance of the rod. Reels are made of all sorts of
metals; very light ones are made of aluminium.

363

Attaching a line to the drum.

A line slips round if tied to a smooth drum. It is best to attach about 18 in of waxed line permanently to the drum, having a loop at the end large enough to pass the reel through it. Make a loop on the backing and you can easily loop it on or unloop it when necessary.

Never fill your reel too full of line. If in doubt of its capacity, first wind the casting line on the reel, then add sufficient backing to fill the spool level, clearing the bars and reel plate easily. You can then reverse the line so that the casting line shall come on the top.

For *stream* fishing the capacity of a reel should not be less than 50 yards, *viz*: 30 yards casting line and 20 yards backing.

For *lake* fishing the capacity should not be less than 100 yards, *viz*: 40 yards casting line and 60 yards backing.

The inner faces of the drum should be straight or vertical, not concave or 'dished.'

If they are at all dished, the line tends to climb up the dishing on one side, and at last a coil falls on the centre portion forming a loose loop, which is liable to become locked and cause trouble.

Revolving rollers on the pillars save the wear on the line. They are a luxury, however, and are not absolutely necessary.

The line should have a clear run off the drum. In most reels this is through the 1st and 2nd pillars.

An adjustable check on a casting reel is very useful. The check should not be too hard; so long as it prevents over-running this is all that is necessary. When, however, heavy fish are expected, a stiffer check is advisable, also a brake on the drum is a very useful addition to a reel when salmon fishing.

When you take the reel off a rod, tie the end of the line to one of the pillars; this prevents the end getting under the coils and causing trouble.

a. SPINNING REELS

There are three styles of spinning reel, *viz:*

1. The freely-revolving drum, or centre-pin, type controlled by the hand (*e.g.*, Nottingham, Aerial).

2. Multiplying reels, equipped with drag and ratchet check, in which the drum is geared to the handle in a ratio of about 3 : 1 to give rapid recovery, and in which the line is automatically wound on evenly by means of a ' level-wind ' device.

3. Fixed-spool reels, in which the line uncoils off a non-revolving spool placed across the line of the rod and is recovered on to the spool by a revolving arm, or bale, or pick-up, which is geared in a ratio of about 3 : 1 to the handle. These reels usually have a ratchet check and an adjustable slipping clutch which allows fish to take line. They work most efficiently when filled with fine lines and almost to capacity.

Both multipliers and fixed-spool reels enable a relatively unskilled fisherman to cast much greater distances than with a centre-pin.

I prefer the Aerial type of reel (without a line guard), fitted with a strong check on the outgoing line. The check is light when reeling in. Never put too much line on the drum; when winding in be careful to have the line evenly distributed.

SECTION 5
Lines

a. MEASURING THICKNESS OF LINES

For many years I have used the standard wire gauge (S.W.G.) for measuring the thickness of fishing lines and in the first edition of this little book the thickness of all lines has been referred to in terms of SWG.

As there are various kinds of wire gauge, *viz:*

The Birmingham wire gauge (B.W.G.).

The Standard wire gauge (S.W.G.).

The Brown & Sharp wire gauge (B.& S.) etc, etc.
this is liable to lead to some confusion, so I have found it simpler to use a micrometer (which records 1,000ths of an inch) for measuring the thickness of all lines, gut and wire.

It is most useful when comparing the thickness of one line with another, or when ordering a line of similar taper or thickness to an old one.

Further, many of the leading tackle makers have now adopted this method of describing the thickness of their lines in terms of 1,000ths of an inch.

In measuring a dressed or an undressed line, it should fit easily into the gauge without any forcing.

The micrometer only measures the actual thickness, as regards the quality of the line it pays to purchase from a reliable maker and to insist on the best material procurable.

b. THE STRENGTH OF A LINE

In testing the strength of a line, you should put on a steady even pressure, no jerk or chuck. You can break most lines with a sudden jerk or snap.

When a line is wet it loses 10% of its strength.

When you cast a knot on a wet line, the line loses quite 20% of its strength.

A knot weakens a thin line much more than a thick line.

Some methods of testing a line:

1. Put the required weight in a reel bag. Take 3 or 4 ft of line and knot a loop at each end, stand on a

chair, and lift the weight steadily (no jerk) say 18 in off the ground.

2. Take about 20 ft of line, knot a loop at each end, hang it over the staircase, and lift as in 1. In this case you can also test the elasticity of the line (*see page* 368).

3. Take a length of line with knotted loops at each end. Put one loop over the hook of a spring balance and the other over a smooth round stick. Apply pressure steadily pound by pound.

In each of the above methods it will be found that in almost every case (7 out of 9 times), the break will occur at one or other of the knots.

Some kinds of knots may stand a little more strain than others, but not much.

Manufacturers test their lines with a machine (a dynamometer) with no knots on the line at all, and in this way arrive at the advertised breaking strain. If, however, in the methods 1, 2, 3 above described, the loops are whipped and not knotted, the result will be almost the same as if a dynamometer was used; anyhow it is sufficient for all practical purposes.

The breaking strain.

The following table is just a rough guide shewing what strain ordinary *undressed lines* of various diameters should stand.

The breaking strain depends on the quality of the line, the care taken of it and the time it has been in use, etc.

Most lines of superior quality will stand a much greater strain than that given below.

Thickness :

·013 should stand a strain of at least					3 lbs
·017	,,	,,	,,	,,	,,	6 ,,
·020	,,	,,	,,	,,	,,	8 ,,

·022 should stand a strain of at least 10 lbs.

·024 ,, ,, ,, ,, ,, 12 ,,
·028 ,, ,, ,, ,, ,, 15 ,,
·032 ,, ,, ,, ,, ,, 20 ,,
·036 ,, ,, ,, ,, ,, 25 ,,
·040 ,, ,, ,, ,, ,, 30 ,,

As regards the breaking strain of tapered *dressed lines*,

    (i) That of a trout line should be at least 5 lbs;
    (ii) That of a salmon line should not be less than 10 lbs.

With a dressed line and an undressed line both of the same thickness, the dressed line will have a breaking strain of a few lbs less than the other owing to the dressing.

The *elasticity* of a line is very important.

If you put a strain on a line, it stretches until the elastic limit is reached, when the strands become tightened and a permanent 'set' occurs in the material.

A line strained to breaking point is weakened by losing some of its elasticity.

In judging the strength of a line one must decide the amount of strain the line will stand without losing its elasticity. In fact a line should have the maximum of elasticity coincident with reasonable breaking strain.

The amount of strain which is required to move a sulking fish :

It has been proved by experiments:

    (*a*) That a fish weighed out of water is 6 times heavier than when weighed in the water.
    (*b*) That a 16 lb fish in the water has a resisting power with its fins of about 2 lbs. Therefore a 16 lb fish which is sulking or stationary can

be lifted or made to move by putting on him
a strain of 3 lbs. Ex: $\frac{1}{6} \times$ (16 lbs plus 2 lbs
fin resistance) $= \frac{18}{6} = 3$ lbs.

Of course a *moving* fish is quite another matter.

If an 18 lb salmon moving at the rate of 20 ft a
second is pulled up dead short, this would cause a
sudden strain on the tackle of about 60 lbs. Ex:
$\frac{18}{6} \times 20 = 60$ lbs.

But then the bend of the rod and the give of the
line running off the reel do not allow the fish to put
on all this strain in ordinary play.

C. DRESSED LINES

There are roughly two types of dressed lines:

1. The line with a smooth shiny enamelled surface, which when new feels rather stiff in the hand.
(Ex: the Kingfisher line, the Corona line, the Heron
line, etc.)

2. The line with a dull surface – not at all shiny –
waterproofed under pressure, and rather pliable.
(Ex: the Halford line, the Optimus line, etc.)

I prefer the latter type, No 2.

In purchasing a dressed line it pays to buy the
best procurable and take proper care of it.

In the evening when you have finished fishing,
always rub it down with a dry rag to remove all
grease, scum, dirt, etc. Dry it well before putting it
back on the reel.

Never allow a wet line to remain on the reel over-
night.

To dry a dressed line use a line drier, if you have
not got one, try this way:

Hold the reel in the right hand and with the left
hand draw off line, making it into loops of about two
feet in diameter in the left hand, see that all the

loops are about the same size, then hang them on the reel-seat to dry.

To get the line back on the rod put the loops over the back of a chair.

With an *undressed line* this way is not satisfactory, it is best to use a line drier.

If the dressing is at all chipped or worn, the water will get in and rot the silk unless the line is re-dressed.

At the end of the fishing season put away an oil dressed line (not a rubber dressed one) in a tin box and sprinkle it with a little of the following powder, *viz* equal parts of talcum powder and fuller's earth. This prevents the line becoming sticky. Some fishermen bury their lines in this powder. Others prefer to hang up a dressed line in loose coils on a wooden peg when not in use. I think, however, that sprinkling it with powder as described above is the better way.

Do not keep a dressed line (especially a thick one) too long on the reel, as it gets 'coils' in it and is liable to kink. It should then be taken off and stretched. By 'too long' I mean putting it away on the reel for say a month or two.

Thickness of tapered lines :

A line should be tapered to suit the rod used and according to requirements. The following is a rough guide as regards the taper of lines for fishing under normal conditions:

1. For a trout line
   From ·020 to ·028 at the point.
     ,, ·030 ,, ·048 at the centre.
2. For a salmon line
   From ·032 to ·048 at the point.
     ,, ·050 ,, ·080 at the centre.

For undressed lines (*see page* 374).

The line must suit the rod. Never use too heavy a line.

If, when casting, a line feels at all heavy, change it for a lighter one.

A rod is very uncomfortable to cast with when it is under- or overlined.

The tendency of most rod sellers is to underline a trout rod and to overline a salmon rod.

A greased line collects scum and dirt off the surface during a day's fishing, especially in still water (*see page* 35).

You should apply grease to a dressed line when you want:

(*a*) To make it float
(*b*) To prevent it getting waterlogged
(*c*) To cause it to shoot better
(*d*) To make it run easily through the rings
(*e*) To enable you to pick the line off the water more easily.

Never apply grease to a wet line. If the line is at all wet rub it down with a piece of amadou or leave it in the sun for a bit to dry.

Solid mucelin is the best grease for a line; put some on a rag and rub it in, going over the line two or three times (*see also page* 34).

To treat a very sticky line.

When a dressed line is very sticky and feels like treacle, some say burn it, but before doing so try this method of restoring it:

Put the line in a bowl with just enough acetone to cover it, leave it for about fifteen minutes until all the dressing is off, then wash it well with soap and water.

Stretch the line between two posts where it will not be interfered with and when quite dry, paint it with Ripolin paint of a suitable colour, thus,

Take a bit of soft leather about 4 in square and smearing it with the paint, apply a thin coat to the line, allow this to dry, then in the same way apply as many coats as are necessary to bring the weight back to the line.

Finally, let it dry for about 48 hours and you should have a smooth, flexible line with a good polish.

To attach backing to a dressed line.

This is usually done by splicing the two (*see* page 329). But it will be found very convenient to splice a yard of undressed line on to the dressed line with a loop at A. Then make

Dressed line   A B Backing a loop at the end of the back-
ing B (large enough to pass the reel through). This allows for the backing being easily separated from the reel line without having to cut it.

A piece of gut at the end of the reel line:

It is a good plan to splice a bit of stout or twisted gut 18 in long to the end of the reel line, whipping a 3 in loop at the end at B.

Reel Line   18″   B This enables a cast to be changed quickly and easily, and does away with the usual knot.

Soak the 18 in of gut well before use or it is liable to crack. This attachment should last a whole season, not longer.

d. A HEAVY LINE

1. It is easier to cast with but makes rather a splash on the water, especially on a windy day.

2. It is useful for casting a long line, for shooting the line, and for casting against the wind.

3. It is rather visible in the water and sinks deep.

4. Lifting and casting a heavy line is rather hard on the rod.

A rod which has a stiff top and a certain amount of spring in the butt playing down to the hand, is best for casting a heavy line.

5. When casting, the line tends to lead or go beyond the gut cast as it is extending over the water, causing the cast to fall in a heap round the fly, and in a stream a belly is produced in the line before the fly begins to fish properly.

6. The strike is a little slow, owing to the added weight of the line to be moved.

e. A LIGHT LINE

1. The line falls slowly on the water with very little splash.

2. It is not easy to cast against the wind.

3. It is more difficult to cast quite accurately.

4. It is useful for short casts as in upstream fishing.

5. It is not very visible in the water.

6. It is suitable for a rod with a supple top and stiff in the butt.

f. TAPERED LINES

1. The centre or thick part of a tapered line is heavy chiefly to make the rod bend to do its work.

2. The length of the taper is usually 4 yards.

3. A tapered line for dry fly work should be heavier in the centre than a tapered line for wet fly fishing.

4. A tapered line is not so hard on a rod as a level one.

g. LEVEL LINES

1. You can cast a long line with a level line.

2. A level line is useful in boat fishing, when you cast a long line down-wind with fairly large flies.

3. It is harder on a rod than a tapered line.

4. Two yards of stout gut attached to a level line is a good substitute for a taper; but with this long length of gut you must be careful that the loops or knots do not get stuck in the rings when you have a fish on a short line before landing.

h. UNDRESSED LINES

An undressed line should be plaited and solid, not hollow, or on a core, and not too tightly woven.

In comparing lines by thickness you should take into consideration the fact that some lines may be woven or plaited tighter than others and some may be stretched from constant use, etc.

A useful thickness for undressed spinning lines is:

For trout ·020
For salmon ·025 to ·030

depends on the river and size of fish expected.

An undressed line should always be greased before use, otherwise

1. It retains the water
2. Wears out quickly
3. Flattens in parts
4. Kinks and rots soon.

Ceroline (solid) is the best grease to use.

The line must be quite dry. First rub it clean with a dry cloth. Then rub it over two or three times with a rag soaked in ceroline (it is best to warm the ceroline, it soaks in better).

Rub it gently with a cloth to take off superfluous grease.

Always rub an undressed line the same way.

After a line is wound on the reel, test it by turning the reel the reverse way; the line should then fall on the ground. If it sticks or is carried round the drum through being over-greased, it should be rubbed down again until all inclination to stick has been removed.

Frost is very hard on an undressed line; the line freezes, and cuts very easily. Without great care a new line can be ruined in a few hours' fishing.

After a day's spinning, the last 6 ft or so of a line is liable to get worn, flattened and overstrained; test it carefully and break off the damaged part.

At the end of the season hang up the line in coils on a peg in a dry place, and not exposed to light or dust.

To re-spool a line, put a pencil through the spool and put a pin in one side of the spool as a handle, then wind the line on to the spool.

Undressed lines made of flax or hemp are all right for trailing, but are unsuitable for spinning purposes, as they are very liable to kink. They have the advantage of being cheaper than silk lines, are very strong, and if taken care of will last a very long time.

SECTION 6

Landing Nets

A net should be deep and almost square at the bottom, not pointed.

It should be roomy;

The mesh must not be too large;

A small stone or a ½ oz lead attached to the extreme bottom of the bag causes the net to sink at once in the water, and is a very convenient addition.

Of the many patterns of short folding or expanding net handles and carriers, etc, on the market a short handled folding net carried on a strap over the shoulder is very handy; but it is useless as a wading staff. And a wading staff with a net or gaff attachment is very necessary on some rivers.

Here are some suggestions for such an implement. There are many patterns of wading staffs on the market which combine most of these suggestions, *viz*:

1. You want an ash handle about 50 in long to steady you in a heavy stream;

2. It should be possible to attach the handle to your body and trail it behind you, or to sling it over your shoulder;

3. It should have a spike and hook screwed into the lower end: the spike to get a firm hold on the bottom, the hook for releasing a cast from branches, etc (*see F below*).

4. A handy form of net which can be folded and carried in the fishing bag is one on a folding metal ring (14 in or 16 in in diameter) which is made to screw into the top of the handle, at A. There can be two cords attached to the handle, thus:

(*a*) One attached to a brass eye screwed into the handle at B with a 2 in spliced loop at C;

(*b*) The other with a 2 in spliced loop to fit round the screw of the metal at A.

The end D can be fastened to loop C

with a slip knot, so that a sharp tug will release it when carried across the shoulder.

5. A piece of cork at E to float the whole thing is a useful addition in some waters.

6. It is convenient to mark off a portion of the handle in feet and inches.

For boat fishing you want a longer handle, say 6-ft, made of ash or hazel, and a folding metal ring 20 in in diameter. You don't have to carry it about.

These metal folding rings are only suitable for landing fish up to about 10 lbs. They are not strong enough for bigger fish.

A net for salmon :

For heavy fish you must have a deep and roomy net with a strong v-shaped wooden rim. The screw of the net should fit at least 4 in into the handle. This is heavy to carry; but you have a ghillie.

A string out of the centre of the bottom is useful to control a deep net, otherwise it may turn inside out when placed in the water.

SECTION 7

Gaffs

The handle should be 4 or 5 ft long.

It should be slightly tapered and the gaff screwed into or lashed to the thinner end.

The handle should be light but strong. It should not be varnished, it is better to oil it. Ash or hazel wood make a good handle.

When fishing from a boat it is handier to have the handle only 2 or 3 feet long, as with the shorter handle it is easier to get a good upward lift with the gaff when the iron is home.

The gape of the hook AB should measure at least 3 fingers (1st, 2nd, 3rd fingers of the hand).

The point may be a shade bent off as at A.

The iron should be slightly curved as at C. Many Irish gaffs have this curve exaggerated:

The point of the gaff must be kept very sharp.

A good protector is a champagne cork attached by a loop of string round the iron at B.

There are several slings or attachments on the market for carrying a long handled gaff while bank fishing or wading (*see also* Wading Staff, *page* 376).

An improvised pocket gaff is useful at a pinch (*see diagram*). Lash securely a large hook or a gaff

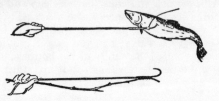

hook to about 4 ft of stout cord. Lash the hook roughly to a twig with a bit of twine. The stout cord between the hand and the hook must be stretched quite taut when in use.

A short telescopic gaff to carry in the fishing bag is useful, especially when you have to depend on gaffing your own fish.

But a good long handled light gaff is the best weapon for general use.

SECTION 8

Tailers

A tailer is light, strong and easily carried.

It is composed of a steel tube flexible for about half its length and a cable noose or snare.

Slip the noose over the tail of the fish and draw it towards the head (not towards yourself) you get a better grip in this way.

The most convenient make has a screw to fit into an ordinary gaff handle.

It is very useful when the gaff is prohibited, or when kelts are about.

Book VII: SUNDRIES

Part VI

NOTES ON VARIOUS SUBJECTS

SECTION I

Notes on Various Subjects

a. THERMOMETER FORMULÆ

Fahrenheit is most generally used in Great Britain.
Centigrade is used chiefly for scientific work.
Réaumur is now seldom used.

			Freezing	*Boiling*
Fahrenheit (F)	.	.	$32°$	$212°$
Centigrade (C)	.	.	0	$100°$
Réaumur (R) .	.	.	0	$80°$

Formulæ:

$$F = \tfrac{9}{5} C + 32 \quad C = \tfrac{5}{9}(F - 32) \quad R = \tfrac{4}{5}C$$
$$ = \tfrac{9}{4} R + 32 \quad = \tfrac{5}{4}R \quad\quad\quad = \tfrac{4}{9}(F - 32)$$

Ex: Q: What degree Fahrenheit is 20° C?
     A: $F = \tfrac{9}{5} 20 + 32 = 68°$

b. RIGHT AND LEFT BANK OF A STREAM

Face downstream.
The right bank is on your right.
The left bank is on your left.

c. WADING A RIVER

Cross a river diagonally downstream thus, from
A to B.

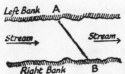

Have a good stick with a
cord attached and fasten this
cord to yourself somewhere.
If the current is heavy,
plant the stick downstream
of you and try walking slowly
from A to B with your body
sideways to the current. Never cross your legs but
always keep the lower leg downstream.

Loss of footing when wading a stream :

Scramble along with your hands on the bottom
until you can get your head above water; then and
only then stand up cautiously and walk backwards,
slowly; steady yourself with a stick or rod planted
downstream of you. Shoulder straps on waders are
better than a belt.

Loss of footing in deep water :

Lay yourself out flat and swim; you can swim
easily but slowly with waders full of water; let your
waders get full at once, it is your best chance. If
you are wearing a belt loose it as soon as possible.
Don't fight against the stream – the current will
usually take you to the side.

To prevent rheumatism :

Dust powdered sulphur into your shoes and stock-
ings before going out in the morning.

d. TO EXTRACT A HOOK

To extract a hook from your flesh.

1. With a pair of pliers break off the barb or com-
press the barb flat, and draw out the hook. This is
useful for double or treble hooks.

2. With a single hook it is best to cut the shank
with pliers and pass the shank back through the flesh.

To extract a hook from a fish's throat.

A small hook can usually be removed with a
disgorger. With a large single hook, pull it out
through the gills and wind the cast two or three
times round the bend of the hook, then draw the
hook by the bend out through the mouth.

To extract a hook from Cloth.

Insert a pin between the thread of the cloth and
the outside of the barb. Press the pin close to the

hook, pushing back the cloth to clear a hole for the
barb. Holding the pin in this
position, with the inside of the
barb resting against the pin,
push out the hook.

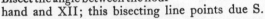

e. USING A WATCH AS A COMPASS

To find true N. with a watch :
Point the hour hand at the sun.
Bisect the angle between the hour
hand and XII; this bisecting line points due S.

f. TO LAY OUT A RIGHT ANGLE

Take a piece of string and mark it off into 12 equal
parts (a tape measure will of course do).

Put a mark at the 4th and 7th part, thus:

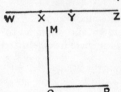

Take 3 pegs, M, O, P.
Attach X to O.
    ,, Y to P.
Join the ends W and Z.
Move peg M about until
it coincides with the point
where W and Z join.
    MOP = a Right angle.

The principle being: $(MP)^2 = (MO)^2 + (OP)^2$

When MP = 5 units
       OP = 3 units
      OM = 4 units

g. TO MEASURE WIDTH OF RIVER

Select a mark A on opposite
side (a tree, a bush).

Mark with a stick a point
B just opposite to A.

Place a stick at C some
yards along the bank (CB
must be at right angles to BA).

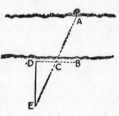

Continue in a straight line along the bank, putting a stick at D, and making DC = CB.

Walk from D at right angles to BD.

When C and A are in line put a stick at **E**.

Measure ED = width of river.

SECTION 2

Notes on Fish

a. MINNOWS
(*Phoxinus Lævis.*)

In *winter* they remain in deep water and pools.

In *summer* they move to shallow easy water in side streams for spawning purposes.

The males prepare the spawning bed or patch of gravel chiefly by churning up the water and cleaning the gravel.

The female deposits her little amber coloured ova in the spaces between the gravel and then leaves when the operation is over and the male has fertilised them.

The male hangs about to guard the spot.

Eggs hatch out in about 4 days.

Fry have a yoke sack attached for 15 days; after that they swim freely.

Chief food is vegetable matter.

To keep minnows bright :

Put them in a receptacle the interior of which is painted white, as they try to harmonise their colour with their surroundings.

To catch minnows (see Baits, *page* 268).

b. STICKLEBACKS

Two fresh water species:

    1. Three spined stickleback (*Gasterosteus Aculeatus*),

2. Ten spined stickleback (*G. Ringitius*).

The habits of both are similar.

The three spined stickleback is common everywhere in the British Isles.

Spawn in May and June. Fry hatch out in 8–10 days; depends on temperature.

Male makes nest of weeds and bits of stick, then invites females to deposit ova in it, which he fertilises.

Female goes away after spawning. Male remains about nest to guard eggs and young until they are able to fend for themselves.

Food is chiefly ephemera and small larvæ and even alevins.

A stickleback can be transferred from fresh water to sea water without any injury.

C. EELS

There are two sorts of eels in the Atlantic, and in appearance they are very similar, *viz*:

1. American eel (*Anguilla Rostrata*)
2. European eel (*Anguilla Vulgaris*).

Both deposit ova in very deep water in region of the Sargasso Sea, S of Bermuda, and both are hatched out there; both lay an enormous number of eggs, some say 10,000,000 (?) each.

When hatched out the tiny elvers ascend gradually towards the surface and start off on their long journey to American and European waters.

The European eel. The elvers guided by the gulf stream take about 3 years to cross the Atlantic. They arrive off the British Isles in December each year, and commence to ascend the rivers the following May. They are then 2 in or 3 in long, and their arrival each year is remarkably punctual. All predatory birds and most fishes feed on elvers.

The adult eel has few enemies, except the otter and the heron.

The females go high up the river and into the burns, pools, ponds, etc, while the majority of the males remain in the lower reaches.

In addition to other foods, eels eat great quantities of the spawn of other fish.

In winter they cease feeding and hibernate, and on the first touch of frost they bury themselves in the mud.

Some eels have been known to remain in fresh water 15 or 20 years. These would be barren fish, specimens of which have been caught from time to time in different parts of the British Isles weighing 20 or 30 lbs. But as a rule male eels remain in fresh water 5 or 6 years, while females remain 7 or 8 years. They then become silver eels (ready for the spawning migration), the yellowish belly becomes quite silvery.

The male eel is seldom more than $1\frac{1}{2}$ ft long and has a pointed nose. The female eel grows to quite 3 ft long and more, and has rather a flat nose.

The silver eel commence to descend towards the sea in the autumn and usually start on dark stormy nights. So great is their breeding instinct that they will travel short distances overland from one piece of water to another on their way down to the sea. They usually select a time when there is a heavy dew on the grass.

They travel in vast shoals across the Atlantic to the spawning grounds in the vicinity of the Sargasso Sea.

The male and the female die at sea. They never return to fresh water.

To kill an eel, first stun him with a sharp blow on the *tail*, then with a knife cut the spinal column just below the head.

To catch eels, first of all stir up the bottom and make the water muddy, this helps to make them

move about and take notice. Then break an egg (any
sort of fresh egg will do) and throw it in the water,

Or, throw in the gills of a fish or any piece of flesh
with blood on it (eels are attracted by the smell or
taste of blood). They will soon collect and you can
catch them with a worm.

Hold an eel under the second finger of the hand
pressed against the first and third fingers, this grip
helps to prevent him slipping.

The blood of an eel is poisonous and causes
inflammation if it gets into a scratch or wound.

Favourable conditions for eel fishing are, when
the water is warmish and when the day is dull and
cloudy, eels dislike light of any sort.

d. SPRATS
(*Clupea sprattus*.)

Is a northern fish – North Sea, British Isles, etc.
Ova is pelagic.

A gull always swallows a sprat head first on
account of the spines on the belly.

Sprats are much used when spinning for salmon,
pike, etc. A sprat is similar in appearance to a young
herring or a sardine; to distinguish between the
three, hold the fish up by the dorsal fin.

A *herring* balances evenly, has a smooth belly,
has a patch of teeth on the vomer.

A *sprat*, the head hangs lower than the tail, has
spines on the belly, has no teeth on the vomer.

A *sardine*, tail hangs lower than the head.

e. WHITEBAIT

Whitebait is composed:

In February and March of 7% herring fry, 93%
young sprats.

In June and July, 87% herring fry, 13% young
sprats.

SECTION 3

To Dry Long Rubber Boots

Put a piece of cardboard or a folded newspaper in each boot so that the top protrudes about 6 in and does not quite reach to the bottom of the inside of the boot.

Place the boots in a draught. A current of air is directed by the cardboard down the inside to the foot portion and soon dries the boots.

Or, stuff the boots full of old newspapers and they will dry in a night (*see also page* 393 d.).

SECTION 4

Amadou

Amadou is a timber fungus which grows on the trunks of old trees; the best is found on old birch wood.

It is soft and very absorbent; is used by surgeons and dentists.

In the Highlands of Scotland it is called 'Spoung' and after treatment with nitre is used as tinder.

Commercial amadou chiefly comes from Norway.

The Latin name is *Fomes (Polyporus) igniarius*.

The name 'Amadou' is said to be derived from the Latin *ad manum dulce* (soft to the hand).

French – Amadou.

German – Zunderschwamm.

It is best obtained from a store supplying dental accessories.

Very useful for drying a fly or a line, or for cleaning grease off a line or cast. It absorbs oil and water, so when you dry your fly with it you should re-oil.

SECTION 5
Packing Fish for Transit

When you catch a fish which you want to send away, handle it as little as possible.

If in a boat keep it in the shade covered with a damp cloth.

If by the waterside, wrap it in a damp cloth in a fish basket: a bag crushes a fish and makes it soft.

Do not carry fish in a bag with a waterproof lining, especially in hot weather.

After a fish has been landed, it should not be washed or put in water again *until just before cooking*.

A fish that has been cleaned at once will keep much longer than one which is carried about all day and cleaned or gutted in the evening.

The method of packing a fish depends on the weather and the time it will take in transit.

In close warm weather and when the journey takes 2 or 3 days, the following method should be adopted:

Gut the fish, removing the gills, leaving the blood and slime; the blood acts as a preservative, so just wipe out the inside with a dry cloth. It is also well to pick out with the blade of a knife most of the bits of black stuff or blood which adhere along the spine.

Sprinkle a little salt in the inside, down the spine and about the mouth and head where the gills were. I met a distinguished angler at Loch Maree who always used powdered charcoal or cold ashes from a wood fire instead of salt, it appeared to be a very messy method, but he assured me charcoal was an excellent preservative.

Wrap in clean waterproof paper and be sure the fish do not touch one another. Put in a frail of suitable size, sew up with packing needle and string (not too tightly), and your fish is ready for post. Tie on two labels: one often comes off in the post.

See that the frail is long enough; it spoils a fish to double any part of it. A 5 lb trout requires a fish bag 22 in long and 8 in deep at least.

Never pack fish in green grass, rhubarb, dock or cabbage leaves; any vegetable wrapping hastens decomposition.

Dry straw, hay or bottle covers give a taste to fish.

Dry nettles are said to preserve the colour of the fish, but are troublesome to use.

Some people sprinkle the fish with pepper instead of salt; never do this as it gives it a horrible taste.

If the journey is short (say 24 hours) and the weather is cool: Strip the fish by pressing the fingers down the belly to the vent. Dust a little salt about the gills and mouth. Wrap in clean paper and put in a bass fish frail, or make a cigar-shaped parcel of it with green rushes (the rushes allow for ventilation).

Nearly all preservatives – Milton, borax, glasioline, formaline – alter the taste of a fish, so use them very sparingly. Before cooking, all fish treated with preservatives must soak for two hours in cold water.

If you must use preservatives I think the following are best:

One part Milton and fifty parts cold water,
Or, ½ oz borax to 1 pint cold water.

Just dip the fish in the mixture and hang it up to dry in a cool place.

Salmon do not require such elaborate treatment. They are not soft like trout and sea trout, and have little or nothing in their intestines. It is usually enough to put the fish in a large frail or matting bag and strengthen the parcel with laths or a piece of board. A perforated box is of course best.

In the case of all fish which have a long journey (especially salmon) they smell rather strongly when opened; this smell can be removed by washing the fish in a very weak solution of vinegar and water.

A specimen fish for setting up : Strip the vent, wrap in white paper, tie to a flat board to preserve the shape, put in a box or make up into a brown paper parcel.

A fish sent for examination should be wrapped in damp blotting paper, just as it is (without removing any mucus or growth on it), rolled in waxed paper, put in a box or made up into a parcel.

SECTION 6

Notes on the Otter

He is a nomad of the wilds, living among the rocks etc, in unfrequented places.

In the *winter* months his diet is composed chiefly of fish.

Sluggish fish such as bream, carp, tench, etc, fall an easy prey. He follows the migratory *salmonidæ* and brown trout on to the spawning beds.

One of his methods of attack is to drive a lot of fish into the shallows or on to the shore and catch them there.

In some Asiatic countries the natives train otters to drive shoals of fish into their nets.

He has a great partiality for eels when he can get them (most eels hibernate in winter).

In the *summer* months his diet is much more varied.

In addition to visiting the streams and loughs he will take long journeys across country and over the moors after rabbits, grouse, ducks, waterfowl.

An otter eats the whole fish if he can manage it, leaving only a few scales and a fin or two. A 2 lb or 3 lb trout is a nice meal.

He does not always bring his prey ashore to eat it.

When, however, he has had enough or is not hungry, he will take a bite or two out of the shoulder, leaving the rest of the fish on the bank; but this is the exception, not the rule.

Otters which frequent the estuaries of rivers frequently fish in the sea.

SECTION 7

Insect Bites

Midges are most troublesome when the weather is warm and muggy, particularly in shady places and under trees.

If you can manage to keep in the wind or hot sun they won't bother you much.

They dislike red or yellow and avoid objects or persons dressed in these colours.

There are many lotions on the market which profess to keep off midges, flies, etc. Hardy's 'Anti-midge' and Farlow's 'Mosquito lotion' are quite effective.

After applying any lotion wash your hands well before handling your flies or lures.

When bitten it alleviates the pain if you rub in undiluted Milton or if you rub the place with a paste made of fresh tobacco or cigarette ash, the carbon in the ash neutralises the acid in the bite or sting.

When wearing trousers brown paper rolled on the legs like a puttie inside the trousers will prevent insects biting.

SECTION 8

Notes on Waders

(a) Trouser waders should be roomy at the hips and come well up to the fork.

(*b*) Here is one way of putting them on,

    (i) Put on a pair of waterproof socks over your own stockings, then a pair of thin woollen socks,

    (ii) Draw on the waders and put on over them a pair of thick socks,

    (iii) Then put on your brogues or boots,

    (iv) Roll down the tops of the thick socks to prevent them working down about the heels of the brogues.

(*c*) Both the waders and waterproof socks when taken off should be turned inside out and thoroughly dried, as the perspiration tends to rot the fabric. The outsides of both can then be dried.

Some anglers turn their waders inside out and wear them in this way on alternate days.

(*d*) Long rubber boots or short waders have a strap for attaching to one of the two buttons on each side of the trousers.

It is a small matter, but it pays, to put an extra button very securely sewn on between the two for attaching the strap to, as the ordinary trouser button soon becomes loose and falls off owing to the extra strain (*see also page* 388).

Book VIII

THE SALMON FAMILY

Book VIII: THE SALMON FAMILY

Part I

THE SALMONIDÆ.

SECTION I

The British Salmonidæ

The badge of the family of *salmonidæ* is two dorsal fins, one of which is an adipose or dead fin. The diagram below gives the names of the fins of Salmonidæ.

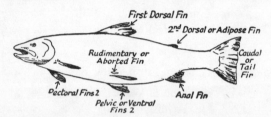

As regards the ancestry of these sporting fish, scientists now consider that they are derived from a trout.

They maintain that the original primitive trout was developed in the Arctic regions during the Eocene period and from it are descended all salmon and other trouts.

Thousands of years ago, some of these primitive trout passed from the Arctic into the Pacific Ocean through the Behring Straits, forming a Pacific species, while others passed from the Arctic into the Atlantic Ocean, forming the Atlantic species.

The classification of the Atlantic species of *salmonidæ* found in the British Isles is given on the following page.

The British genus *Salmo* may be conveniently divided into

    (*a*) Migratory Fish – *S. Salar, S. Trutta.*
    (*b*) Non-migratory – *S. Fario.*

Tate Regan and other authorities consider that there is only one trout in the British Isles, *viz*: *S. Trutta*, and that *S. Fario* is just a non-migratory sea trout.

Salmonidæ

Salmo	Salvelinus	Coregonus	Osmerus
S. Salar	*S. Alpinus*	*C. Clupeoides*	*O. Eperculans*
S. Trutta	(Char)	(Gwyniad)	Smelt)
S. Fario		*C. Vendesius*	
		(Vendace	Thymallus
		C. Pollan	*T. Vulgaris*
		(Pollan)	Grayling)

There are several species of gwyniad, pollan, vendace and smelts, all of which have white flesh and in some localities are called 'white fish.'

a. TO TELL ADULT SALMON FROM TROUT
(say 24 in and over)

1. Count the scales between the back part of the adipose fin and the medial line.

The line of scales runs in an oblique direction towards the head.

S. Salar = 10 to 13 scales (usually 11-12)

S. Trutta $\Big\}$ = 13 to 16 scales (usually 1.$\frac{4}{5}$).
S. Fario

It is very exceptional to find a fish in which the number of scales differ from those given above.

2. Examine the maxillary bone close to the mouth of the fish when the mouth is closed. In *S. Salar* the bone only extends to a vertical line through the pupil of the eye, so the mouth appears small. In *Salmo Fario* and *S. Trutta* the bone extends to, and frequently beyond, the vertical through the posterior edge of the eye itself, so the mouth appears large.

3. The caudal peduncle of *S. Salar* is more slender and the tail is stiffer than that of *S. Trutta* and *S. Fario*.

The tail of a *trout* will slip through the hand when the fish is held up by the tail.

b. TO TELL ADULT BROWN TROUT FROM ADULT SEA TROUT

1. Spots on a sea trout are blackish and like x x x x. Spots on a *S. Fario* are circular and reddish or pinkish.

2. *S. Trutta* has a yellowish tip on adipose fin. *S. Fario* has a pinkish tip.

3. Scales of *S. Trutta* are loosely put on. Scales of *S. Fario* are firmer.

4. When *S. Trutta* enter the river from the sea they are silvery in colour, but when the male fish has been in fresh water some time and is ripening to spawn, it becomes dark in colour and develops reddish spots.

c. TO DISTINGUISH BETWEEN SMALL TROUT, AND SALMON PARR OR SMOLTS

In a small *trout* 3 in to 6 in long:
1. The maxillary bone extends to below the back of the eye and often beyond it.
2. The spots on the gill cover are in a group.
3. The outer edge of the adipose fin is tipped red.
4. The anal fin is edged with white and a dark stripe behind it.
5. The tail is rather blunt.

In a young *salmon* in the parr or smolt stage, 3 to 6 in long:
1. The maxillary bone extends only to below the pupil of the eye.

2. There are one, two or three spots on the gill cover, if three they are always more or less in a straight line.

3. The adipose fin is of a slaty colour.

4. The anal fin is of a pale colour throughout, almost transparent.

5. The tail is distinctly forked.

A parr has eight or more *regular* blue-grey blotches or parr marks on its sides, while in a trout the blotches are *fewer* and very *irregular* in shape.

The scales of a parr come off very easily, those of a young trout are more firmly put on.

A parr when lifted out of the water at the end of a cast struggles vigorously, wriggling his head as much as his tail.

A trout is much quieter; he wriggles with his tail but scarcely moves his head at all.

d. MEASURING A FISH

Lay the fish on a flat board. Mark points A and B with pins. Remove the fish and measure AB.

Here are two methods of measuring:

1. In the case of *Salmonidæ*, measure from the tip of the nose to the end of the middle rays of the tail, thus:

2. The international method of measuring all fish with forked tails is, to measure from the tip of the nose to a perpendicular drawn

between the flukes of the tail when spread out naturally on the board, thus: AB.

All *baits* (Gudgeon, Sprats, Phantoms, etc) are measured in this way, also when there is a rule that fish of a certain size have to be returned to the water their length is usually measured in this way.

e. WEIGHT BY MEASUREMENT

1. The Sturdy scale given below is based on the assumption that a 36 in salmon weighs 20 lbs, and an 18 in trout weighs 2½ lbs. Measure from tip of nose to end of middle ray of tail:

Salmon		Trout		
Inches	*lb*	*Inches*	*lb*	*oz*
30	11·574	9		5
31	12·770	10		7
32	14·046	11		9
33	15·404	12		12
34	16·848	13		15
35	18·379	14	1	3
36	20	15	1	7
37	21·713	16	1	12
38	23·522	17	2	2
39	25·428	18	2	8
40	27·435	19	2	15
41	29·544	20	3	7
42	31·759	21	4	0
43	34·082	22	4	9
44	36·516	23	5	3

Salmon		Trout		
Inches	lb	Inches	lb	oz
45	39·063	24	5	15
46	41·725	25	6	11
47	44·506	26	7	8
48	47·407	27	8	7
49	50·432	28	9	6
50	53·584	29	10	7
51	56·864	30	11	9
52	60·274			
53	63·819			
54	67·500			
55	71·320			

2. Another method, $W = \dfrac{(L + \frac{L}{8}) \times G^2}{1000}$

L = Length on a flat board in inches from tip of nose to middle ray of tail.

G = Girth in inches taken just in front of the dorsal fin. This is accurate for fresh run salmon in prime condition, netted or caught near the estuary.

For fish that have been a certain time in fresh water (usually rod caught fish) deduct $2\frac{1}{2}\%$ to 5% from the weight according to time they have been in the river.

Any fish which is in very poor condition deteriorates in his girth while his length remains the same.

f. WEIGHING A HEAVY FISH

Suspend a stick from a point one-third of its length; say the stick is 3 ft long, then suspend it at B one foot from one end. Attach the fish at A. Attach a spring balance at C. Pull on the spring balance until the stick is level. Double the reading on the spring balance = the weight of the fish. (Ex: spring balance shows $25\frac{1}{2}$ lbs, therefore weight of fish is $2 \times 25\frac{1}{2} = 51$ lbs.)

Weighing a fish without a spring balance :

Take a stick ED and an article of known weight A (say 7 lbs).

Attach the fish at E. Attach the article A at D. Ascertain the point C on the stick where they balance.

Measure EC = 18 inches

CD = 36 inches

Then 18 in: 36 in: : 7 lbs: x

x = 14 lbs = weight of fish.

g. CONDITION FACTOR

A useful method of comparing one fish with another:

1. Weigh the fish accurately. W = weight in pounds.

2. Take exact length on the flat from the tip of the nose to the end of the middle ray of the tail. Do this on a measuring board or lay the fish on a tape stretched flat. L = length in inches.

$$\text{Condition Factor} = \frac{W \times 100 \cdot 000}{L^3}$$

Condition factors vary in different rivers. The following are only approximate:

Shannon salmon,	CF	= 46
Wye salmon	,,	= 38
Dee salmon	,,	= 36
Test trout	,,	= 42
Blagdon trout	,,	= 45

A salmon with a CF below 30 is usually a kelt.

The formula $CF = \dfrac{W \times 100 \cdot 000}{L^3}$ is useful to find

the weight when the length and CF are known.

$$\text{Weight} = \frac{L^3 \times CF}{100 \cdot 000}$$

h. LOSS OF WEIGHT AFTER CAPTURE

Loss of weight in a fish depends on whether

1. There has been much loss of blood,
2. There is much wasting at the vent,
3. The fish has been very roughly handled,
4. The fish has been exposed to the sun and wind for any length of time.

If salmon or trout are exposed to any of the above, the loss of weight would be about 2% in 6 hours.

Coarse fish lose more weight in proportion than the *salmonidæ*.

As regards spring salmon, Hutton mentions that they should not lose more than 1 to 1·5% in the first 24 hours, and a further 1% in the following 24 hours.

i. HANDLING LIVE FISH

1. Cause no loss of blood; he can ill afford to lose a drop. The weight of blood in a fish of 1 lb is only $\frac{1}{4}$ oz.

2. Don't squeeze a fish; if you squeeze him until he squeals you kill him, as you have burst the air bladder.

3. When handling fish, wet your hands well to prevent rubbing off any of the slime with which the skin is covered.

4. Don't injure the gills; if they bleed it is fatal.

5. It is best to remove the hook with a forceps.

6. When returning a fish to the water don't fling it in; liberate it from your hand.

To liberate an undersized fish, don't lift it out of the water; just run your hand down the cast, grasp the hook firmly; he will struggle and the chances are he will liberate himself. A wounded fish has a much better chance of recovery when the water is warmish than when it is very cold.

The Food of Salmonidæ

The main difference between the food of salmon and trout is:

A *salmon* feeds chiefly on organisms which float or swim in the upper water layers of the sea (*see page* 442).

A *trout* feeds chiefly on organisms which live on or near the bottom of a stream or lake. Underwater food is really the beef and mutton of a trout's meal, while surface food is only the caviare.

I think there is a good deal to be said in favour of Mr. Griswold's theory which he mentions in his book, namely 'That square tailed fish are generally bottom feeders and have the local habit, while forked tail fish are generally surface feeders and travellers.'

SECTION 3

The Senses of Fish

What is the instinct that prompts a salmon which is resting quietly some distance upstream to go and see what is exciting his brothers in a pool lower down? It cannot be his sense of vision, as he lies facing upstream.

Throw a handful of worms or prawns into a pool where salmon are; they at once commence to nose them and investigate them. After two or three minutes, fish from upstream, well above the point where you threw in the worms, will come down and join in the investigation.

Is it that the nervous system of one salmon plays on the nervous system of another by some sort of

telepathy, or is it through the lateral line sense or
the hearing sense that they are enabled to detect the
presence of the worms?

Eels will act in a similar manner.

Fish have at least seven senses (possibly more):

1. Lateral line sense
2. Hearing sense
3. Feeling sense
4. Smell sense
5. Taste sense
6. Vision sense
7. Mass control sense.

A deficiency in one sense is compensated by acute-
ness in others.

The same applies to man. (Ex: During the war
blind men were employed to use delicate sound
ranging instruments.)

a. LATERAL LINE SENSE

The lateral line and the skin surface carry very
sensitive nerves communicating with the brain.
These are very highly developed, and they register:

1. Vibrations in the water
2. Direction and strength of the current
3. Resistance and pressure of the water. (We
   know that water resistance is greater the
   nearer the water is to a solid body; this fact
   enables blind fish to avoid obstacles.)

b. HEARING SENSE

The hearing sense is closely connected with the
lateral line sense.

Fish do not hear as we do, they are conscious of
vibrations in the water, just as listeners in a ship can

detect vibrations of the propeller of another ship miles away by means of special instruments.

Fish can detect these vibrations by two organs, *viz*:

    1. The nerves in the lateral line and skin

    2. The ears and the otoliths (*see page* 416).

Fish have no outer or middle ear, they only have an inner ear, which in a minor degree is sensitive to vibrations and is mainly used as a balancing organ.

Any vibrations made in the water by any substance in connection with the water, such as the noise of the rowlocks of a boat, the noise made by iron shod brogues in a boat, out-board motors, etc, are 'heard' by the fish.

But in the case of noises in the air, where there is no connection with the water, such as the sound of a bell or the discharge of a gun, this is quite a different matter and it is open to question whether fish can always 'hear' these noises. In many cases there may be local conditions assisting the passage of certain pitches of sound into the water, causing all sorts of anomalies and apparent contradictions.

c. FEELING SENSE

Fish have little sense of feeling as we know it, but from perceiving vibrations they have an 'extended touch' or feeling.

A fish touched gently under water (*i.e.* tickled) shows no sign of alarm, but if vibrations are caused in the water, or the body of the fish is at all displaced from its position of rest, it at once becomes alarmed (*see page* 438).

d. TASTE AND SMELL

Most fish bolt their food and don't trouble about the taste of it.

The carp species have taste bulbs on the palate

which afford them some sense of taste. These bulbs
are, however, absent in the *Salmonidæ*, so we must
assume they have no sense of taste as we know it.
Ronalds has proved this by the following experiment: he smeared flies with different ingredients
including cayenne pepper, and he found that the
fish took every fly without distinction.

Salmonidæ possess olfactory organs and it is certain that they have the faculty of smell and that they
are attracted or repelled by certain odours; but the
exercise of this faculty differs from that of air breathing animals in that it is not connected with the
machinery or function of respiration.

e. SENSE OF VISION

All fish see best in shaded or diffused light. Shade
is essential for their true vision. A strong light has a
blinding or dazzling effect on a fish. It is suggested
that one of the reasons of the shoal formation of fish
(herrings, mackerel, etc) is the mutual shade thrown,
which enables food to be more easily seen.

The fish's eye has no protection. In the human
eye the pupil can expand and contract, there are
eyelids and eyelashes for shade, and a man can avoid
a strong light by moving his head and eyes. In a
fish's eye the pupil is in a fixed state of dilation. He
has no shades for the eye, and cannot move head and
eyes to avoid light.

They have no binocular vision and have little
or no power of judging distance by the eye as a
man has.

A fish, in common with many of the lower animals,
has panoramic vision (no power of focusing both eyes
on an object). Movement of the object plays a most
important part in the panoramic vision of a fish. Of
course they also judge an object by its size, shape,
and the amount of light it transmits.

The eyes of a fish are placed laterally in the head with a tilt upward and forward; this limits the view from below and behind.

When a fish sees a lure he generally raises himself in the water until he gets almost in line with it and just below it, as he can best appreciate objects in an upward and forward direction (*see also page* 141).

A fish can see an object better against a dark background than against the sky, the light dazzles him.

When fishing downstream (even with the sun behind you) and the water is broken by wind, rain, etc, the fish's vision is blurred and he can't see you well, always provided your shadow does not fall within 5 ft of the fish.

The deeper a trout lies in the water the larger the cone of light, and the shallower he lies the smaller the cone. This cone is called the fish's window or cone of vision (*see also page* 316).

In the cone of light a fish sees *surface food* like a silhouette blurred against the light. Outside the cone he sees surface food against the reflection of the bottom on the undersurface of the water, with only the hook or bits of hackle sticking through. He can, however, perceive the splash a long way off.

Inside the cone of light he sees *underwater food* rather blurred and indistinct. Outside the cone he sees underwater food against the reflection of the bottom on the undersurface of the water, and he can see it quite a distance away.

Objects on the bank of a stream appear to the fish on the rim of the cone. The area of this cone of vision is enlarged by refracted rays entering it from objects above and outside the area.

An angler distant 30 ft from a fish is sufficiently veiled if he does not place any part of himself more

than 5 ft above the level of the water. If he is closer
than 30 ft his image will appear to the fish on the
rim of the cone.

A trout cannot see any object directly behind him
which is inside an angle of 30° on each side of his
dorsal fin.

Blindness in fish. Continuous strong sunlight has
a serious effect on a fish's vision. Observers in Scotland report cases of salmon becoming quite blind
after having been subjected to a long period of bright
sunlight in shallow water from which they were
unable to escape. A fish which has been blinded by
exposure to sunlight shews a white patch and
depression in the head over the brain.

A blind fish can still find his way about through
the medium of the lateral line, which registers
greater water resistance when close to a solid body
or obstacle (*see page* 407). In blind fish the skin is of
a dark colour (*see page* 418), and when a salmon or
trout is blind of only one eye, the skin on the side
opposite the blind eye is darker than that on the same
side as the blind eye.

(*Trout Fishing*, by Taverner, Lonsdale Library,
p. 53.)

For a trout's sense of colour (*see also page* 486).

f. NIGHT VISION

Salmonidæ can undoubtedly see our fly in the dark
when we cannot see it. How do they do it? Here
are three reasons, Nos 2 and 3 are I think the most
likely.

1. *Projected light rays.* There are many light rays
in water which we cannot see. These rays are col-
lected by the fish's eye upon the reflector (*tapetum
lucidum*), which organ fishes possess in common with
the cat and tiger, etc, and from which light is

reflected upon the object observed. (Ex: the cat's eye shining in the dark.)

2. *Amount of light.* The primary colours of the spectrum are red, orange, yellow, green, blue, violet, and ultra-violet. Man's sense of visible light is limited from red to violet; beyond this all is darkness to him. It is proved that the owl, the tiger, the cat, etc, have considerably more than our range of vision.

The *salmonidæ* are all predatory nocturnal feeding animals, and like such animals they possess this extra power of vision that owls and the feline animals enjoy.

3. *Fluorescence.* Dr. Spencer has an exhibit in the Natural History Museum which demonstrates fluorescence, and is of interest to men who fish at night. The exhibit is a box lit up by a lamp producing ultra-violet rays. Some hen's hackles, heron's feathers and mole's fur are put in the box. The lamp is extinguished. For a few seconds the objects are invisible and in complete darkness. Suddenly (actuated by a light invisible to the human eye) the objects glow and glisten with wonderful colours. This is fluorescence. Some physicists give the following explanation of it:

'The objects have the power of absorbing the invisible ultra-violet rays which are of short wave lengths, and when these objects are in darkness they give off visible rays of longer wave lengths.'

It is proved that some furs and feathers fluoresce while others do not. It is also proved that those which fluoresce will do so in water in exactly the same way. So for night flies fishermen should use material which does 'fluoresce.'

It may be asked: when the sun has set, whence is the origin of this ultra-violet light? The reply is 'no night is absolutely dark to night feeders with their sense of vision of ultra-violet light, which to us is darkness, because our sense of vision does not react to the ultra-violet rays of the spectrum.'

If we had the eyes of an owl, tiger or cat, how surprised we should be to see a field mouse or a mole gleam and glisten like a glow-worm in the darkness of the night!

g. MASS CONTROL SENSE

This sense is as highly developed in fish as it is in some gregarious birds, etc. It is a sort of thought transference of which very little is known. Take for example:

A school of minnows: If a pike attacks the one lowest down in the stream, they will all scatter at once; the same will occur with a shoal of herrings, mackerel, etc.

A flock of starlings will rise, swerve and keep station as one bird.

A cloud of locusts, so thick that they darken the sun, will swerve or change direction as one insect, under some guiding influence.

SECTION 4

Respiration of Fish

A man obtains life-giving oxygen from the air through the lungs. A fish obtains it from the air dissolved in the water passing through his gills.

When respiring, a fish opens his mouth, drawing in a little water, and then almost immediately he closes it, driving the water out through his gills.

In the *salmonidæ* there are four gills on either side of the head, set on bony gill arches. On these gill arches are:

(*a*) A double row of red filaments
(*b*) A row of gill rakers.

These are used by the fish during respiration as follows:

(*a*) In the red gill filaments there are minute blood vessels with exceedingly thin walls, so that the blood is brought into intimate contact with the water passing through the gills. This blood is charged with waste products in the form of carbon dioxide. As the water passes over the filaments, the blood gives off the carbon dioxide and absorbs the oxygen, which is then distributed all over the body of the fish.

(*b*) The inner edges of the gill arches are provided with stiff gill rakers. These are used as filters for food particles passing through.

The process of respiration is really two-fold:

1. The extraction of oxygen from the water by means of the red filaments.

2. The filtration of the water for food particles by means of the gill rakers.

Since respiration is nothing more than the exchange of gases through the blood, most fishes make this exchange through the gills. A few, however, adopt other methods, *viz*:

(*a*) Some fish have 'air sacs' or bladders for storing the air for respiration

(*b*) Eels respire chiefly through the skin

(*c*) The loach passes air through his intestines and out at the vent, extracting oxygen on the way.

The maximum quantity of oxygen which water can contain under normal atmospheric conditions is only $\frac{1}{2}\%$ by volume as against 21% in the air; consequently a considerable weight of water has to be pumped through the gills of a salmon or a trout in order to extract quite a small quantity of oxygen (*see also page 422*).

In very fast water a fish prefers to allow itself to float down tail first. It will only swim with its head downstream when the current is slow enough and its own speed is great enough to enable the water to pass through its gills in the right direction.

SECTION 5

Balance in the Water

The following organs and 'motions of the body,' etc, all help a fish to keep its balance in the water:

(*a*) It can keep on an even keel by the muscular motions of its body, fins and tail.

(*b*) The inner ear, which is connected with the air bladder, also helps as a balancing organ.

(*c*) The air or swim bladder functions as a hydrostatic organ, enabling the fish to accommodate itself to the varying pressures encountered at different depths, by increasing or diminishing the volume of gas which is contained in the bladder.

SECTION 6

Do Fish feel Pain?

F. Brunner divides the nervous system of a fish into two kinds, *viz*:

1. The sensory nerves (in the gills, the skin along lateral line, etc); if these are severed pain is felt.

2. The motor nerves (in the fins, mouth, gullet, stomach, and lower surface of the fish between the pelvic fin and vent, etc); if nerves in these are severed little or no pain is felt.

It is restraint rather than pain from the hooking that alarms a fish. Being entangled in a net frightens a fish much more than being hooked in certain parts.

Cases are reported in the Press of the same fish having been caught and liberated two and even three times in half an hour. This appears to show that the fish did not suffer much pain from being hooked in the mouth anyhow.

In this connection, I have heard it suggested that when a fish has been taken out of the water and exposed to the air, it very soon becomes unconscious or drunk from excess of oxygen and consequently does not suffer pain.

When one considers that the amount of dissolved oxygen in the water in which a fish lives is only $\frac{1}{2}\%$ by volume and that the air contains as much as 21% of pure oxygen, there would appear to be something in this suggestion.

In any case it is more humane to kill a fish at once when landed.

SECTION 7

Otoliths or Earstones

These are found in all fish in two cavities at the back of the brain (with which they communicate). They are sensitive to vibrations in the water just as the human ear is sensitive to vibrations in the air, and are also made use of by the fish for balancing purposes.

In appearance they are small white bones on which, when held up to a strong light, or examined under a microscope, concentric rings can be seen, some dark coloured, some light coloured. These rings denote the summer and winter zones of growth; count them and you can tell the age of the fish! The light coloured rings denote the summer life and the dark coloured rings the winter life.

The shape of the otoliths vary in different species of fish.

SECTION 8

Fish Burying Themselves

There have been many cases reported in England and elsewhere of carp, tench, pike, perch, roach, burying themselves during a drought when the bed of a stream or pond becomes dry, and reappearing when the stream or pond fills up again; the larger fish bury themselves earlier and deeper than the smaller ones.

On the first touch of frost most eels go into the mud and remain there for the winter.

Some rainbow trout bury themselves during a very cold winter, and many rainbows when very old (7 or 8 years) go blind, bury themselves in the bottom, and die.

Brown trout in India have been found during a severe drought one foot down in the gravel of a dry river bed, and from there have been dug up alive and transferred elsewhere.

SECTION 9

Colouring Matter in Fish

The presence in the skin of certain colouring agents in the shape of minute granules of pigment of a black, yellow, or reddish hue, is the main factor in the production of colour, and the blending or the combination of these primary pigment cells produces different shades when required.

As regards the *salmonidæ*, I will just mention two of the most important colouring agents, *viz*:

1. Melanine (black pigment)
2. Zoerythrine (red pigment).

1. *Melanine* is a waste product of the body. It is a black pigment in the skin, the granules of which

have the power of rapid contraction or dilation when
affected by light or the absence of it on the retina of
the eye (*see page* 420).

> (*a*) The effect of light is to collect the granules
> of the pigment into a tiny mass and cause the
> skin to become a light colour. With dead
> fish pressure in the fishing bag causes the
> granules to collect and the skin to become
> light coloured.
>
> (*b*) The effect of the absence of light is to dis-
> perse the granules and make the skin of a dark
> colour. In blind and unhealthy fish, the
> granules are dispersed and the skin is dark
> coloured. But all dark coloured fish are not
> necessarily blind or unhealthy (*see page* 485).

2. *Zoerythrine* is not a waste product and is not
found in all fishes. It is a red or orange pigment
derived from carrottine; it is found in crustaceans,
shrimps, etc. (The shells of some crustaceans contain 'albumen of carrottine' which turns red when
subjected to heat.)

When the *salmonidæ* eat these crustaceans, etc, the
red pigment affects the colour of the flesh, making it
of a pink colour.

When the red and yellow pigment is well developed
and the black and brown are absent in a fish, a golden
colouring is produced, as in the case of the golden
orfe, gold-fish, golden tench, etc.

The colouring of the *salmonidæ* is not due entirely
to pigments. There are the iridescent and prismatic
hues characteristic of most fish. This is due to the
presence of a reflecting tissue, *i.e.* guanine.

Guanine is a waste product of the body; it is composed of very minute alkaline crystals (white) which
adhere to the scales and skin and other parts of the
body; its principal feature is the power of reflecting

light and causing iridescence. Examples: the
silvery sheen of the bleak and the *salmonidæ* (particularly smolts of salmon and sea trout). It is
abundant at spawning time in all *salmonidæ*.

a. PROTECTIVE COLOURING

Fish are protected or camouflaged in roughly
four ways:

1. By counter-shading
2. By reflected light from the scales
3. By a colour change controlled by the eye
4. By marks or stripes on the body.

1. *Counter-shading*. Most fish have dark backs,
light sides and white bellies. Viewed from above the
dark back blends with the dark colour of the bottom.
Viewed from below, the white belly has a close
resemblance to the surface of the water with the sky
beyond, and is toned down by the reflection from
the dark bottom. This obliterative shading helps
to conceal a fish from its natural enemies.

2. *Reflected light from the scales*. The scales act
like a mirror. A silvery fish on an even keel is a
mirror of its surroundings, causing the fish to appear
indistinct or ghostlike.

When a fish on an even keel turns over on its side,
its scales reflect the light from above, and the flash
gives away its presence (*see Guanine, page* 418).

3. *The effect of light on the eye*. Light, or the
absence of it, on the retina of a fish's eye, gives the
fish the power of camouflaging itself to 'tone in' with
the colour of its environment (*see also page* 418).

If a fish is near green weeds it assumes a greenish
hue; if near rocks it reflects the dark colour of its
surroundings.

The following is roughly the way a colour change is controlled by the eye. 'A sensory impulse travels along the nerves running from the eye to the visual centres of the brain, from where a motor impulse is transmitted to the granules of pigment in the skin, causing them to undergo expansion or contraction until the desired effect is obtained' (J. R. Norman, *S & T Mag*, No 63, 1931).

Here is an example of this colour change. On a sunny day you will often see trout resting in the shallow water, the bottom of which is variegated with shadows from overhanging trees, etc. The fish are difficult to see, as they have become banded or blotched by the shadows. Frighten them! . . . and they bolt upstream to open sunlit water, where their appearance at first is grotesque, until the bands and blotches have faded away in their new surroundings.

4. *By marks and stripes on the body*, which give the fish an obliterative effect by breaking up the outline of the body against the dark or light background. When a fish is striped like a perch and moves about among reeds or rushes, the stripes or markings blend in with its surroundings and help to make it less conspicuous.

SECTION 10

Oxygen and Fish

Feeding fish are often more affected by the oxygen content and temperature of water than by actual hunger. The oxygen content is chiefly governed by:

1. The temperature
2. The wind
3. The barometric pressure
4. Aquatic plant life.

1. *Temperature.* Cold water is capable of containing more dissolved oxygen than warm water. Clean water at a temperature of:

32°F contains 10 c.c. of oxygen per litre
39°   ,,   9 ,, ,, ,, ,, ,,
50°   ,,   8 ,, ,, ,, ,, ,,
59°   ,,   7 ,, ,, ,, ,, ,,
68°   ,,   6 ,, ,, ,, ,, ,,

In water containing a normal amount of oxygen (*i.e.* 7 c.c. per litre) fish are lively and feed well.

In water having a paucity of oxygen fish are sluggish, out of breath, and off their feed; while an excess of oxygen in water causes discomfort and tends to produce skin and eye diseases. Mature fish are more sensitive to oxygen deficiency than are yearlings or fry.

In water deprived of *all* oxygen a fish will 'drown' and die quickly.

2. *Wind.* Wind (warm or cool) produces evaporation and cools the surface of the water, causing it to take up oxygen from the air. 'White horses' and 'white water' under a weir have a similar effect.

3. *The barometer.* With a *low* or falling barometer there is reduced or decreasing pressure of air on the water, and the water at the surface gives off oxygen to the air. Fish tend to go deeper or to the bottom, where the water is better oxygenated.

With a *high* or rising barometer there is a greater or increasing pressure on the water, and the water at the surface absorbs oxygen from the air. Fish then come towards the surface where the water is better oxygenated.

4. *Aquatic plant life.* Growing green aquatic plants under strong sunlight consume carbon and give off oxygen to the water. Decomposing plants and organic matter use up the oxygen from the water.

A fish extracts oxygen from the water as it passes through his gills (*see* Respiration *page* 413). In order to sustain life comfortably, and as warm water holds less oxygen than cold, a fish must pass more water through his gills when that water is warm than when it is cold.

It has been proved by experiments that an 8 in trout (to exist comfortably) has to pass water through his gills at the rate of 20 c.c. a minute, when the water is at a temperature of 43°. While, if the water is at a temperature of 60° it must be passed through his gills at the rate of 44 c.c. a minute.

To be comfortable, active fish like *salmonidæ* require to extract more oxygen from the water than roach and fish of the carp species.

SECTION II

Notes on Fresh Water Biology

This Section deals with the relation of animals and water plants to their surroundings and to one another.

The ultimate supply of food for animals comes from plants, chiefly the very small plants, *i.e.* algæ, etc, which float in or on the water, adhering also to the rocks and stones of the bottom and to the stems and leaves of living water plants.

These algæ are consumed by very small animals, *viz*, water fleas, shrimps, larvæ, etc. These in their turn are consumed by larger ones; and so on until we come to fish.

The growth of plants is affected and controlled to a great extent by light. The green colouring matter of plants (chlorophyll) enables plants to absorb energy from the sun's rays, and they use this energy to build up organic matter.

To build up this organic matter they also require

a supply of mineral salts, nitrates, phosphates, silicates etc (just as the supply of manure affects the growth of plants on land). These salts are obtained from the water and from the mud or soil of the bottom.

The respiration of animals and plants, and also the decomposition of organic matter by bacteria, produce carbon dioxide gas, which is held as a dissolved gas in the water.

Under the action of sunlight, plants convert this carbon dioxide into sugar, starch, etc, releasing oxygen from it to the surrounding water. This oxygen is respired by animals and is also used by bacteria to oxidise and break down organic matter into simpler substances and mineral salts.

Every year the plants build up living organic material from carbon dioxide, water and mineral salts, the energy for this process coming from sunlight.

This living organic matter which is built up by the plants in the summer (under sunlight) dies or decays during the winter months, when it is attacked by bacteria and broken down again into its constituent parts of mineral salts, etc, and these become available for reconstruction into living matter in the summer months.

Where sewage pollution is introduced into water in any quantity, the activities of the bacteria in breaking it down will consume so much oxygen from the water that other forms of life will be destroyed and die from want of oxygen.

To sum up the situation roughly: Plants are mainly the 'producers': Animals are mainly the 'consumers.'

Carbon dioxide is produced by the breathing of all forms of life, as well as by the various processes of decay, etc. Plants absorb this CO_2 gas, retaining the carbon to build up their tissues and restoring the oxygen to the water for further use by the animals.

If a body of water can support the requisite number of plants, the entire microscopic population will be great, but not otherwise.

The abundance of fish is definitely related to the quantity of microscopic life present.

SECTION 12

Pollution of Water

There are two principal kinds of pollution, *viz*:

1. Poisonous matter (effluent) from industrial premises (oil refineries, tanneries, cement works, sugar factories, paper and pulp mills, plating works, etc.), from sheep dipping, tar washings off roads, and agricultural fertilisers and sprays.

2. Sewage from septic tanks and insufficiently treated sewage from sewage works, etc.

Most pollution acts by absorbing the oxygen from the water and rendering it unfit for fish life, killing the fish food and the fish, or driving the latter up- or downstream. (Salmon have not been caught in the Thames since 1820.)

Crayfish, fresh water mussels and shellfish are very susceptible to pollution of any sort; when they leave a stream you may be sure that the water is polluted in some way.

Perch are very sensitive to pollution of any sort. (For natural pollution *see page* 428.)

The presence of creosote or chlorine in water renders fish uneatable; chlorine causes fish to taste of iodoform. There is also a sort of worm (*Balanoglassus*) which when eaten by a fish causes the flesh to taste of iodoform.

a. ACIDITY OF WATER

The following are some of the causes:

(a) Boggy peaty soil round the banks of a stream

(b) Floods from sphagnum moss beds

(c) Floods after cutting spruce and fir trees near the banks

(d) Streams running through woods and forests are generally acid

(e) Mountain streams flowing through granite districts are usually acid

(f) The refuse from pulp and paper mills makes a stream acid.

Acidity varies with the rainfall. After a flood of acid water salmon and sea trout cease to run up a river until it subsides.

Acid water is a very poor food producer.

Trout and salmon will not spawn in very acid water; it kills the ova.

Trout in acid water are usually small and dark coloured with big chocolate spots.

Examples of acid water areas: the non-limestone waters of Devonshire, Wales and Scotland; Donegal, Connemara and Kerry.

In some rivers the head waters may be quite acid from passing through boggy and peaty ground, while lower down as the stream passes over limestone soil the water becomes alkaline. A good example of this is the upper waters of the River Liffey, which are derived from granite mountains covered with peat; the water is very acid and the trout are small. The lower parts flow over limestone and limestone-bearing gravels; the water is alkaline and the trout are of a large quick growing type.

The following do well in acid water, *viz*:

1. Leeches

2. The water wood louse (*Anselus Aquaticus*)

3. The fresh water limpet
4. Some mosquitoes, sedges and caddis. (The
   ephemeridæ are not so numerous as in
   alkaline waters.)
5. Sphagnum moss, peaty plants, wild ranun
   culus, water celery, star wort, milfoil and
   pondweed.

Experiments prove that a worm or snail from
alkaline soil will die if put in acid soil.

Pike, perch and rudd are seldom associated with
acid water.

b. ALKALINITY OF WATER

In streams which pass through limestone or chalky
soil, the water is alkaline (calcium carbonate and
other salts are formed in the water). Ex: the chalk-
streams of the South of England, Blagdon lake, the
limestone rivers of County Limerick, Derbyshire
and Yorkshire.

It is the presence of calcium which provides the
bone forming and flesh building element for fish.

Most flora and fauna thrive in alkaline water. The
following especially do well: freshwater shrimps,
snails, most mollusca, crayfish, caddis and larvæ,
beetles, boatmen, water fleas, plankton, protozoa and
algæ.

Algæ are usually green in alkaline water and a
bluish green in acid water. The minutest forms of
animal life (protozoa, etc) live on algæ, and must
have suitable clean water free from pollution.

In alkaline water, trout are usually healthy, well
fed, of good size and colour, and often silvery, as the
food which is rich in oils and fats produces guanine
(*see page* 418).

The scientific way of measuring the acidity or
alkalinity of water is to determine its hydrogen-ion

concentration or p H. I have found the following method quite satisfactory:

Get a small bottle of 'universal indicator for testing the reaction of water' from the British Drug House, City Road, London.

Put two teaspoonfuls of the water in a test tube. Add 2 or 3 drops of the indicator. The label on the bottle gives the p H for the colour produced.

These colours vary according to the colours of the spectrum from red (very acid) to violet (very alkaline).

Water from a limestone area is alkaline in reaction with a p H ranging from 7·6 to 8·4 (*see page* 484).

Water from a non-limestone area is acid in reaction with a p H ranging from 4 to 6·8 (*see page* 484).

Water with a p H of from 6·8 to 7·6 is usually due to mixing of water from limestone and non-limestone areas.

Most water plants thrive in alkaline water, especially those which depend on the river bed for their nourishment.

The following are the best to cultivate or encourage in a stream or lake:

As there are several varieties of some of these plants I have been careful to find out and add the Latin names of the suitable plants.

For the deeper parts of the water :

    Lakewort (*Litorella Lacustris*)
    Water moss (*Fontinalis Antipyretica*)
    Lobelia (*Lobelia Dortmanna*).

For the sides and margins :

    Crowfoot (*Ranunculus Aquatilis*)
    Water Celery (*Apium Nodiflorum*)
      ,,   stonewort (*Chara Flexilis*)
      ,,   plantain (*Alisma Plantago*)
    Forget-me-not (*Myosotis Officinale*)

Starwort (*Callitriche Aquatica*), does best in a muddy bottom.

Milfoil (*Myriophyllum Spicatum*), thrives on a stony bottom; spreads very quickly, must be kept in check.

Pondweed (*Potamogeton*), does best on a muddy bottom, spreads quickly.

For the inflow of a small burn:

Watercress (*Nasturium Officinale*)
Marsh marigold (*Caltha Palustris*)
Willow herb (*Epilobium Angustifolium*)
Arrow head (*Sagittaria Sagittifolia*)
Sweet flag (*Acorus Calamus*).

SECTION 13

Marsh Gas

Is formed from decomposing vegetable matter deposited on the bottom (leaves, weeds, grasses, etc, which form a black evil-smelling mud). This mud will not support plant life. It is classed as 'natural pollution.' In hot weather gases rise to the surface in bubbles; the formation of these gases uses up oxygen from the water.

Certain water-weeds contain a percentage of sulphur, which on decomposition forms sulphuretted hydrogen, using up oxygen and causing injury to fish life, *viz*:

Watercresses
Ranunculus
Flannel weed
Retted Flax, etc.

SECTION 14

Fungus Disease

This disease has two stages. First of all the fish is attacked inwardly by a bacillus (*bacillus salmonis pestis*), which gains access through abrasions, etc, in the skin and invades the tissues, making the fish unhealthy and causing secretions of dead and diseased matter. This bacillus can be transmitted from dead and diseased fish to others in the same water.

Secondly, the fish is attacked outwardly by a fungus (*Saprolegnia ferax*), which grows on the unhealthy and diseased parts. This fungus is a vegetable organism common in nearly all waters and is capable of attaching itself to all dead or diseased matter.

Cold water is much more favourable to its growth than warm water, indeed experiments with goldfish and the carp species have proved that water at a high temperature has a very healing effect.

Fish sometimes die of multiplication of the bacillus alone and sometimes of the fungus alone. A fish may be cured of the fungus and may afterwards recover from the bacillus. The bacillus thrives in salt water while the fungus does not. Healthy fish free from wounds or abrasions are seldom attacked.

Some of the contributory causes of the disease are:

(a) A very dry season, with low water in the river
(b) Pollution (*see page* 424)
(c) A sudden fall of temperature in the water
(d) Unhealthy, wounded fish, or fish that have been roughly handled, are very vulnerable.

Fungus can often be cured by rubbing the fish gently with a flannel soaked in a 10% solution of salt and water.

Another method is: first remove the fungus very carefully with a scalpel, then one or two applications of a drug called *resorcinol* will usually cure the fish completely. These treatments are generally carried out with 'tame' fish (*i.e.* in a stew or similar enclosure).

a. FURUNCULOSIS DISEASE

(*Bacterium Salmonicida*.) In appearance it is a sort of inflamed tumour, or soft patch under the skin, which when cut shews pus mixed with blood. Patches usually appear on the sides of the body and at the base of the fins. The vent is often enlarged, inflamed and discharging. Infected fish are generally dark coloured, with a cloud-like film on the back of the head; while sometimes the disease attacks the internal organs and there are little or no external signs, rendering it very difficult to recognise.

Experts are investigating this disease; some of the suspected causes are:

(*a*) When a river is overstocked and the water becomes low, fish congregate and are over-crowded in the pools: this may render them susceptible.

(*b*) When fish are in poor condition, after a hard winter and a cold long spring, which retards the evolution of natural food.

(*c*) Salmon after spawning are very susceptible, also when they have to wait some time below a weir or obstacle before ascending; the pools become overcrowded with fish. Salmon are more susceptible than sea trout.

(*d*) When the water is polluted, deficient in oxygen, or very warm. A water temperature of about 65°F helps to develop the disease. It seldom occurs in water at or below 40°F. The disease is not acquired in salt water.

(*e*) Fish that have reached the breeding age appear to be more liable than the younger fish.

(*f*) There is a theory that the germ is in all *salmonidæ* and that it is brought out or

developed when vitality and living conditions
are very poor.

(g) Some *salmonidæ* are said to be 'carriers' of
the disease. So one must be careful not to
introduce any stock likely to contain carrier
fish. Imported fish are suspected of being
responsible for spreading the disease.

(h) Some authorities consider that the bacillus
can lie dormant in the organic débris at the
bottom of a river and infect the fish with the
disease.

In any effort to stamp out the disease, one should
aim at having:

1. Clean, unpolluted water
2. No overcrowding
3. Net out all diseased fish and bury the bodies
4. Allow normal conditions of life and environment. No undue netting or handling.
5. Construct proper fish passes, to allow salmon
   a fair chance of ascending even at low water.

SECTION 15

Hook Worm

(*Echinorhynchus Truttæ.*) It is a parasitic intestinal
worm, conveyed to the intestines chiefly by eating
shrimps and certain mollusca. It is common in
ducks and trout; salmon parr or smolts are seldom
affected. It is not serious unless the parasite is in
very large numbers.

When infected, trout become blackish and will not
respond in colour to changes of light like healthy fish
do (*see page* 419).

The disease in the case of tame fish can usually
be cured by soaking the food in a solution of Epsom
salts.

SECTION 16
Deformities of Fish

In most cases deformity commences in the ova or in very young fry. The chief causes are:

  (*a*) Sudden changes of temperature
  (*b*) Pollution
  (*c*) Overcrowding or poor food
  (*d*) Parasites.

Deformities are more prevalent in non-migratory fish than in migratory fish.

In the ova, dropsy or 'water swollen yoke' causes:

  1 Pug headed or stunted fish
  2. One eyed fish
  3. Defective gill covers, etc.

A parasite is often the cause of:

  1. Bent spine by the tail
  2. Staggers, vertigo
  3. Stunted head.

a. MORTALITY OF FISH

Here are a few of the causes of death:

  1. Pollution from sewage or poisonous matter in the water (*see page* 424).
  2. Excessive marsh gases (*see page* 428).
  3. A very heavy pea soup flood will choke and kill fish. It also covers the reeds with mud and kills the ova.
  4. Various diseases, furunculosis, fungus, etc.
  5. Severe concussion, when the body sinks to the bottom. In cases of mild concussion the body floats on the surface.
  6. Many fish are killed or drowned fighting one another. One seizes the other by the tail or fins and tries to pull him downstream and

drown him, or he seizes the other by the lower jaw, which, if injured, is fatal to respiration.

7. Many are killed by birds, otters, etc. The scales act as a sort of protection or armour against the teeth of their enemies (the teeth slip on the scales).

SECTION 17
Autopsy of a Fish

To carry it out properly you require blunt pointed scissors and a pair of forceps (a knife is not satisfactory). Cut with scissors from vent to the gills. At the upper end of this incision, the triangular-shaped and pink coloured heart is seen.

Behind the heart is a dark red organ, the liver.

Behind the liver is the stomach, usually somewhat hidden in fat. The roe in a hen fish is on either side of the stomach. The swimming bladder is beneath the stomach. The spleen is near the vent. The intestine is the short tube between the stomach and vent.

To remove all these (except the heart), pull down the stomach with the forceps, exposing the white tube or gullet. Cut the gullet and the whole abdominal contents can be pulled down. Cut the intestine near the vent and everything comes away easily.

SECTION 18
Do Fish Sleep?

Mr. J. R. Norman in his *History of Fishes* puts it in this way: 'Although it is impossible for a fish to shut its eyes to impressions from the outside world, there can be little doubt that all fishes spend at least a part of the day or night in a state of suspended animation.'

Boulenger, who has ample opportunities for observation, describes in his book how different

fish take up different positions while sleeping, some
even lying on their sides on the bottom.

To Photograph a Fish

Lay the fish out on a piece of white paper as a
background. Put a foot-rule or watch by it. Get
directly above it by standing on a chair. See there
is a good light on the fish. The back or dark part
should be well lighted.

You can suspend the fish by the head or the tail,
but before doing so it should be allowed to 'stiffen'
or there will be a certain amount of distortion in the
belly.

A leafy hedge makes a good background, but see
that the hedge is out of focus or you may lose the
outline of the fish.

When photographing a fish from directly above it,
I think it sometimes shews up the outline and
appearance of a fish better if it is laid out in a bed of
hay or grass than if it is laid flat on a board or on a
sheet of paper.

SECTION 20

Poaching and Destruction of Fish

The following are only a few poaching methods,
the details of which I have obtained from various
sources; there are I am afraid many others.

I make no apology for referring to them in a book
on fishing, as some knowledge of them is often
useful to owners in dealing with cases of poaching
in their water.

1. *Cross Lines.* Two boats are used, about 100
yards apart (*see* diagram). There is a short very stiff
rod or a pole in each boat connected with a line,
having a cork at A to float it. On the line there are

about 70 'foot links' alternately 3 ft and 6 ft long,
with 8 in of strong gut attached to each. The flies

(size about No 6 or No 7) are knotted on to each bit
of gut.

The boat is rowed very slowly, and when the
poacher sees a rise, he strikes at once with a vigorous
pull on the inside oar. When he has hooked two or
three fish, he takes in line into the boat.

This method was explained to me some years ago,
when it was legal, by a local fisherman on Lough
Derg. The taking-in and paying-out of line obviously
required great care on account of the numerous
hooks.

2. *Otter Board.* Usually worked from the shore.
It is a board about 2½ ft long x 3 in deep with a lead
keel. Strings of unequal length
are attached. About 50 yards
of line is attached at A. When
the line is pulled tight, the otter
tends to move away, as the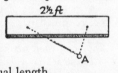
string attachments are of unequal length.

On the line are about 25 flies arranged as for cross
lining (*see above*). The poacher walks slowly along
the shore, the otter-board keeping the line taut. He
strikes by giving a firm tug to the line.

3. *Lime.* A method sometimes adopted by poachers
during 'the trouble' in the South of Ireland was to
sink a carboy of unslaked lime, corked, with a small
hole in the cork to let in water, in the upper end of a
holding pool. It killed all fish in the pool.

Another method sometimes adopted was to fill a
soda water bottle (with a glass ball stopper) about a
quarter full with lime, add water until the gas pushed

up the ball and corked the bottle, and then throw it into the pool; in a short time it burst.

4. *Spurge*.   Spurge (*Euphorbia hibernica*) is a marginal plant which thrives in peaty boggy soil. Poachers in Ireland use it in a stream, when the water is low and the weather is warm, to stupefy and catch fish.

They fill a sack with pulped spurge, place the sack in the stream at the top end of a pool where fish are, and stamp well on the sack to press out the milky juice. After two hours all fish in the pool become fuddled or stupefied and can be taken out by hand.

In spurge there is a strong alkali, and if used in very strong solution it will kill fish. You can usually tell a salmon which has been killed by spurge as the gills are of a very pale pink colour.

5. *Seeds*.   Called ' fish seeds ' (*Cocculus Indicus*), from the Malay Archipelago. Several tons of these seeds are imported yearly into the British Isles.

A teaspoonful of powdered seeds is mixed into a ball of bread paste about the size of an egg. Fish eat it greedily and become fuddled and intoxicated. They can then be easily caught by hand.

These seeds are also used for catching birds.

6. *Night lines*.   A night line is about 30 yards long, with ' foot links ' every yard or so, having hooks attached baited with lob worms. A lead weight at the end enables the poacher to throw it out diagonally downstream. He sets it after dark and gathers the fish at dawn. A most deadly method of poaching.

7. *Killing cannibal trout*.   Three or four large minnows are put in a glass pickle jar and its top covered with muslin. The jar is then lowered into a pool which the wanted fish is known to frequent and after about three-quarters of an hour, by which time the fish is attracted, a live minnow bait is dropped near the jar. Then you have him.

8. *Stopping salmon running up a river.* I heard of a ghillie using the following method at the mouth of a tributary to prevent fish running up it and to divert them to his own beat in the main river.

He put a wire across, staked it well down under water and attached several small dead dogs (reddish-coloured). The fish took them for otters (presumably) and would not pass.

9. *Electric Current.* German scientists discovered that fish swim in the same direction as a direct electric current sent through the water, with their heads towards the positive pole; whereas they swim at right angles to an alternating current. Accordingly they adopted the following means of clearing their preserves of cannibal fish.

A copper cable connected with one pole of the current at the source was sunk lengthways along the bottom of a lake 500 yards long and 50 yards broad. A second copper cable supported by floats and connected with the other pole was stretched across the breadth of the lake, and was pulled slowly by men at each end along the whole length of the lake. The strength of the current employed was 350 volts.

All fish within about 10 yards on either side of the advancing cable were stunned, lay on the surface and could be lifted out with a landing net. None were killed or suffered any physical injury, and all recovered completely in a short time.

A modified version of the method, employing portable electrodes, is now widely used in this country by River Boards and clubs, especially to clear coarse fish from trout preserves. It is successful only in comparatively shallow water.

10. A favourite method with poachers in some districts is to put some salmon roe in a small muslin bag, sink it in a stream; trout soon collect round the bag and they can be caught with a worm.

11. *Stroke hauling or snatching*. The poacher's outfit is a powerful stiff rod, a thick line and a very strong cast about 8 feet long, it is weighted with leads at intervals along it. (In some districts this is called the lash.)

At the end of the lash are three large hooks (size about 10°) tied back to back forming a triangle.

The line is cast or thrown out beyond where salmon are lying, the lash is allowed to sink over the fish. It is then drawn across their backs; an expert can tell where to strike or draw the hooks home.

Some poachers use only a line and lash with hooks attached which can easily be carried in the pocket.

The locality for the operation must be carefully selected, the bottom must be clean and free from obstacles.

12. *Tickling trout*. A person who catches trout by tickling them must have a knowledge of the water and the usual lies of the fish.

He has to work cautiously and very slowly, searching for the fish under the bank, a ledge of rock, or in a loose weed-bed, moving deliberately, causing no disturbance or vibrations in the water (*see page* 408) and making sure the trout cannot see him.

When he is in position he feels about carefully until he feels a fish. Then he tries to slip his hand very gently from its tail towards the head, keeping his fingers under its belly and his thumb above it until the dorsal fin is felt.

A sudden firm grip behind the gills then usually has the fish out, but he has to be careful not to touch the gills before he grips it, as a fish is very sensitive in these parts.

A hot sunny day when trout seek shelter from the sun is usually a favourable time.

Book VIII: THE SALMON FAMILY

Part II

THE SALMON

SECTION 1
Atlantic Salmon

Genus: *Salmo*. Species: *Salar*.

The range of Atlantic salmon in the sea is limited by the temperature of the water. In the Northern hemisphere the limit is 40° N latitude. In the Southern hemisphere the limit is 40° S latitude.

One of the chief characteristics of a salmon's life is its apparent irregularity. To predict exactly what a salmon will do at any stage of its career is a difficult proposition

There are certain generally accepted rules as to his movements, etc, but to almost every rule there are occasional variations, for instance in the matter of

   (*a*) Its migration from river to sea
   (*b*) Its return from sea to river
   (*c*) Its age of maturity
   (*d*) Its reason for spawning
   (*e*) Its sea growth and migration
   (*f*) Its behaviour after spawning
     and even the colour of its flesh.

SECTION 2
Pacific Salmon

Habitat, west coast of Canada and U.S.A. Genus: *Onchorhynchus*. Species: Five as under, *viz*:

1. *O. Quinnat* – also called chinook or king salmon. When very large (about 60 or 70 lbs) called Tyee salmon. A very game fish.

2. *O. Kisutch* – also called Coho salmon. Smaller than No 1, but a very game fish, many in Campbell River, Vancouver.

3. *O. Nerka* – Sockeye salmon. The red canned salmon of commerce, chiefly from

the Frazer River.   Also called Blueback
Salmon.

4. *O. Keta* – the Dog Salmon, very ugly at
   spawning time. Head large, jaws have big
   fangs, a fierce looking fish.

5. *O. Gorbuscha* – Humpback salmon. A small
   fish usually about 4 lbs, seldom over 10 lbs.

None of the above five species is found on the
Atlantic Coast. Although they are called salmon,
they are not even classed in the same genus.

The life history of the Pacific salmon may be
divided into three chapters:

1. Early life of young fish in fresh water

2. Period of growth in the ocean

3. Return to fresh water to the spawning
   grounds.

They seldom, if ever, live to spawn a second time,
as owing to the great length of the rivers between the
spawning beds and the sea and the very rocky and
turbulent nature of the water throughout the whole
length, few, if any, survive.

SECTION 3

Life and Food in the Sea

(Atlantic Salmon)

Nature prompts a smolt to leave fresh water and
go to the sea where food is more abundant. The
majority of salmon return to fresh water after about
a year, some remain at sea two, three or four years,
and return as very big fish. A 70 lb fish found dead
on the bank of the River Wye had been five years in
the sea without returning.

While in the sea, their chief food is composed of
organisms that float or swim in the upper layers of
the ocean, such as pelagic crustaceans, the fry of

herring and haddock, sprats, sand eels, pilchards, capelan, etc.

The North Atlantic, almost up to the Arctic Circle, holds most of the favourite feeding grounds. Where food is plentiful a salmon will increase in weight at the rate of about one pound per month.

After leaving his native river some 'sense' or instinct guides the smolt to a good feeding ground.

Observers have noticed that the growth of West Coast salmon during their first year in the sea is considerably greater than that of East Coast fish, which indicates that they do not frequent the same feeding grounds.

The fact that a salmon in a river will take a red boiled prawn seems to indicate that at some period of its sea life its feeding grounds are in deep water where the natural prawn is red in colour.

This is confirmed by the correspondence which has appeared in *The Field* and also in *The Fishing Gazette* of 5th April, 1924, in which it is definitely stated that men engaged in research work under the Fisheries Laboratory, Lowestoft, frequently find prawns of a light orange or red colour in the deep waters of the Atlantic and indeed in parts of the North Sea.

On the other hand experts (including Professor Knut Dahl) consider that 'a salmon lives and feeds only in the surface layers of the ocean,' but surely there is no reason why he should not occasionally visit the abysmal depths where he can meet prawns of a reddish colour.

a. RANGE IN THE SEA

The stock of smolts which go to the sea each spring from a river form a separate 'pack' or colony while in the sea.

When nature prompts them they return (as a

general rule) to the river they were bred in. In very exceptional cases some odd ones may lose their bearings and go elsewhere; for instance, a fish marked as a smolt in the River Spey was caught in the River Eden near Carlisle some 600 miles away. It is of interest that the furthest known recovery of a salmon tagged in a Scottish river was made off Greenland.

Their time of return may be delayed or altered by marine currents, amount of food available, etc.

The movements of salmon in the sea are influenced a good deal by marine currents or flows of warm or cold water. These sea currents are influenced by solar and lunar forces which act on the tides. These tide-generating forces vary, and are at their highest at intervals of nine years.

The chief flow of current in the Atlantic is the Gulf Stream (which is very saline, warm, and much preferred by fish life). The shoals of herring fry, etc drift with this ocean current, and the salmon follow the food.

In some years the drift of this Gulf Stream passes our coasts far out at sea and the fish food is carried with it, while salmon and other schooling fish follow the food and remain with it far out at sea. This means a poor salmon fishing year, because the fish miss the inspiration to run up a river prompted by the taste of the fresh water off the coast; they are also disinclined to leave the good feeding grounds and make a long cold journey to the river mouth, so presumably only those fish with a very strong urge to spawn would come in to do so.

In other years the drift of the Gulf Stream passes close to our shores, bringing the fish food and the following salmon. This should mean a good salmon fishing year.

As regards the cycle of nine years already referred to, during which the ocean currents vary from 'close

to' to 'far off from' our coasts, the following statistics
dealing with the British Isles as a whole rather show
that there may be something in this 'nine-year
cycle' theory which was first mentioned by Mr.
Griswold in connection with Canadian salmon, and
later confirmed by Professor Otto Petersson, of
Gothenberg, in connection with salmon in European
waters.

> 1905 – Drift was far off, poor season
> 1914   ,,   ,,   ,,   ,,   ,,   ,,
> 1923   ,,   ,,   ,,   ,,   ,,   ,,
> 1932   ,,   ,,   ,,   ,,   ,,   ,,
> 1941 should be a poor season.

1927 was a good year so 1936 should be a good
season (I hope!).

SECTION 4
Periodical Runs of Salmon

Assuming that in every case the fish have spent
two years in fresh water before migrating to the sea
as smolts, the various runs of salmon in a river may
be roughly divided under six headings as follows:

Class	Years in River	Sea	Approximate age in years
Grilse	2	1+	3½
Small spring	2	2	4
Small summer	2	2+	4½
Large spring	2	3	5
Large summer	2	3+	5½
Very large spring	2	4	6

Observers have noticed that a good run of small
spring fish (two years at sea) is usually followed the
next year by a good run of larger fish (three years at
sea), while a poor run of small fish (two years at sea) is

445

usually followed the next year by a poor run of large spring fish (three years at sea).

a. SOME REASONS FOR A SHORTAGE OF SALMON IN CERTAIN YEARS

1. Fluctuations of marine currents (*see page* 444).

2. Mortality from marine upheavals on the feeding grounds.

3. Mortality among the smolts owing to river pollution, or unfavourable conditions when they first reach salt water, such as: extremes of temperature of the sea or insufficient salinity, scarcity of plankton, small crustaceans or other food on which smolts depend.

4. Mortality from disease in the sea or from sudden changes of temperature during exceptionally cold spells.

5. Serious over-netting in the estuaries and off the coast, especially in the autumn when they are running up to spawn.

6. Drought, and lack of spates in a river at the proper time. The vibrations from motor boats and refuse oil from steamers off the coast are liable to put fish off from running up a river.

7. Exceptionally heavy floods which wash out the redds, or severe frosts and low water rendering the ova infertile. The effect of this would be felt about four years later.

SECTION 5
Life in Fresh Water

The home of the salmon is in the sea. When by good feeding he has stored up in his tissues sufficient fats, etc, to bring him up to a certain standard, Nature prompts him with a desire to spawn.

As the ova of salmon cannot live in salt water, the fish 'runs up' a river some distance into the clean fresh water, where the fry can thrive and be fairly secure from its numerous enemies. Many answer this call of nature to spawn after about a year in salt water, while some remain in the sea two, three, four and even five years.

There are three main runs of salmon during the year:

1. The spring run, January to May
2. The summer run, June to August
3. The winter run, September, October.

As regards the age and size of fish when they return to fresh water, the following is a rough outline of what occurs:

The ova hatches out, say, in 1916
The parr migrates as a smolt in 1918
Returns as a grilse in 1919
Returns as a small salmon in 1920
Returns as a large salmon in 1921
Returns as a very large salmon (a 6-year old fish) in 1922.

From the time a salmon enters fresh water until its return to the sea after spawning, the fish loses about $\frac{1}{5}$ of its weight.

a. EFFECT OF WIND AND TEMPERATURE

When in fresh water salmon usually move against the wind, accordingly they prefer a downstream wind when running up a river. When in the sea, however, they move with the wind; a wind blowing on to the coast causes fish to come inshore.

When fish are about to enter a river, the temperature of the water is very important. If the temperature is much below 56° F few fish will run up.

Salmon prefer that the temperature of the water of the river they are going to enter shall be about the same as that of the sea they are leaving.

Rivers fed from melted snow are always late rivers.

In cold weather their rate of travel upstream is slow (about three miles a day), while in warm mild weather a fish will do as much as fifteen miles a day.

When there is a strong spate salmon keep close to the banks to avoid the current.

Salmon won't enter any river the water of which is badly polluted or devoid of oxygen. (Ex: The Thames, Clyde, Mersey, etc.)

b. SURMOUNTING OBSTACLES

The tendency or desire for salmon to go up a weir or fall depends a good deal on the temperature of the water. When it is very cold fish seldom try to ascend. It is only in mild weather and when the water is fairly warm that they attempt to do so.

Provided there is deep water below a fall and the fish can get a run at it from the bottom, a salmon (or a big sea trout) will get up a weir 8 or 9 ft high. He prefers to pass through 'the black water,' he avoids very broken water. He swims and leaps chiefly by flexion of the body; the action of the tail is used to help the movement. He prefers a rising spate to a high flood.

When the water is very low at a weir, it helps fish to ascend if a board is put diagonally across the falling water; this enables him to 'slither' up it.

The colour of an artificial salmon ladder should be brownish or greenish, not light coloured. The flow of water should be smooth with no undue disturbance producing aeration.

c. JUMPING AND THROWING THEMSELVES

Salmon will often jump out of the water or show themselves from one of the following causes:

1. When hunted by a seal, otter, or attacked by an eel.

2. When he has a loose hook or gut cast on him.

3. When irritated by intestinal or other parasites.

4. When alarmed or excited by an unusual looking lure.

5. When confined in a pool for a long time he becomes restless and will splash or 'slung' about.

6. Before attempting to surmount a weir or obstacle, he will often jump out of the water to get his bearings.

7. With a falling barometer or when a spate is expected he becomes lively and shows himself.

8. When fighting or chasing other fish, through jealousy as to places in a pool, etc.

9. A kelt generally throws himself on his side. A 'fish' usually throws himself on an even keel.

d. FOOD IN FRESH WATER

Whether a salmon feeds in fresh water or not is a much debated question.

(*a*) G. H. Nall in his *Life of the Sea Trout* sums up the situation as follows:

'Salmon may occasionally feed in fresh water; their feeding is not regular nor do they digest, absorb and utilize the material so as to nourish the body adequately. No such feeding is necessary. They live on their accumulated stores of fat.'

(*b*) Some authorities consider that when a salmon does take a minnow, prawn or worm he just chews or pulps it, swallowing the juices and ejecting the solids as he cannot easily digest solid food when in fresh water.

(c) If all the salmon in a river were to commence feeding to assuage hunger, the young trout and parr would be exterminated.

I think it may be safely said 'that the amount of minnows, worms, etc, that a salmon eats in *a month* while in fresh water, would not equal the amount of herring fry, etc, which he gobbles in one day in the sea.'

SECTION 6

Notes on Spawning

A well-conditioned salmon fresh from the sea does not spawn until it has gone through a period of wasting and until its genital organs are matured. Most fish mature in fresh water and some may take months to do so, a few, however, mature in the sea and spawn in the lower reaches of a river.

Before spawning a hook or lump grows on the lower jaw of the male; both male and female become a dirty orange or red colour and are ugly and slimy.

After spawning all fish are feeble and weak and in this condition many are washed down by floods, wounded against the rocks, become diseased and die. Very few cock fish survive to spawn again.

In short, easy-flowing rivers more fish survive to spawn again than in long, rocky rivers where the waters are strong and turbulent.

Most salmon spawn once. From 5% to 15% (not more) spawn twice. About 1% spawn three times. It is rare for a fish to spawn four or five times. In Norway only 4% spawn twice.

Salmon spawn in winter between November and February (November and December are favourite months).

Perhaps the following are some of the reasons why they choose the winter months to spawn in:

1. After spawning, they can themselves return as kelts to the sea, arriving there about March or April when sea food is fairly plentiful and they will meet the inshore migration of herring fry, etc, about the estuaries.

2. Nature tells them that in winter most of the eels (which are the worst enemies of salmon ova) are hibernating.

3. About the end of March insect food is becoming plentiful at the time when the young fry are becoming active feeders.

Salmon lay fewer ova than any salt water fish, and nature prompts them to deposit those few ova in a place that is free from the numerous enemies met with in the sea, and that place is in fresh water far up a clean stream or burn.

When the water is low the spawning grounds are overcrowded and late spawners cut up the redds already made. There is usually a great waste of ova in a season of low water.

a. THE OPERATION OF SPAWNING

The hen fish selects a gravelly shallow with a current of clean fresh water over it. The gravel should be coarse (about 2 in in diameter) and unlikely to be shifted by floods.

The following is roughly the way in which a 'redd' is made.

A female fish makes the redd or hollow in the gravel by violent effort of the body and tail. Fish are most active between sundown and midnight.

When the hollow is made, the hen fish emits her ova over the upstream end. The cock fish who is just above her in the stream (or alongside of her)

flushes the ova with milt. The hen then covers the
milted ova by working her body and flapping her
tail vigorously, stirring up the gravel and causing
the stream to distribute it over the hollow, thus
covering up the ova.

The whole process may take from three to ten
days; a night's frost hastens the operation.

The redd when complete is about two yards long,
and from the bank looks like a trench about 8 in
deep with a mound of gravel below it.

The cock fish, when he is not assisting the hen to
cover the ova with gravel, is busy fighting other
males who are hanging about the redd. In these
fights males are often badly wounded and even
killed. The cock fish has also to drive off and fight
the numerous trout and other fish which hang about
downstream eating the ova.

Male parr sometimes develop their milt and have
been seen on the redds fertilising the ova of full-
grown salmon.

It is presumed that this only takes place when
there is a scarcity of male fish about.

b. NOTES ON OVA

The number of ova found in three salmon were
counted by hand and were found to be:

1. A 6 lb fish had 4,500 ova, and the ova were
   small, average per lb 750.
2. A 10 lb fish had 6,200 ova, average per lb 620.
3. A 16 lb fish had 8,000 ova; the ova were large
   and very fertile, average per lb 500.

Ova are like balls of rubber, very elastic and not
easily crushed. They are protected from their
numerous enemies when they fall into the crevices
among the gravel.

The ova of salmon is destroyed at once if put in salt water.

The period of incubation or hatching out varies with the temperature of the water, and may be 36, 60 or even 120 days in very cold water.

The ova becomes 'eyed' about half-way through the period of incubation.

There is an enormous loss of ova every year from various causes, *viz*: Other fish, birds, non-fertilisation, floods, pollution, water insects, etc.

According to some authorities a pair of salmon will only produce four adult fish and of these two are caught by some means and only two are left to breed. If all the ova of salmon came to maturity the river could not hold the fish.

C. ALEVINS

Alevins (from the French *aleviner* to stock with fry) are tiny little fish just after being hatched out and while they still have the umbilical or yolk sac attached. They are about $\frac{1}{2}$ in long and wriggle about in the gravel at the bottom of the stream. They retain the yolk sac for from three to six weeks, this being their chief source of food; they are then about $1\frac{1}{4}$ in long.

During a heavy frost alevins suffer considerably from the cold and it is not uncommon for them to lose the lower ray of the tail.

Birds and other fish eat a great number of the alevins of salmon, sea trout and brown trout.

d. FRY AND PARR

Fry are the little fish after they have absorbed the yolk sac. They are about $1\frac{1}{2}$ in long, usually go about in shoals, and feed chiefly on plankton and very minute insects.

Parr are about 3 in or 4 in long; they have 6 or 8 bars or 'parr marks' on the body, and are spotted and marked like a small brown trout.

In winter they hide among the stones at the bottom and do not feed much (if at all). In the summer months they are very lively and feed greedily on small insects, etc.

A short undersized one-year old parr, usually turns out a poor and rather old smolt with poor growth in the sea, while a long first year parr will turn out a good smolt which will grow well during its sea life. The length of the first year parr is really the index of its growth through life.

The scales of a parr come off easily when handled.

e. SMOLTS

A time comes in the life of a parr (usually when about 5 in or 6 in long) when they think about migrating to the sea. They drop down the river towards the estuary and collect in some large pool or broad stretch of deep water just above the tide level. Here they assume their silvery dress. When conditions are favourable and when the temperature of the tidal water is about the same as that of the river water they go off to sea.

The age at which a parr matures for this migration varies considerably. In northern rivers parr do not mature until after two, three, or even four years of river life. Knut Dahl says the further north one goes the longer is the river life of smolts. Four-year old smolts have been caught in Norway $8\frac{1}{2}$ in long. On the Conon (where food is scarce) cases are reported of smolts in their fifth year being caught.

In the rivers of the south of England, where the food supply is good and the temperature of the water seldom very cold, parr mature in about 15 months;

they seldom stay in fresh water until two years old. The Hampshire Avon is a good example.

In May and June of each year parr drop down to the estuary of a river. They move in shoals, not singly.

Instinct appears to tell them that food is more abundant in the sea they are making for than in the river they are leaving.

> *The first flood in May*
> *Takes the smolts away.*

The progeny of one salmon do not all go to the sea together as smolts, some remain in fresh water longer than others. Observers on the Tweed say about two-thirds of the smolts go to sea when two years old, and one-third remain in the river three years or even longer.

The longer a parr remains in fresh water, the shorter the time he will spend in the sea before again returning to fresh water, and vice versa. A three-year old smolt will only remain a short time at sea and return as a small fish, while a one-year old smolt will remain at sea much longer, returning as quite a big fish.

Experiments in America tend to prove that the smolts' silvery dress is Nature's armour-plating to protect the fish from the pressure of the deep water at sea. A parr was put in very deep water and died almost at once. A smolt was put in very deep water: it lived and appeared to suffer no inconvenience.

f. GRILSE

Grilse, from Swedish *gralax*. In some parts of Ireland grilse are called peal or first fish.

A grilse is a fish that having migrated as a smolt has spent one winter in the sea before returning to the river (*i.e.* about 1¼ or 1½ years in the sea). Smolts

migrate in the spring, so the following is roughly
what would happen:

A smolt	migrates	to	sea		spring	1927
"	"	remains	in	sea	summer	1927
"	"	"	"	"	autumn	1927
"	"	"	"	"	winter	1927
Returns as a grilse .			.		spring	1928
"		"	.	.	summer	1928
"		"	.	.	autumn	1928
Returns as a full salmon or 'fish'					winter	1928
					spring	1929
					summer	1929

The best way to tell a grilse from a full salmon is
by scale reading (*see page* 465). The following points
may help:

A grilse is more slender and graceful, has a smaller
head, a more deeply forked tail; has thinner scales
which come off very easily. A grilse after thirteen
months in the sea will weigh 4 or 5 lbs, while after
seventeen months it will weigh quite 10 lbs.

The grilse is a fish of the North and West coasts of
the British Isles; very few are found in the rivers
of the South, chiefly because in most southern rivers
the smolts go to sea when about seventeen months
old and remain at sea two or more winters, returning
as full salmon.

Of late years the number of grilse even in northern
and western rivers has decreased and the number of
spring salmon has increased. The decline is not confined to any particular type of river (rapid, sluggish,
polluted or unpolluted). Some authorities think
that they are being exterminated by over-netting, etc.
This opens the much debated question 'Do grilse
breed grilse, and do spring fish breed spring fish?'

There is at present a growing belief among some
authorities (although as yet there is no real evidence

to support it) that the hereditary principle operates through succeeding generations of salmon, and that the progeny of early running fish and late running fish will themselves be early or late running.

After all, we accept the fact that most salmon return to spawn in the river in which they were born, so why should not the hereditary principle operate through succeeding generations of salmon? (Report of Salmon and Freshwater Fisheries, 1932.)

The term 'grilse' and 'maiden salmon' should not be confused. A grilse is certainly a maiden salmon, but a fish can be a maiden salmon after having spent two or more years in the sea. For instance, three maiden fish (six years old) were caught in 1928 on the Wye, 40, 42, 44 lbs.

On first arrival in tidal water, grilse have very tender mouths and require careful handling when hooked.

g. KELTS

A kelt is a salmon that has spawned and is dropping down the river towards the sea. They are called 'slats,' 'spent fish,' etc. A male kelt is called a 'kipper,' 'a red fish.' A female kelt is called a 'black fish.'

The longer a fish remains in fresh water before spawning the more dirty and discoloured it becomes as a kelt.

Fish which enter the river in the autumn are very often quite a brightish colour after spawning.

A kelt will take flies and other baits greedily, and is often a nuisance to anglers. I do not think they catch many parr or young trout, perhaps these are too quick for them.

When in the water a kelt 'flashes' a dead whitish colour, while a clean fish flashes a bright silvery colour.

To distinguish a kelt here are some points to note:

(a) A kelt is usually lanky, lean and discoloured. The head looks large in proportion to its body.

(b) Its body is slimy with a very fishy smell.

(c) The tail is usually frayed at the end.

(d) The vent is inflamed and protruding.

(e) There are maggots in the gills (*see page* 463).

(f) Most kelts are full of flatulence; shortly after being landed the flanks collapse or cave in.

(g) The eyes of the kelt are bulged outwards from the top and have a downcast appearance; there is also a semi-circular hollow over the upper half of the eye.

(h) The teeth are sharp and firmly embedded in the jaw.

(i) A kelt 30 in long weighs about 7 or 8 lbs. A clean fish 30 in long will weigh about 11 lbs.

(j) The flesh is soft and oily, of a whitish or very pale pink colour, and is unclean to eat.

(k) When in the water a clean salmon will remain quiet for hours in the same spot, while a kelt is much more restless and constantly cruising about.

(l) A kelt when hooked seldom jumps, and seldom runs upstream against a strong current.

(m) The contours of the back and belly of a kelt are nearly parallel, while with a clean fish (no matter how thin) the contours are convex.

After spawning kelts are very exhausted and emaciated. Some rest a little in the deep pools others drop down quietly to the sea by easy stages. When the temperature of the water is low or during a frost they are inclined to collect in the pools.

h. A WELL-MENDED KELT

A 'well-mended kelt,' or as it is sometimes called 'a not much deteriorated kelt,' is a fish that has not shed all its spawn; what is retained is absorbed into the system and helps to nourish and restore the exhausted fish more quickly. All well-mended kelts are females, the male always sheds the whole of his milt.

In appearance they have many of the distinguishing marks of a kelt (but not always very pronounced). I have seen kelts on the Test which looked bright and silvery and at first sight were difficult to distinguish from clean fish.

i. A BAGGOT

A baggot or 'rawner' (Irish *noclath*) is a fish that has matured, but for some reason (constitutional or otherwise) has not managed to spawn and is hanging about in the river. They are usually met with when the spawning season is well over. In many rivers they are scarce. On the Tweed there are quite a number in the river some years.

In appearance they are silvery and look in fair condition, but the belly is rather extended and when the fish is held up by the tail the ova sags towards the head.

After capture the fish remains flabby and does not become stiff and firm like a 'clean' fish; the belly also falls in and becomes flat.

Some ghillies tell you that a baggot is 'a fish' all right, but when it is cooked you will soon find that it tastes oily, insipid, and the flesh is soft and flabby.

It is uncertain what exactly does happen to a baggot; some say they all die, some think they recover and return to the sea.

Condition and Appearance of a Clean Fish

A well-conditioned fish is silvery, with a greenish hue on the back. An hour after being killed it should still be plump in the body and become stiff and rigid.

A fish retains its flavour best if allowed to bleed. If, however, many scales are removed by rough handling the flavour of the fish is impaired and it will not keep well.

A maiden fish (male or female) has only about two spots on the gill covers and none below the lateral line. In fact the whole belly below the lateral line is clean, silvery and spotless.

The teeth are few and lightly stuck in the jaw.

A maiden fish, fresh run from the sea, with sea lice on it, is the best salmon for the table.

A fish that has spawned has several spots on the gill covers, and the spots on the sides extend well below the lateral line. The flesh is usually a little paler than that of a maiden fish.

After a week or so in fresh water, a salmon gets a purplish hue on the back and sides, and after some time in peaty water they become brownish. They are of course still clean fish, but the flesh is rather soft and pale in colour when cooked and inclined to taste a little muddy.

With a brownish salmon or sea trout you can restore the silvery colour by dusting the dark parts with a little salt and then wrapping the fish in a wet cloth or damp moss, in about 6 hours the brownish colour will have disappeared.

Even without the salt, if the cloth is kept well wetted, the silvery colour will return if the fish is not too dark.

a. CONDITION OF NETTED FISH

Fish caught in sweep nets are usually better for the table than those caught in stake nets, as in the latter a fish gets very much knocked about.

Fish caught on a rocky shore are better eating than those caught on a sandy shore. As on a sandy bottom food is usually plentiful, there are lots of herring fry, sand eels, etc which are easily caught and the fish become lazy and soft. While on a rocky coast food is not so abundant, so fish have to work hard for their food and are more energetic and virile, the flesh is firmer and better for the table.

The flesh of salmon caught in a strong running stream is firmer and better than that of fish which have been in still water for any time.

b. CONDITION OF FROZEN FISH

When a salmon has been frozen, the whole fish is rather flabby when thawed and the skin has a dull darkish colour. When cooked the flesh is hard, with not much taste, and round the bones of the spine it is discoloured (reddish). This is the case with most fish that have been frozen stiff. If, however, a salmon is kept at an even temperature of 34° F. and not allowed to freeze, it will remain at its best with curd between the flakes for a week or even longer.

SECTION 8

Sex of Salmon

To distinguish a cock from a hen fish examine:

1. The length of the head,
2. The shape of the gill covers.

The *head* of a cock fish, measured from the centre of the eye to the tip of the snout, is proportionately

461

longer than that of a hen, and this length increases as the season advances. Take for example a cock and a hen fish each 29 in long, caught in the autumn. It will be found that the snout of the cock fish, measured as above, is 3 in while that of the hen fish measures only 2 in.

The *gill cover* of a cock fish is pointed posteriorly, while that of a hen fish is more rounded.

If you look at the head of a hen fish, you will see it is shaped like a gull's egg (rounded at one end and pointed at the other), the point being the mouth end and the gill covers the rounded end. The head of a cock fish is as if you cut two eggs of a gull in half and fitted the two pointed ends together. The mouth end is very like the hen fish's head in front, while the gill covers behind are also the shape of the pointed end of the egg.

As the season advances towards spawning time the cock fish grows a beak or knob on his lower jaw and the head gets proportionately longer. After spawning this knob is absorbed on the journey to the sea. Opinions vary as to the use of this knob. One theory is that it is provided to prevent the teeth from seriously injuring other males during the numerous fights which take place on the spawning beds, when they seize one another by the small of the tail or fins, using the beak as a good hold. Another theory is that it comes from the wasting of the back part of the jaw, owing to efforts in spawning and the consequent filling up of the forward part.

A considerable number of the very large salmon that are caught are males. It is known that very few male fish survive to spawn a second time, so these large male fish must be on their first visit to fresh water after a long period in the sea. Here are three examples which according to scale reading were all maiden male fish:

51 lb killed on Tweed 5½ years in sea
47 ,,   ,,   ,, Thurso 5   ,, ,, ,,
56 ,,   ,,   ,, L. Awe 4   ,, ,, ,,

SECTION 9
Parasites on Salmon

1. Fresh water parasites, Leeches
2.   ,,   ,,   ,, Lice
3.   ,,   ,,   ,, Gill Maggots
4. Salt   ,,   ,, Sea lice.

1. Leeches are about 2 in long. They drop off when the fish is taken out of the water.

2. Fresh water louse (*Argulus Foliaceus*). Oval body ¼ in long, no tail, powerful suckers, a free swimmer. They attach themselves to salmon after it has been in fresh water about 14 days.

3. Gill maggot (*Lernæpoda Salmonea*). Bred in fresh water, free swimming. Attaches itself to the gills of salmon after they have been some time in fresh water. Always found on kelts. They can live but cannot breed in sea water. Kelts sometimes go to sea with gill maggots and return again to fresh water with them still on. These maggots are now much larger (quite ½ in long) and the gill is usually much eaten away. Some consider that the presence of these large gill maggots is good evidence of previous spawning.

4. The sea louse (*Lepeophtheirus Salmonis*). Bred in the sea, free swimming. They have no suckers; the body acts as a sucking disc, but they also have four claws to hold on by. The male is about ¼ in long. The female is 1 in long and has a white tail or string of eggs. A sea louse is whitish in colour when in the sea, but becomes blackish after a few days in fresh water or when dying. In cold fresh water they

will remain on five or six days. In warm water they
will fall off after a few hours. In fresh water the
females will drop off first, while the male will hang
on the longest. So a sea louse with egg strings on
a fish means a very fresh run fish.

SECTION 10

Age and Mortality

The Atlantic salmon is a short lived fish, seven or
eight years is about his limit and few attain that age.
The oldest and largest fish are those that have been
longest in salt water.

While in fresh water up to the smolt stage, the
mortality is very heavy from cormorants, herons,
other fish, otters, pollution, etc. While in salt water
the salmon also has enemies, *e.g.* seals, grampus,
other large fish and even sharks (a 14 ft shark which
was caught off Aberdeen had eight salmon inside it).

Gannets also kill an enormous number of salmon
and sea trout smolts when they pass from the
coloured water of a river over the shoals to commence their sea life.

After the act of spawning large numbers of salmon
die (*see page* 450). The mortality is highest during
the first month, and varies considerably in different
rivers. A fish that enters a river in October or
November and spawns, has a much better chance of
surviving than a spring fish which passes about three-
quarters of the year in fresh water before spawning.

Mr. Hutton calculates that out of every 10,572
salmon which enter the River Wye,

9,689 will die after the first spawning
  809   ,,   ,, second ,,
   72   ,,   ,, third ,,
   2 fish only will survive to spawn a fourth time.

SECTION 11

Scale Reading

The salmon while in the sea eats less in winter than in summer (even if food is available); it is this fact that makes scale reading practicable and of value.

The fish scale is a transparent plate, two-thirds of which is embedded in the skin and one-third of which is exposed; it is the portion which is embedded that carries the marks or rings that help in scale reading.

A parr (when about an ounce in weight) has the same number of scales as he will have when he is a full grown salmon of 20 or 40 lbs; the only difference is the scales are larger and have grown by ridge-like additions (or rings) to the edges. These rings form concentric lines round a central whorl, which is the original scale of the young fry. Some of these lines are close together, others are wider apart having the appearance of dark and light bands on the scale. (Two represent a year's growth.)

The dark bands represent the slow growth in the winter caused by the cold and paucity of food consumed. The light bands represent the quicker growth in the summer caused by warmth and the abundance of food.

Scale reading is a separate study (these notes only deal with the broad principles), and an expert in scale reading can tell:

1. The number of years passed in fresh water
2.   ,,   ,,   ,,   salt water
3.   ,,   winters passed in the sea
4.   ,,   times (if any) a fish has spawned.

When studying a scale the expert first makes a microphotograph of it in order to make the lines clearer.

When removing scales from a fish for examination, Hutton gives the following very useful instructions, *viz*:

Take a dozen scales from the shoulder with the point of a knife, and while moist lay them between two pieces of clean paper; they will then dry flat. Give also the following details:

Date and where caught, weight in pounds, length in inches from tip of nose to central ray of fork of tail measured on the flat, girth in inches round body measured just in front of the dorsal fin.

A corroboration of scale reading can be obtained by making a section of an otolith or earstone (*see page* 416) for it shows lines of yearly growth, just as we can tell the age of a felled tree by counting the rings which are defined by the contrast between spring wood and summer wood.

The scales of salmon caught in the sea are rather loose, but when the fish enters fresh water the scales become more firmly attached.

The following is the usual notation adopted by scale readers in describing the life of a salmon:

A figure before a full stop, thus '3.', means years of parr life.

A figure after a full stop, thus '.2', means maiden years.

S.M. means spawned once. 2 S.M. means spawned twice.

+ denotes a period of less than one year

2.3 + means $5\frac{1}{4}$ years old

3.2 + 2 S.M. + means $\left\{\begin{array}{l} \text{3 years parr life} \\ \text{2 years maiden} \\ \text{Spawned next two} \\ \quad\text{years} \\ \text{Age } 7\frac{1}{2} \text{ years.} \end{array}\right.$

SECTION 12

Land locked Salmon

The term 'land locked' is applied to colonies of small salmon which at some remote epoch have been voluntarily or involuntarily land locked, and have acclimatised themselves to fresh water. These fish form a dwarf race of salmon.

No doubt the comparative scarcity of large food forms (such as the fry of herring, haddock, etc) prevents greater growth. These small land locked salmon are found in certain waters of Europe and America.

Here are just two examples:

(a) S. Salar Sebago in certain lakes of New Brunswick and Nova Scotia, many of the fish are only 12 inches long when 5 years old.

(b) S. Salar Hardinü or Belga in Lake Wenern and in Byglands-fjord (Norway). The fish are only 12 inches long when 7 years old. Professor Dahl considers that these Belge have existed as a land locked race for about 9,000 years.

In this connection it is interesting to refer to an experiment carried out by Earl Buxton and described in the *Salmon and Trout Magazine*, No 69, December, 1932. He managed to produce dwarfed salmon, by putting some 18 months old parr into a fresh water lake from which they could not escape.

He found that most of them lived quite comfortably for about 7 years and were then only 14 inches long when they all died.

Book VIII: THE SALMON FAMILY

Part III

THE SEA TROUT

SECTION I
Various Names

There is only one trout in the British Isles, *viz*:
S. Trutta. The brown trout (*S. Fario*) is a non-
migratory member of that species (*see page* 399).

Sea trout (*S. Trutta*) are known by various names
in different parts of the British Isles according to
their age, size, colour, spawning marks, etc.

In the *smolt* stage, when they are about 7 in long,
they are called:
> Yellow fin
> Orange fin
> Silver whites
> Tecon
> Black fin
> Black tail
> Sprod (N. of England).

In the *grilse* stage, on first return from sea when
about ½ lb to 1 lb:
> Sewen (Wales)
> Whitling (Scotland)
> Herling (Scotland)
> Finnoch (Highlands—*Fionach*, white fellow)
> Cochivie (R. Tees)
> Mort (Cumberland)
> Lamasmen.

In the *adult* stage, second summer after migration,
when about 1½ lb and over, they are called:
> White trout (in Ireland)
> Sea trout
> Salmon trout
> Peal (Devonshire)
> Truff (Devonshire—fish that have spawned)
> Sewen (sometimes in Wales)
> Breach fin (in Ireland).

When they have spawned several times and have become large, coarse, dark in colour with many spots, they are called:

> Round tail
> Grey trout
> *Salmo eriox*
> Bull trout
> Brith Dail (Wales, 'The spotted one')
> Scruff (R. Tees).

As growth and length of fish advances the tail becomes less forked and more rounded.

The multiplicity of local names for sea trout causes such confusion, that it is simpler to class them in connection with their first migration to the sea as smolts, *viz*:

> (*a*) Before migration call them fry, parr, smolts
> (*b*) About a year after migration call them whitling
> (*c*) In the second summer after migration they can be called adult sea trout.

A bull trout is an overgrown sea trout (*see page* 476).

Blacktails are fish which after having migrated as smolts, have only been two to five months at sea, and have returned to fresh water. These little fish have a dark band on the end of the tail.

The name 'round tail' is given to sea trout in some localities.

But in general terms one may almost say:

> 1. All trout up to 20 in long have forked or concave tails,
> 2. Most trout between 21 in and 29 in long have square tails,
> 3. All trout 30 in long and over have convex or rounded tails.

SECTION 2

Notes on Ova and Alevins

The time the ova takes to hatch out depends on the temperature of the water. In warm water they will hatch out in 30 days. In cold water they take as long as 90 days to hatch out.

Alevins retain the yolk sac for one month.

a. FRY, PARR, SMOLTS

In the fry and parr stage sea trout remain in fresh water from one to five years (average about three years). It depends on the temperature and food supply.

In southern rivers the parr stage is short and growth in fresh water is rapid. In northern rivers the parr stage is relatively long and growth in fresh water is slow.

It is difficult to tell a sea trout fry or parr from a young brown trout of the same size.

The chief migration of smolts to the sea takes place in March, April, May, when the parr puts on his silvery coat and goes off.

The time of migration is fairly constant, but the age of migration depends chiefly on temperature and food supply as already mentioned.

The smolts which go to sea in any one year are not all of the same age and are drawn from different 'hatches.' Nature would appear to arrange this in order to provide for a bad hatching season.

The sea trout smolt is a little larger and longer than a salmon smolt, chiefly because he is older and remains longer in fresh water. When the growth in the river is slow, the growth in the sea is rapid.

In fresh water the fry and smolts keep much more together in little colonies or shoals than small brown trout do.

HH   471

SECTION 3

Life in the Sea

Sea trout of all ages, when in the sea, congregate in some favourite spot, usually on or near shallows or banks off the coast, where food is plentiful; they run into fresh water at irregular times during the season; their habits vary in different districts. In some cases the feeding grounds may be a good distance away and their visits to fresh water would not be so frequent.

The age of return to fresh water and the age of spawning are different. They may return to fresh water several times before they return to spawn. A few may run up and spawn six months after their first migration as smolts. They have, if possible, a more exact homing instinct than the salmon. The majority spawn eighteen months after their first migration. Some may spend two, three, or four years at sea before spawning.

While in the sea they keep together in communities or shoals.

A spate in a river encourages them to run up (when the tides are suitable).

On some rivers it is possible to arrange an *artificial spate*. The best time to let the water down is when the wind at the estuary is blowing on to the shore. The flood water should reach the estuary at the time of high tide and of course there must be fish in the salt water waiting to run up.

Under similar conditions an artificial spate can be arranged for salmon.

Prof. Dahl is of opinion that many sea trout do not remain in the sea all the winter, some of them hibernate in the brackish water of the estuaries.

They usually commence to run up the rivers in May. In most localities the larger fish (3 and 4 lb) run up first, and as the season advances the size of the fish as a rule decreases until say August when they may average about 1 lb.

In exceptional cases sea trout travel some distance in the sea from their native river. Recently one was marked in the N.E. of Scotland and was caught in Ireland. Sea trout marked in Scotland have been re-captured on the Dutch and Danish coasts.

During the year there are two principal 'runs' of sea trout in most rivers, *viz*: one in the summer and one in the autumn months. They include fish of all sizes, some mature, some immature. The fish of the summer run are as a rule larger and in the best condition.

Roughly speaking, after migration as a smolt, the life and movements of a sea trout year after year consist of feeding and growing in salt water, and at intervals moving into fresh water.

Their food in the sea is similar to that of the salmon (*see page* 442).

SECTION 4

East and West Coast Fish

Mr. G. H. Nall in his book, *The Life of the Sea Trout*, points out that there is a difference of habitat and environment on the east and west coasts. On the *east* coast generally speaking the coast line is unbroken, sandy and shallow. The rivers are comparatively long, with sandy estuaries.

The sea trout are nearly all coastal fish, and assemble in common feeding grounds in the sea in the shallow water, where there is plenty of winter feeding, herring fry, sprats, etc. Example, the Beauly Firth.

In very stormy weather fish are unable to enter the estuaries owing to the maelstrom of sand on the bar.

The flesh of these fish is comparatively soft and rather light coloured, and the fish are not so robust as those on the west coast that lead a more active life hunting for their food.

On the *west* coast, generally speaking, the coast line is rocky and indented. The rivers are comparatively short, flowing out of or through fresh water lochs. The estuaries are rocky with long narrow salt water bays and the adjacent sea is deep. These walls of rock tend to confine the fish, and cause them to remain in the estuaries of their own rivers, leading an estuarial life. There is little evidence of any winter feeding or common coastal feeding ground.

The rivers dry up soon, and fish run up quickly (on a spate) to the fresh water lochs, where they remain until the urge of spawning drives them up the small streams.

West coast fish mature slowly, live long, are bigger, the flesh has a rich red colour owing to an active and healthier life.

Compared with the sea trout of Scotland, Wales and England, those on the west coast of Ireland (although abundant) are rarely very large. Nall puts this down to scanty feeding. The water deepens rapidly on the west coast, herrings do not spawn there, and the supply of similar small fish is scanty; while on the south-east coast at Waterville, there is a large area of shallow banks which provide good feeding grounds, and the fish are larger.

SECTION 5

River Life and Spawning

When fish mature and are ready to spawn, they enter the river and pass quickly up into the burns and small streams for that purpose. The older a sea trout smolt is when it first migrates to the sea the earlier it will return to spawn. They spawn about October and November. The redds are made higher up in the small streams than salmon redds.

The operation of spawning is similar to that of the brown trout (*see pages* 500–501).

When once a sea trout spawns, it generally spawns annually afterwards. The oftener they spawn the coarser and more spotted they get, the tail becoming less forked, until it gets square or even convex at the end.

Sea trout certainly do feed in fresh water, but they do so more intermittently and with less robust appetite than the brown trout.

The sea trout is the most active and sporting of all the *salmonidæ*. They run up a river much faster and in shallower water than salmon do.

Some sea trout occasionally remain in fresh water lakes (finding the food plentiful and suitable) and become acclimatised and non-migratory fish. These acclimatised sea trout are found in many of the hill lakes of Connemara, *viz* Lough Illany, near Maam, etc. Also in Lough Melvin, where they are known as 'Sonachen trout.' In appearance they are steely coloured fish with a few blackish spots. After a year or so in fresh water they closely resemble brown trout. But in the spring of each year they become quite silvery for a short period.

SECTION 6

Age and Mortality

The mortality after spawning is comparatively small. Unlike salmon, the sea trout feeds in fresh water and soon recuperates. Mortality is very heavy in the fry, parr and smolt stages. But it is a curious fact that ordinary pollution in a river does not affect the mortality of sea trout smolts so much as it does salmon smolts.

As regards mortality in early life, G. H. Nall, in his *Life of the Sea Trout*, estimates that out of every 1,000 ova, only 7 fish reach the smolt stage and of these 4 only survive to become whitling.

The age limit of sea trout in the British Isles is about 13 years; few live to this age.

Exceptional cases are reported such as the 19 year old fish weighing 12½ lbs which was caught on a fly in Loch Maree in 1928. It had spawned 11 times according to its scales. There is also the 29 lb sea trout which was caught in Orkney on a bait meant for sea fish. I do not know the age of this fish.

Bull Trout

The name bull trout is applied to different species, in different localities, by different persons. For instance, the slob or estuary trout, which by reason of frequent spawning have become coarse, big and spotted, are in some places called bull trout. In some Scottish rivers salmon on a second or third spawning journey are called bull trout. In some localities these fish are incorrectly called *S. Eriox*.

The true bull trout (or round tail) is just a type of sea trout. It is not a separate variety at all.

Tate Regan and Nall consider that there are two types of sea trout, *viz*:

1. The sea trout that goes far out to sea, to the good feeding grounds, where they feed largely and rapidly become sea trout of abnormal growth. These are the true bull trout which one meets in such rivers as the Tweed, Coquet, etc.

476

2. The other type is the sea trout of ordinary growth, whose range in the sea is limited.

In appearance a bull trout is a deep fish, looks short and stubby, is much spotted, the tail is almost square, and often convex. The flesh is a sort of faded pinkish yellow colour; it is dry, rather insipid, with a muddy taste.

A bull trout plays heavy, slow and deep; he seldom takes a fly or lure near the surface. You seldom see a small one, just as you seldom see a small *S. Ferox* (*see page* 480).

Book VIII: THE SALMON FAMILY

Part IV

THE BROWN TROUT

Varieties of Trout

Although Calderwood, Tate Regan, and other authorities have decided there is only one species of trout in the British Isles, it is convenient to divide British trout into two species, *viz*:

1. Migratory fish - sea trout.
2. Non-migratory fish – fresh water trout which have lost the migratory habit.

The non-migratory species varies in appearance according to food, soil, water, nature of bottom, spawning habits, environment, locality, etc. The following are some of the names these varieties of trout are commonly known by.

a. *Salmo Fario*

Brown trout, brook trout, lake trout, yellow trout. Have red spots on body and a red tip to adipose fin. Sandy bottom produces a yellow or golden bellied trout. Colour varies with nature of food, bottom and environment.

b. *Salmo Ferox*

Are cannibal trout, food is chiefly fry – minnows, gudgeon, etc, in preference to flies, snails, shrimps, larvæ, etc. Usually old and degenerate trout become cannibals. The head is long and pointed, the mouth large, the teeth sharp. You seldom see a small *Ferox*.

c. *Salmo Stomachus*

Called Gillaroo – *goilla ruadh*, the red fellow; also called in Ireland Boddac, Boddah.

Food is chiefly snails and mollusca. They develop a hard lump or gizzard (full of snails and shells) in

the stomach. When overcrowded they pass the shells
out through the vent. The gizzard will disappear if
fish are fed on different food, so it is all a matter of
food. The change may take a couple of years.

d. *Salmo Negripinius*
Salmo Cornubiensis

Black-finned trout, are usually found in the Welsh
and Cornish mountain streams, also in Ireland,
Lough Melvin, etc.

They have long and black pectoral fins, and the
ventral fin is black on its outer half. The tail is a
little larger than that of an ordinary brown trout.

They are quick risers and fight well. In a lake
they usually keep together in shoals.

e. *Salmo Estuarius*
Salmo Galwensis
Salmo Orcadensis

These slob trout are brown trout which in times
of drought or from paucity of food in the river have
dropped down and taken to living in brackish water.
There is no evidence whatever that these slob trout
move along the coast from river to river as was at
one time supposed. They just remain in the brackish
water of their own river.

f. *Salmo Levenensis*

Trout from Loch Leven, sometimes called *S.
Cæcifer* owing to the large cæcal intestine developed
by rich food. Its chief food is the larvæ and fly of
the bloodworm and water snails (in the shape of a
catherine wheel, which are very abundant).

A silvery fish, with numerous dark spots close
together and very few red spots.

Scientists think that Loch Leven trout are the
descendants of sea trout which became land-locked.

There appears to be some doubt as to when this occurred, some authorities say in the seventeenth century; others consider that they became land-locked many centuries ago.

g. IMPORTED AMERICAN TROUT

1. The English rainbow trout (*Salmo irideus*), were first introduced into England from America about 1882. Many of these fish were a cross between the true American rainbow (*Salmo Shasta*) and the steelhead (*Salmo Gairdneri*).

Salmo Shasta is a non-migratory fish and is a native of California, in the region of the McLeod river.

Salmo Gairdneri is a migratory fish, similar in many respects to *S. Shasta*, but with much smaller scales, and is a native of the Pacific coast rivers.

The habitat of both these species is west of the Rockies.

2. *Salmo Salvelinus Fontinalis*, or the American brook trout, is a species of char. Its habitat is east of the Rockies. It has been tried in the British Isles, but does not do well. They must be well wired in as they try to escape.

h. RAINBOW TROUT

Many of the rainbow trout of Great Britain (*S. Irideus*) are a cross between *S. Shasta* and *S. Gairdneri* (*see above*).

Salmo Irideus is a heavy feeder and eats twice as much as a brown trout. They have a tendency to develop liver complaints and should not be fed on artificial and fatty foods. Natural foods such as snails, shrimps and insects are best. Normally a rainbow's liver is three times as big as that of a brown trout.

When food is plentiful they will gain about one pound in weight each year. They thrive best in alkaline water (with a p H value of 8); acid water does not produce enough good food for them (*see pages 425–484*).

When confined, or 'wired in' in a water, they show a strong desire to try to escape.

German authorities consider that having consumed most of the natural food from a stretch of river, they just drop downstream in search of new feeding grounds without any intention of migrating to the sea. In some cases this may be so, but the fact that many of them are related to *S. Gairdneri* (a migratory fish), may also account for their roving tendency (*see page* 482).

They spawn in April and May, but when settled down and acclimatised in a water they tend to spawn earlier.

Never put rainbows in water which gets very cold; they rise best when the temperature of the water is over 61°. They thrive in water at a temperature of 77°, while brown trout would probably die when confined in water of this temperature for any time.

In winter they suffer from the cold and shortage of food and try to escape. In a very cold winter they bury themselves in the mud, and some are suffocated, while others are killed by the marsh gases at the bottom.

They live only about five or six years, at the end of which period they generally become blind, go into the mud, and die. In their last year a film comes over the eye; this is the commencement of total blindness. At Blagdon they have been caught with a landing net in a semi-blind and dazed condition, among the weeds close to the shore.

The Natural Colour of Trout

The colour of a fish is in the skin, in which are deposited cells containing pigments of various colours. The colour of trout varies considerably, no two individual fish are exactly alike. The colour and markings are chiefly influenced by

1. The quantity and quality of the food
2. The nature of the soil, the bottom, and the acidity or alkalinity of the water
3. Ill health or disease.

1. *Rich feeding* produces brilliant spots and ocellated rings. With very rich feeding the rings are often joined together. Foods which are rich in fats and oils produce an alkaline substance called guanine, which gives a silvery colour to the fish (*see page* 418). The number and size of the spots and rings on a trout vary with age and food. The colour of a trout can be artificially changed by altering the food.

2. Alkaline or chalky *limestone water* (with a p H ranging from 7·6 to 8·4) (*see page* 427) is rich in vegetable life, fish food, crustaceans, etc. Fish are silvery, well fed and in good condition, with a few brilliant red spots.

Very chalky water produces very silvery fish (Ex: L. Cara Co. Mayo, where the trout look like herrings and even the flesh is impregnated with lime).

Acid or *peaty bog water* (with a p H ranging from 4 to 6·8) (*see page* 427) is not so prolific in fish food (such foods as snails, shrimps, etc, do not thrive in it at all).

(*a*) In streams and rivers where the bottom is soft and peaty with swampy margins, the trout are usually small and black, with dark stains on the belly, chocolate-coloured spots on the sides, and the scales are loosely put on.

(b) In streams with hard peaty bottoms, the fish are of a more brilliant and well defined colour, with deep red spots. They are usually larger and in better condition than in (a).

In large lakes the colour of trout varies considerably. In some parts where the bottom is muddy and peaty the fish will be of a dark colour, while in other parts where the bottom is sandy they will have golden bellies and sides with numerous brilliant spots. This is very noticeable in the Irish lakes, where you get golden bellied, dark coloured, greenish coloured and steely-grey coloured fish in different parts of the same lake.

In very deep water, in caves and deep holes, trout assume an almost black coloration.

3. *Ill health and disease.* Trout become black and in some cases a very pale colour under the following conditions:

(a) When infected by internal parasites (tape worm, hook worm, etc: the host of both these parasites is the fresh water shrimp).

(b) When suffering from certain liver and stomach complaints.

(c) When suffering from blindness (*see page* 418).

(d) When wounded in certain nerves.

(e) From the effect of pollution, paucity of food, or unsuitable food.

(f) From old age and from anything which upsets the proper working of the machinery which enables a fish to adapt its tone or colour to its surroundings.

Black trout are best removed from the water.

a. A TROUT'S SENSE OF COLOUR

Dyers and artists divide colours as follows, *viz*:

(1) *Primary colours*

Brilliant red

    ,,   blue or violet

    ,,   yellow

(2) *Secondary colours* – a mixture of two primary colours

Green – blue and yellow

Orange – red and yellow

Purple – red and blue.

3) *Tertiary colours* – a mixture of two secondary colours

Brown, olive, grey,

A fish living in coloured surroundings and feeding on coloured creatures must have some sense of colour and cannot be colour blind. 'Colour sense' is a mental physical phenomenon which can be improved by practice or dulled by disuse. Take the case of a man, he can sharpen or improve his 'colour sense' by matching coloured articles for ten minutes a day. But a trout does this for his living, for several hours a day every day of his life, so his sense of colour should be good.

A trout's eye is more used to tertiary or dull colours, which are the colours of the world he lives in, *viz*: greys, olives, browns. Primary colours dazzle him when they appear among the blended tertiary colours of his surroundings. He sees a primary colour really as a tertiary one, but of startling brilliance.

Dunne very rightly says 'Never use primary colours for artificial flies as the colour of all natural flies is tertiary.' A fly of tertiary colours reminds a fish of some sort of food and he takes it as such. A fly of primary colours attracts or excites a fish's curiosity or pugnacity, and he goes for it to investigate or to destroy it.

A trout in a shaded spot (say under a bridge) is far more discriminating than one in the open sunlight, as he can see the colour and form of your fly so much better.

SECTION 3

How a Trout Feeds

In the case of small trout which feed on plankton and minute organisms these are sifted by or arrested on the gill rakers when the water is sucked into the mouth and passed out through the gills. All food which is sifted in this way is compacted until just moist before being swallowed (*see also page* 414). A fish swallows very little if any water.

As trout grow older the mesh of the gill rakers becomes larger and they are unable to arrest minute particles of food. An exceptional case is reported of a two pound trout on L. Derg which retained a very small mesh and was able to sift minute organisms.

The usual methods adopted by adult trout when taking surface and underwater food are referred to on pages 48, 49.

a. THE FOOD OF TROUT

Trout must have a mixed diet – some surface food, some mid-water food, some bottom food. They soon tire of only Mayflies, only minnows, only snails and larvæ. The chief food is:

Ephemera	
Diptera (two-winged flies)	
Crane flies and gnats	
Perlidæ (stone flies)	Which fall on or are born in the water.
Trichoptera (sedge flies)	
Coleoptera (beetles, etc)	
Hymenoptera (lacewings, etc)	
Spiders and caterpillars	

Crustaceans and *mollusca*.

Caddis and Larvæ. These are very voracious and feed on small larvæ, snails and algæ; won't breed in mud; must have gravelly bottom and clean water; dependent on certain kinds of plants to live and breed on.

Crayfish eat snails greedily. The water must be absolutely free from pollution, and not too warm.

Shrimps eat snails greedily; they thrive in running alkaline water.

Snails eat green algæ, prefer sluggish water, and thrive in watercress beds. The two sorts trout like are *Limnia Peregra* and *Limnia Stagnalis*.

Water louse
Water limpets
Leeches $\left.\vphantom{\begin{array}{c}1\\2\\3\\4\\5\end{array}}\right\}$ These thrive in acid water.
Mosquitoes
A few snails

Minnows
Sticklebacks $\left.\vphantom{\begin{array}{c}1\\2\end{array}}\right\}$ Too many in a water are not good.

Worms
Fish Ova
Perch fry, other fry, and elvers.

As a rule there is far more cannibalism among trout in still water and deep water than there is in running water or shallow water.

When trout reach more than ordinary size they become underwater and bottom feeders.

Shallow loughs produce most food and biggest fish. In very deep loughs food is more scarce and fish are smaller. Like the salmon, all brown trout consume much less food during the cold winter months than they do during the rest of the year. The winter bands on the scales indicate this (*see page* 465).

June–July is the breeding season of many insects (when they are very active), snails, beetles, shrimps, etc.

During August and September insects hatch out and go into the mud. Shrimps and snails go among weeds and under stones. Minnows and sticklebacks congregate in backwaters.

Green weeds and plants in a water increase the general well being of a stream or lake. They act chiefly as follows, *viz*:

(*a*) During daylight they produce oxygen and aerate the water (*see pages* 421–2).

(*b*) They afford shelter and a home for the food of the fish.

(*c*) They help to consolidate the bottom.

(*d*) They collect on themselves minute plants, animals and other substances which are food for the 'trout food.'

(*e*) They thrive better in clear water than in muddy, clouded water, as the former allows the light to penetrate better.

As regards (*a*) daylight also affects the movements in the water of snails, caddis and other larvæ, etc. This is referred to by Dr. Eve in a very interesting article in *The Field* of the 4th January, 1933. He noticed that during daylight the snails, caddis, etc, in his aquarium remained on the green weeds, while at night they all left them. The reason being that during daylight green water weeds give off a certain amount of life-giving oxygen, while at night they absorb oxygen, giving off carbon dioxide gases. When this happens the insects leave them.

Accordingly it is worth while considering whether the very early morning (before the insects have returned to the weeds) is not the best time for weed cutting.

When the weeds become too numerous in a stream, very great care should be taken in cutting them. Some patches should always be left for the 'fish food' to live and breed in. If you remove or cut *all* the weeds in a water you eliminate the food of the fish.

A stream, the level of which keeps fairly constant and does not rise or fall suddenly, is best for producing fish food, as it affords a normal stability for the insect and other life in the water.

The chief food of the fry of trout, sea trout and salmon is the larvæ and nymphs of *diptera* (gnats, midges, etc) cyclops, daphnia, etc. When for any reason the hatch of this food is delayed, such as in a prolonged cold spring with high water, there is great mortality among the fry from starvation. Indeed experts maintain that there is often greater mortality among the fry of the *salmonidæ* from starvation than from their enemies.

b. THE FOOD OF THE TROUT'S FOOD

Take a pebble from the bottom of a stream, a piece of water weed or the stem of a water plant; it is covered with slippery slimy stuff: this is composed of very minute animal and vegetable organisms. This minute animal and vegetable life (which is also found held in suspension in the water) is called *plankton*, and it is on this that the trout food chiefly feed. There are two sorts:

        (*a*) Animal plankton
        (*b*) Plant plankton.

(*a*) Animal plankton (*Zoa Plankton*) is composed largely of

      (i) Cyclops (minute crustaceans)
      (ii) Daphnia (water fleas, etc)
      (iii) Protozoa (single cell animal organisms)
      (iv) Wandering suspended animalculæ.

All these form the chief food of shrimps, crustaceans, mollusca, larvæ, water fleas, etc, and also of
very young fry ½ in, and even of some mature fish,
notably Pollan.

Animal plankton lives chiefly on algæ.

(*b*) Plant plankton (*Phyto Plankton*), is composed
of minute vegetable organisms, chiefly algæ, which
form on the bottom and are also held in suspension
in the water. Algæ must have light; when shut off
from light it rapidly decays. In hot weather the
algæ rises to the surface as a sort of scum of various
colours (green, brown, yellow, red, black) according
to the nature of the water and the soil.

The scum is green in alkaline water, blue-green
in acid peaty water.

Shrimps, snails, caddis, etc, eat green algæ
greedily.

N.B. Algæ is one of the best oxygen producers
when exposed to sunlight, and in its largest form is
flannel weed.

Plankton of both sorts can be gathered in a very
fine tow net.

SECTION 4

The Growth of Trout

The size of a trout depends on the amount of good
and nourishing food available for him to eat, and on
the temperature and amount of dissolved oxygen in
the water during the summer months or feeding
season (*see page* 41). In chalk streams trout grow
big, as food is very plentiful. In mountain streams
and burns trout are seldom any size, as food is
comparatively scarce.

Trout food is composed of

1. Surface food
2. Underwater food.

1. Surface food is composed of flies and insects, etc, which are either hatched out in or blown on to the water.

2. Underwater food is shrimps, snails, crustaceans, mollusca, caddis, larvæ, minnows, beetles, boatmen, water fleas, fry, etc. Underwater food is dependent on the condition and quality of the water as regards alkalinity, acidity, floods, pollution.

If you want big fish in your water

1. There must be plenty of surface and underwater food available

2. The water must not be overstocked with fish

3. No pollution, and the water must be suitable for 'trout food' to live and thrive in

4. Trout will grow big, live long, and be more game and healthy if they are developed gradually and not pushed on and overfed. If heavily fed they will certainly grow large, but will soon deteriorate. A diet of sea mussels will soon produce big trout.

With trout a paucity of food dwarfs the fish; with other animals it leads to starvation and death, not dwarfing.

A scale for calculating the size or weight of a trout when its length is known is shown on page 402.

When about 7 years old a trout begins to deteriorate.

Malloch reports the oldest trout he has seen as 13 years. Knut Dahl reports one of 14 years old. Day records a trout which lived in a well for 30 years and only weighed 1½ lbs. By regular and rich feeding, Malloch reared a 2-year-old trout which weighed 2 lbs.

SECTION 5

Rearing and Choosing Trout for Stocking

The usual food for trout in a stew is sheep's liver or horse flesh chopped very fine, chopped carrots, fish meal, mussels. Most of the food given should float – it trains fish to take surface food.

Food that sinks fouls the bottom. Some of the advantages of the artificial hatching of trout fry are set out below, and in most cases when properly carried out the methods are quite satisfactory:

1. The fertilization of the ova is more perfect in a hatchery than in nature.

2. The loss of ova in nature is very great, whereas practically all ova are safe in a hatchery.

3. In nature the young are subjected to very great dangers, particularly in the alevin stage. These dangers can be avoided in the hatching boxes and rearing ponds.

A rearing pond or stew containing fry should be very carefully guarded against herons, king-fishers, etc.

Eels are also among the worst enemies of the young fish.

Fry fed on the natural plankton of a stream are far more healthy than those fed on artificial foods.

With careful rearing from 100 ova you may expect 66 10-in trout.

Wild trout are of course best for stocking, but are not always easy to obtain. If you want to improve your fishing *quickly*, stock with yearlings or two-year-olds. It is, however, better to stock with fry about three months old, although in this case you may have to wait two or three years before the fish are sizeable. Release them about the second week in

May, when the natural food supply of the water is well established.

Put them in the gravelly shallows and side streams (the shallower the better provided they never become dry); distribute them in batches of about ten up and down the water; a watering-can with a large spout is useful for this purpose. Never liberate a whole lot in the same spot. The season should be mild and the water not too cold; the temperature of the water should be about the same as that in the can from which they are liberated.

SECTION 6

The Habits of Trout

In a lake, trout usually travel up wind about 18 in below the surface when feeding or moving from place to place. They have no resistance of current to overcome and lots of time to examine food carefully; they can have a good meal and retire to the bottom to rest; they tend to become slow and lazy; so to tempt them your lure should accurately resemble some natural creature. A wind is necessary to complete the deception.

If conditions are favourable they move into the shallows at sundown to feed and to get away from the pressure of the deeps.

In winter they retire to the deeps and do not often come to the surface again until spring calls them.

A brook trout must be more alert and active than a lake trout as he has to catch passing food swept by him in the current, his fins are continually working to keep station against the stream, and he has to work hard for his food.

Food is not always abundant so a trout in a rapid burn does not grow very large; a few of course grow big when they find a quiet pool to rest in with plenty of food passing.

Smaller trout (under 1 lb) generally move about in little parties of five or six; when resting on the river bed they lie in sections facing upstream, in order of size, the heaviest at the top of the run or pool and the smaller ones below him in arithmetical progression. There appears to be an unwritten law that each fish has his own beat, and woe betide an outsider who happens to be smaller and tries to encroach on it. When one is caught or killed the next one in order below him takes his 'pitch.'

Old trout become rather solitary and do not join a shoal; they usually occupy a good pitch and stick to it for the season, keeping all others away.

Trout take up their place or pitch in a stream about April below a good spot where food is passing.

In early autumn they congregate at the mouths of tributaries and burns preparatory to running up to spawn. After spawning they drop down to the deep pools and sluggish water to rest until about March, when they appear in the easy water at the sides and in the tails of streams.

During the spawning season particularly trout have many fights, seizing one another by the fins (especially the ventral fins) and small of the tail and rolling over and over in the water.

There are usually more males than females in a stream, the proportion is about five male fish to one female.

SECTION 7

Improving a Trout Water

There are three classes of British trout streams:

1. Chalk streams of the south; plenty of food, and not liable to very heavy floods.

2. The medium flowing streams of the Midlands.

3. The mountain streams of Scotland and Wales; liable to be scoured by sudden floods thus reducing the natural food. The water is often acid from peaty moorlands.

Trout streams may also be classed as 'rain fed' or 'spring fed.'

Rain fed streams are liable to floods, which disturb or wash away much of the fish food: while *spring fed* streams are more constant and regular in their flow, and the vegetation and fish food have a better chance of flourishing.

To improve a stream:

1. Of course try to prevent all pollution.

2. Try to make rapids, eddies, pools, cascades and glides, etc: if necessary put in groins to alter the flow of the streams.

3. Eliminate other varieties which eat trout food.

4. Remove all black and unhealthy fish if you can.

5. Plant suitable waterplants in the shallows – Ranunculus, wild celery, wild parsnip, watercress, starwort, milfoil, etc.

6. A trout stream should carry a stock of 800 or 900 trout of 10 in to the mile, provided there is a reasonable food supply.

7. Stocking with larvæ, snails, etc is a very difficult and uncertain problem. The water must suit the insects introduced and there must be sufficient food for them (*see page* 490).

8. To increase the amount of fly life in a river 'fly boards' are well worth trying. They consist of wooden boards about 4 ft long, one foot broad and one inch thick, pointed

at one end and attached to a projection from the bank in a spot where there is a current.

The upper surface of the board must be above water, dry and free from weeds or deposit of any sort. They enable flies to lay their eggs on the under surface of the board, where they are less liable to be eaten by caddis larvæ than if they were deposited on the weeds at the bottom. The boards can be removed to an area where flies are scarcer.

To improve a lake or pond :

Encourage fauna and flora round the shores and on the bottom. By far the larger part of the fish food in a lake comes from below the surface. Some surface food will hatch out from the bottom, or be blown on from the shore. Bundles of bracken placed in 2 or 3 feet of water and weighed down with stones, make a good hatchery and sanctuary for shrimps, mollusca and other fish food.

Some ideal conditions for a lake :

1. The bottom should be limestone, sandstone, or whetstone, with shingly patches.
2. In-flowing streams should be clean and rapid with gravelly bottom useful for spawning. The water should be more alkaline than acid.
3. An average of 5 to 9 ft is best. In water over 12 ft trout do not rise freely. There should be no large areas deeper than 20 ft. Patches of stones or coarse gravel are useful for fry to hide in.
4. There should be ample fish food for the stock of trout.
5. On the shores and margins cultivate willows, alders, sedges, celery, parsnips, golden rod, loose-strife, ranunculus, starwort, milfoil, quillwort, etc to afford shade and cover.

In the shallows, watercress and kingcups are useful.

On the bottom, lobelia (in 2 ft of water), lakewort (in about 8 ft), water mosses, stoneworts, reeds (not rushes); (*see also pages 427, 428*).

6. It is an advantage to be able to make the water of the lake rise and fall and expose parts of the bottom to the wind and weather. It often pays to dig or plough it up.

7. There should be no overcrowding. If overstocked your fish will be numerous and small. If understocked you will have large, well fed fish.

8. Keep down vermin (cormorants, herons, otters, mergansers, etc).

9. In an artificial reservoir after a time (say five or six years) the bottom is liable to get covered with silt and slimy deposit from floods which eventually kill much of the vegetation and fish food.

a. TROUT AND OTHER FISH IN THE SAME WATER

In a lake where there are deep water and shallows and plenty of room, trout and other fish will do well together. If there are perch and roach in a lake they are an easier prey for a pike than trout, as they are a shoaling fish.

In a small confined pond, trout and other fish (especially pike) should not be together. It is indeed best to have only trout in a small lake or pond if it can be managed.

Migratory and non-migratory *salmonidæ* do not thrive well together, especially if the former are at all numerous. The fry of salmon and sea trout are liable to eat up the food of the small brown trout.

Do not mix rainbows and brown trout unless the food is very plentiful, as rainbows are heavy feeders.

SECTION 8
To Tell the Sex of Trout

It is fairly easy to tell the sex of a trout about 1 lb and over, but it is more difficult in the case of smaller fish.

The head : Measure from the eye to the tip of the nose, a male trout has a longer and larger head. He also has larger fins.

The gill cover : In the cock fish it is pointed. In the hen fish it is more rounded (*see also page* 462).

The body : The cock fish looks longer, has less depth of body than the hen, and is broader across the shoulder. The hen fish is deeper and more shapely.

The belly : Between the vent and the pectoral fin the cock fish is rather narrow, flat, square and hard, while the hen is broad, softer and more rounded.

Colour : A cock fish generally has more numerous and brighter spots, and is more slimy to handle. Many are of a golden tint, while hens are more of a steely or silver tint.

SECTION 9
Spawning and Spawning Beds

The spawning season: Trout spawn between October and January. The legal close season is 92 days.

As the ova are developing in a trout the fish loses muscle and intestinal fats.

Trout run up streams to the higher reaches and into the small burns for the purpose of spawning. They choose running water that is shallow, clean and pure. They know that the higher up they go, the safer the fry will be when hatched out, because there are fewer big fish to interfere with them. Trout as a rule 'run up' a stream after dark.

Observers on Lough Corrib have noticed that the large male trout from the lake enter the river first, the small males follow later; they both hang about the stream and join the females as they pass up.

Lake trout after spawning usually return to their old locality, although they may have gone 5 miles or more to their favourite spawning grounds.

In a mild season trout commence to run up earlier than in a cold season. Mild weather followed by a spate is a favourable time to run up. Cold weather or frost will keep the fish back even if there is a spate.

Suitable ground for spawning: A spawning bed should consist of a layer about 1 ft deep of gravel (not smaller than ¾ in). Gravel of this size protects the alevins and allows free passage of water through it. In fine gravel or sand, the alevins have some difficulty in getting out, also sand is easily shifted in a spate, while mud rots the ova. A hard bottom or one matted with weeds or roots is no use at all. (Notes on Alevins *see page* 453.)

a. MAKING THE REDDS

Having found a gravelly bottom in pure running water, the female fish (assisted very leisurely by the male) makes the 'redd' or hollow in the gravel, by violent efforts of the body and tail. The redd when completed is about 6 in deep x 12 in wide x 18 in long.

The female sheds her ova (a few at a time) while the male (often several males) fertilises the eggs with his milt. This operation usually takes from two to four days. The temperature of the water has much to do with the time taken. During a hard frost trout have been known to shed the whole of their eggs in one night.

The redd is then partially covered in, the male not helping much in the work of filling in. When it is completed, the female drops downstream exhausted, followed later by the male fish.

b. THE OPERATION OF SPAWNING

The male gets parallel to and alongside the female, making vigorous motions of his body and tail, occasionally butting her with his nose to make her eject her ova, sometimes she presses her sides against the gravel to expel the eggs. As the eggs are expelled they fall among the gravel on the bottom. The male then covers them with milt, which is heavy and sinks down between the gravel on to the eggs.

c. NOTES ON OVA

A hen fish carries about 1,000 eggs to the pound. A 3 lb fish should deposit about 3,000 eggs.

The period of incubation varies with the temperature of the water; it would be about

$$32 \text{ days if average temperature is } 54°$$
$$47 \text{ ,, ,, ,, ,, ,, } 50°$$
$$89 \text{ ,, ,, ,, ,, ,, } 43°$$

Cold water retards growth of ova, warm water promotes growth of ova.

If the ova of a brown trout is milted by a salmon or sea trout the result is a hybrid trout. Hybrids of the *salmonidæ* are of low vitality and seldom come to maturity or turn out well. This crossing is rare under natural conditions; it is sometimes achieved in hatcheries.

It is not true hybridization since both types belong to the same species.

The artificial spawning of 'wild fish' requires to be very carefully carried out, or it will cause serious injury to the fish. With 'trout farm bred' fish, the effect of artificial spawning is not so injurious.

A hen fish when ripe is spawned by passing the ball of the thumb over the soft part of the belly between the pectoral fin and the vent and pressing out the ova. With a cock fish the milt is pressed out with the forefinger and thumb. The hand holding the fish should be wrapped in flannel or other soft material during the operation. Sometimes the fish is strapped very lightly to a board and the head is covered up when pressing out the milt or roe.

The best and most fertile ova are obtained from a fish say $1\frac{1}{2}$ to 3 lb in weight; the ova are large and produce healthy fry.

The growth of a trout is largely influenced by the size of the ovum from which it is developed; large ova produce large fry which ensures the little fish a good start.

The size which the trout attains afterwards depends on the food supply, the environment, and whether the water is overstocked or not.

d. EGG-BOUND FISH

I have not personally caught many egg-bound trout. I understand that they get in this condition more frequently in some localities than in others.

The following are some of the suggested causes of brown trout becoming egg-bound:

(i) Want of good and convenient spawning beds, or possibly old age.

(ii) Mr. E. R. Hewett writing in the *Fishing Gazette* of 5th October, 1935 considers it is caused by the fish becoming too fat from heavy feeding just before spawning time, excessive fat preventing them from performing their proper functions.

(iii) In Kenya Colony and Ceylon, where many of the trout become egg-bound, experts consider that the high temperature of the

water in summer is the chief cause. If this
be so, perhaps a very hot summer in the
British Isles may have a similar effect.

e. APPEARANCE AFTER SPAWNING

After the operation of spawning, a trout becomes
thin, lanky and slimy. The tail is usually rather
ragged at the end.

When food is plentiful in the spring a female trout
will recover its condition and appearance much
more quickly than a male fish.

f. WHY DO TROUT SPAWN IN WINTER?

Why do trout spawn in winter, when food is
scarce, whereas other fresh water fish spawn about
spring time or later in the year when there is plenty
of food available?

The theory is that trout are the descendants of
migratory *salmonidæ*, who ages ago became land-
locked and non-migratory, and they still retain the
habits of their migratory ancestors, to their own
detriment.

A salmon (migratory fish) spawns November,
December, January, and kelts (which do not require
much food in fresh water) drop down to the sea
about April where they find ample food in the young
herrings which then come inshore.

A trout spawns in November, December and
January, when little or no insect or natural food is
about. He has to retire to sluggish pools in a state of
ill health and emaciated, and wait till the following spring until food, insects and larvæ become
active.

It would appear that nature has erred in the case
of the trout.

Pike and perch which spawn in the spring do not
suffer from extreme emaciation, as there is ample

food available for them when they have finished spawning.

SECTION 10

Parasites on Trout

Internal parasites

>Flukes (*Trematoda*)
>Tapeworms (*Cestoda*)
>Roundworms (*Nematoda*)
>Hookworms (*see page* 431).

There is a minute internal parasite which causes whirling sickness and gill trouble – its name is *Octomitis Salmonis* The fish loses its sense of balance, turns over repeatedly in the water, lying on its back with its gills extended.

External parasites

>Fish louse (*Argulus*)
>Leach (*Piscicola Geometra*)
>Fungus (*see page* 428)
>Fresh water louse (*Argulus Foliaceus*)
>A sort of gill maggot (*Achtheres Percarum*).

SECTION 11

Good and Bad Tasting Trout

When killed, a trout in good condition should

1. Have put up a good fight

2. Get stiff and rigid about half an hour after having been killed

3. The scales should be firm, not easily removed

4. Be thick in the shoulder

5. Have brilliant spots and colouring

6. Have a small head and no long sharp teeth.

504

In many rivers trout are not in good condition until they have had a good feed of flies and insects about April or May.

Trout with the best flavour are those of from $\frac{1}{2}$ lb to 1 lb from a clean gravelly-bottomed stream, or from a lake up to say 2 lb. Pink-fleshed trout usually taste best (but not always).

Fish which are fed on shrimps, mollusca, crustaceans, and other foods containing calcium have pink flesh and the ova also are a rich pink.

Trout fed chiefly on minnows, gudgeon, and sticklebacks, usually have whitish flesh, and the ova are very pale. From old age or repeated spawning the flesh of all the salmonidæ becomes paler.

There is carrotine in nearly all crustaceans; this gives a pink colour to the flesh.

In some trout farms they feed trout on chopped mussels and sea mollusca to make the flesh pink.

If young fry are fed on crushed carrots the flesh becomes pink.

The tongue of a trout indicates the colour of the flesh: A reddish tongue indicates pink flesh, a whitish tongue indicates white flesh.

Trout which have been feeding on frog spawn or tadpoles taste very nasty. (Blagdon.)

In very hot weather trout caught in shallows among weeds (especially if they are decaying) have a strong muddy taste whether their flesh is pink or white.

The muddy flavour of trout can sometimes be got rid of

1. By cleaning them at once after capture
2. By putting them for a few hours in a solution of salt and water before being cooked.

SECTION 12

To Cook a Trout by the Waterside

Make a good bright fire of gorse. Wrap the trout in greased paper. Cover it with the hot embers; do not, of course, put it in the blazing fire.

For a 2 lb trout leave it in the hot embers for half an hour, when it will be properly cooked.

APPENDIX ON NYLON

The introduction of nylon has provided the fisherman with a new material for spinning lines and traces, and for casts used in fly-fishing.

SECTION 1. CHARACTERISTICS

Nylon is a plastic produced from coal, air and water. It is stiffer than well-soaked gut, but generally not as stiff as gut before soaking.

For the fisherman it exists in two forms—(*a*) monofilament, a single strand, available in various thicknesses; (*b*) braided, when several strands are spun together. Braided nylon is available at various breaking strains.

Both braided and monofilament nylon can be used for spinning lines. Most fly-fishing casts, and nearly all traces for spinning, are made of the monofilament variety.

Nylon is produced for fishing purposes in Britain, America and France. The qualities of the different countries' products vary in some degree. Another synthetic material which is in use for fly and spinning lines is Terylene.

SECTION 2. PROPERTIES

Nylon is translucent and colourless. Most varieties are almost immune from ' flash ' and do not reflect sunlight. Nylon is therefore almost invisible in water.

It is almost completely non-absorbent. This means that water does not rot it.

For the same reason nylon lines require no care and maintenance in the shape of greasing and dressing.

It has a high tensile strength. It does not fray.

SECTION 3. DISADVANTAGES

Despite its strength in resisting a direct pull, nylon tends to be brittle and under some conditions breaks easily when bent. This leads to possible weakness and unreliability at the knots.

Hence, when using nylon, special knots which avoid this danger must be tied. No others will do.

Nylon is elastic. There are three results of this:

(*a*) Stretch occurs in the water when a fish is being played or when the weight of the stream bears on the line after a long cast. In the first case the elasticity adds to the cushioning effect of the rod, and to this extent helps the fisherman. In the second case it militates against firm, accurately timed striking. It is necessary to use extra force when striking a pike.

(*b*) ' Spring ' occurs at the knots, which thus tend to untie themselves. This is another reason why knots specially devised or recommended for nylon must always be used.

(*c*) ' Spring ' may also occur at the reel resulting in ' bird's nests ' at the lower ring when casting and making a level wind difficult on the retrieve. This tendency grows less as the line becomes well-used. It is a fact that some brands of nylon line are more pliable than others and hence less liable to ' spring ' at the reel.

Some anglers believe that nylon is prone to kink when used as a spinning line. It is probable that nylon kinks no more easily than silk, but when it does so the comparative stiffness and elasticity of the material may magnify the results.

Some brands are less stiff than others. When buying nylon, whether for line, casts or traces, it pays to examine a selection and to take that which

straightens itself the easiest when a few loops are
pulled off the reel, other things being equal. Research
progress varies in different countries. One brand
may be the best one year; another the next.

The elasticity of nylon line can have one further
drawback in the use of Nottingham-type reels, *i.e.*
those with free-running drums. The stretch which
develops when the line comes under tension as the
bait is cast operates against full impetus being given
to the drum.

With a heavy bait performance is not affected.
Ultra-light baits are generally better fished with a
fixed-spool or multiplier reel.

SECTION 4. KNOTS

To attach line or cast to swivel or eye on bait the
Half Blood is recommended:

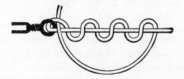

For the same purposes, but when using monofil
nylon this non-slip knot is safe.

To attach a trout fly to a cast this version of the Turle serves.

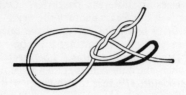

Note the double over-hand knot used in forming the running loop. Compare with the diagram of the Turle knot for use with gut casts on page 324.

For larger flies of the kind put up for salmon and sea-trout this knot, another of Hardy's, is recommended.

INDEX